FROM HOPE TO HATRED

FROM HOPE

TO ...ED

THE FALLS CURFEW

ANDREW WALSH

The History Press

To my wife, Sarah, and my children, Jordan, Jake, Caitlin, Ellé and Dylan.

Dedicated to the memory of my brother and my mother:
Garry Alan Walsh 1970–2012
Mary Jane Reynolds 1937–1987

First published 2013

The History Press
The Mill, Brimscombe Port
Stroud, Gloucestershire, GL5 2QG
www.thehistorypress.co.uk

British Library Cataloguing in Publication Data.
A catalogue record for this book is available from the British Library.

ISBN 978 0 7524 7480 9

Typesetting and origination by The History Press
Printed in Great Britain
Manufacturing managed by Jellyfish Solutions Ltd

CONTENTS

FOREWORD BY DANNY MORRISON

On 27 June 1970 in Belfast the Orange Order planned to march past Hooker Street on the Crumlin Road, where Catholics' homes had been burned down, and up Cupar Street past Bombay Street in the west, which had been similarly razed to the ground.

We know from documents and records that both the British and Unionist governments were told by their own advisers that these marches were provocative and would lead to widespread trouble. But we also know that the GOC of the British Army in the North, Sir Ian Freeland, made the following remark to the Joint Security Committee:

> It is easier to push them [Orange marchers] through the Ardoyne than to control the Shankill.

As predicted, widespread rioting broke out on 27 June and ended up in gun battles and loss of life in various parts of Belfast. In Ballymacarett a Loyalist attack on St Matthew's church was repelled by members of the Provisional IRA after the British army refused to intervene. Paddy Kennedy MP approached a British patrol for help and was told, 'You can stew in your own fat.' Several men died, including a Catholic defender, Henry McIlhone, and Billy McKee, a senior IRA figure, was wounded.

The Stormont government took no responsibility for what had happened and blamed Republicans. At the next meeting of the Joint Security Committee, on 1 July, it was decided that they had to 'restore the military image' and put down trouble 'with maximum force'.* This explains the Falls Curfew one week later and the raid and seizure of arms which had never been used against the British army but were there solely for the protection of people who had experienced terrifying government pogroms just ten months earlier.

---

* According to historian Professor Geoffrey Warner there is no such record of the meeting, although this date and meeting also appears in the *Sunday Times Insight Team* report.

On that Friday night, 3 July, I was in my mid-teens, standing outside the Falls Library, with a group of mates from Beechmount. The soldiers were coming into the area in large numbers and were firing gas at whim and wildly. Overhead a helicopter was announcing what was to prove to be an illegal curfew. We were eventually driven back into Cavendish Street with soldiers making repeated baton charges.

That night we listened to the terrifying sound of gunfire coming from the lower Falls and wondered what the poor people were going through. Rumours abounded. We tried to gauge what was happening by eavesdropping on the radio traffic between the RUC and the British army.

I was later told by one young man that he joined the IRA because of what happened to his friends and neighbours that weekend. He recalled the stinging humiliation he felt when on Saturday morning he looked out from behind his bedroom curtains and saw two Unionist government ministers, John Brook and William Long, standing aloft in an open-back army lorry and driving through the area, inspecting the military operation like overlords.

The Curfew, by alienating and politicising a huge swathe of nationalist opinion, was to dramatically change the context of the political situation. When the British army first came on to the streets in 1969 they were welcomed by the majority of nationalists as their protectors. But over subsequent months this benign image rapidly changed as the Brits became a mere tool of Unionist repression, then, later, the enforcers of British direct rule.

Stormont had also been dragging its heels on introducing reforms. Many nationalists – particularly among the working class – were coming around to the Republican view that they couldn't get their civil rights until they got their national rights and that that would involve an armed struggle against the government and the system.

It was this mood that the Republican Movement tapped into and it was after the Curfew that the IRA slowly began its military campaign which was to continue for the next three decades.

Danny Morrison, 2013
(Irish Republican writer and activist)

FOREWORD BY KEN WHARTON

When Andrew Walsh asked me to write a piece for his book on the famous or infamous 'Falls Road Curfew' – depending, of course on which side of the fence one was on – and said that the views of others with whom I would probably disagree would also be included, I was, understandably, hesitant. However, I was asked to write from the British soldier's perspective and I am honoured to do so.

Back in the early days of the troubles, we were a naïve army made up of young boys, plus older veterans of the last war and of course the new career soldiers who had seen action in the trouble spots of the dying days of Empire such as Cyprus, Aden, Singapore *et al.* Many of us had little idea about Northern Ireland, let alone where it was and of the complex dynamics of sectarianism. I had been brought up as a Jehovah's Witness – not of my own choice, incidentally – and my friends were Catholics as well as Protestants. I had experienced a fair amount of religious intolerance at school but was able to largely laugh it off. When I arrived in Belfast for the first time in the very early part of the decade – the 1970s – I was quite unprepared for the hatred and sectarianism which existed and appeared to be institutionalised. When I patrolled the areas around the Cromacs and on a later tour around the Falls and Divis areas, I saw the results of this sectarianism; incredibly substandard housing, overcrowded ghettos and an 'army' of unemployed men and teenagers. However, somewhere along the line, we had gone from being 'liberators' to 'oppressors' and were no longer welcomed in those areas.

Initially, the Loyalist Protestants had seen us as a 'buffer' between themselves and the Nationalist Catholics and when we tried to be even-handed, they, the Loyalists, turned against us. At about the same time, the Catholics saw us as an army of conquest and as siding with their sectarian enemies. The newly formed Provisional IRA was quick to exploit this and together with some over-zealous reactions from soldiers, successfully painted us as thugs and assassins and any chance of a good relationship in those areas were lost; probably for ever.

There is an old adage in Yorkshire – *give a dog a bad name* – and there were, regretfully, individual soldiers and individual units who were of the mindset that if the IRA were going to brand us as thugs, then why not behave like thugs? On the whole, the British Army behaved with professionalism and fairness and although there were examples of overreaction and unnecessary violence, we generally behaved well under extremely difficult and trying circumstances. As an army, we took many years and lost many lives in trying to understand the sectarian mentality and the mindset of both sections of the religious divide. As an author, I have been a major critic of the Provisional IRA and the various violent off-shoots of Republicanism – INLA, IPLO etc – but do not reserve my opprobrium for them; I condemn in equal measure the Loyalist paramilitaries of the UVF/UFF and Red Hand Commando.

In one of my books, I described the troubles of 1969–98 as merely the latest chapter of 500 years of sectarian violence in Ireland. As soldiers, we became simply a part of that on-going and senseless civil war and as such became very firmly 'piggy in the middle.'

Since the 'official' end of the troubles, I have been back twice to Northern Ireland and walked the same streets on which I had patrolled all those years ago. I have to confess a certain nervousness when I returned to the Ardoyne and New Lodge in North Belfast and the Ballymurphy and Turf Lodge estates of West Belfast. I did, however, feel equally exposed when I went in certain pubs and clubs in the Loyalist heartland of the Shankill and the fear and the menace is still evident in certain areas. I visited several areas where the Loyalist paramilitaries had murdered Catholics and walked the killing grounds of the Shankill Butchers, including the site of the former Lawnbrook Social Club. I actually felt a shiver run the length of my spine as I looked at the new housing which has been built on the site of the psychopathic Lenny Murphy's 'romper' rooms and I silently mourned the loss of innocent Catholic men unfortunate enough to be abducted, tortured and then murdered by his gang of 'Butchers'. The following day, I travelled with comrades to Kingsmill, Co Armagh and stood on a lonely, rainswept road where in early 1976 the Provisional IRA murdered ten innocent Protestant workers in apparent retaliation for the earlier sectarian slaying of Catholic men at Whitecross. It was a cold day and there were few cars as we stood on the spot where terrorists poured a deadly hail of automatic fire into men as they lined up alongside their works minibus. The same shiver ran down my back and I felt sick as I stood in that sad place.

This then is what the troubles meant to me as both a soldier and also as a civilian; it is my earnest hope and prayer that the new generation of men of evil can be stopped and that Northern Ireland can one day be at peace, that people on both sides of the sectarian divide can meet without bloodshed or hatred.

Ken Wharton, 2013
(Former British soldier and writer)

FOREWORD BY SIR GERALD KAUFMAN MP

It is more than forty-two years since the notorious – even infamous – Falls Road curfew, but it still resonates in the history of both Northern Ireland and the United Kingdom. Although, following initiatives started by John Major and completed by Tony Blair, Ulster (despite occasional flurries) is no longer a running sore in the body politic, the history of the curfew, re-created by Andrew Walsh with meticulous research and vivid prose, is essential reading if we are to understand what Northern Ireland was like then, and how far it has come since. As Andrew Walsh documents, I, as a relatively newly elected Member of Parliament, was deeply concerned about this episode, both because of my deep interest in Northern Ireland and because of my deep concern about the civil liberties that were flouted and trampled upon: a 'curfew' that was never legally declared but enforced with blatant brutality; thousands of residents repressed, and four shot dead; a claim that the 'curfew' was imposed for 'protecting lives and property' when in fact property was invaded and the relevant Member of Parliament kept out of his own constituency. There had been different, and mutually contradictory, explanations from different ministers. I was naïve enough to believe that, by raising a debate on this matter in the House of Commons, I might get explanations and perhaps even an apology. Instead, an allegedly liberal government minister replied curtly, blusteringly, and attempting to justify the inexcusable. By refusing to acknowledge what had taken place, the Westminster government connived in it. Read this book, and be educated – and dismayed.

Sir Gerald Kaufman MP, 2012
(British Labour Party politician and government minister during the 1970s)

PREFACE

I

The conflict that plagued Northern Ireland for nearly thirty years was a complex mix of religious intolerance, social deprivation, class division and inherent mistrust. Even today, at the time of writing fifteen years since the Good Friday Agreement, society in Northern Ireland is still heavily haunted by its recent past. Walls still divide communities, snaking along interfaces that have been the scenes of inter-communal violence for generations. Memorials of the fallen in the conflict still dot the landscapes of the Falls and Shankill Roads, as do national flags and other emblems of territorial aspirations. Tourists flock to these sites, some remembering the conflict, others too young to remember but perhaps trying to understand. Belfast is a city steeped in a tragic history, a living history, which the population is still living in today.

Every now and then these old animosities boil to the surface, and create conditions that are reminiscent of the days of old. On Monday 3 December 2012 Belfast City Council voted to fly the union flag at its city hall only on designated days. Previous to this the union flag was flown 365 days a year. The decision was seen as a compromise; nationalists wanted it taken down for good. Nevertheless, many Loyalists have seen this decision as another erosion of their culture. At the time of writing (January 2013) protests are still being held, with marches and rallies right across Northern Ireland. Frequently these have degenerated into riots of the sort not seen in Northern Ireland for decades. It is only by sheer luck that so far no one has been killed and one can only hope that the situation will see a peaceful resolution.

Belfast (Beal Feirste, 'mouth of the sandy ford'), the capital of Northern Ireland, is a vibrant, youthful-looking city on the banks of the river Lagan. It only gained city status at the end of the nineteenth century. It has a varied and very successful industrial heritage; the *Titanic* was built in its impressive docks, and it had a successful and profitable linen industry. The population of the city grew rapidly in the late nineteenth century, when many rural families moved into the city and its environs looking for employment. Many famous authors,

musicians, footballers and politicians call Belfast home. Today Belfast is home
to a wide, diverse group of nationalities; it has its own 'Gaeltacht Quarter',
promoting Irish speech, verse and writing, and has world famous institutions
such as Queens University and the Linen Hall Library, a goldmine of historical documents. However, Belfast has also had a troubled and violent past.

A soldier of the 2nd Parachute Regiment describes the Belfast of his youth
in Max Arthur's *Northern Ireland Soldiers Talking*:

> When I was a kid, Belfast was divided up into ghettos. Belfast was actually
> a lot of little Belfasts. They all had their own names, like Shankill or Tiger
> Bay. My personal one was Sailortown, which consisted of about eight streets
> divided by one street, Nelson Street. All the streets running off one side
> were Catholic and all the streets running off the other were Protestant, and
> you'd have found that people would've gone down Nelson Street on their
> side to walk round the district on the other. They kept on the outskirts,
> they'd never walk through. I'm sure there were Protestants born on the
> Protestant side of Nelson Street who had never been to our town. We used
> to go to dances and pubs and the pictures, and we used to meet people, and
> they could tell where you came from. Those little communities were so
> tight-knit they could tell where you came from just by your accent, in the
> same city. It was fear that dominated, fear: keep together.[1]

This fear was innate; it's what young children were taught by their parents.
Keep together, don't mix with the other side, and stay away. Mistrust and
suspicion were rife in 1960s Belfast. Some of his memories of the activities of
the 'B' Specials could however have been tainted with subsequent events and
popular opinions of them.

> Of course when they started the civil rights movement it brought it all home
> to Catholics. Actually, I was quite happy. I mean, I didn't know I was an
> underdog. People were telling me I was an underdog but I didn't realise it,
> 'cos I was a merchant seaman, the same as everybody else. The employment
> situation wasn't all that good but there was always jobs somewhere if you
> wanted them. But the civil rights thing, Catholic people were watching telly
> and asking 'what are these civil rights?' You see, before 1968 a lot of things
> were not reported, like the B Specials. Why they had B Specials in the towns
> I could never understand. B Specials used to carry Sten guns and .38 Webleys,
> big old fashioned pistols, and it wasn't unknown for them just to take out
> their pistols and shoot at people. I remember one time when I was twelve
> I was at a big dance hall above Bellevue Zoo. Something had happened.

I think there'd been a fight, and for some reason the B Specials did a raid and locked everybody in. When they were letting us out they asked me: 'What religion are you?' If you were a Protestant you would get a smack on the lug and sent home, but if you were a Catholic you'd get a ride in a Black Maria. You know, those were the type of things that happened then.[2]

Not only Belfast, but Ireland as a whole has had a turbulent history, one which does not just go back to the late 1960s. The 'Battle of the Boyne' in 1690, almost forgotten in the mindset of Britain and to a lesser degree the Republic of Ireland, is first and foremost in the psyche of the Ulster Protestant, while the 'Easter Rising' of 1916, again an event that does not trigger much emotion amongst Britons, is also of paramount importance to northern Catholics. Even though the British military presence is no longer visible on the streets of Belfast, there is still an air of trepidation in the centre of the city. An ambulance siren wails; part of normal life in any other major city. However, here people stop and look, anxiety quickly showing in their faces. The people of Belfast still show fear and worry about what has passed, and what might yet come again.

The study of the present Troubles is an ongoing process and is often hampered by how recent many of the major events were. The 1970s were the worst period of the Troubles, a mere forty years ago. Many people are still alive who were involved in the early days of the conflict, and for understandable reasons many of them are unwilling to comment on events that in historical terms were only a short time ago. Lack of documentation from government sources, while another understandable aspect of the situation, considering the importance of ongoing investigations by the Historical Enquiries Team (HET), can also be a frustrating issue in researching the conflict. Many historians have written excellent accounts of the conflict in Northern Ireland within these restrictions, from its roots in a divided and sectarian society through its long-drawn-out agony to the various attempts at closure. Others, however, have incorporated the history of Northern Ireland into an all-Ireland analysis using the country's long-standing and often fractious relationship with Britain as a guide. This has sometimes had the effect of 'diluting' the impact that the conflict has had on the people of Northern Ireland.

Moreover, there are many areas of the conflict which lack in-depth study, and are only 'glossed over' in histories of both the Troubles in particular and Irish history in general. For the people involved this can lead to a feeling of alienation from the history of the conflict. It can also play down the importance that these events had. There were many crucial events, insignificant or small at the time they occurred, that had a dramatic effect on the future course of the conflict. The Falls Curfew is one such event.

The Curfew had far-reaching consequences for the Catholic community of the lower Falls. Although there are no official statistics as to how many soldiers were involved in the operation, indeed even the army are not sure, it is argued by many historians that as many as 3,000 troops were on the ground against a handful of IRA men.

This book uses many resources in its attempt to portray the Falls Curfew as it happened, with witness statements from all sides. Archival records have been used, along with academic books, biographies and historical articles. The Central Citizens Defence Committee, organised in August 1969, took meticulous notes from people who were affected by the Curfew four weeks after the event. A small publication was released under the title of *The Belfast Curfew*. The author is allegedly Sean Óg Ó Fearghail, although many believe it to be Mícheál Ó Dathlaoich (Michael Dolley), a lecturer from Queens University.[3] Although a very one-sided account, as would be expected, this gives important information from the period on how the people of the lower Falls reacted to the wide-scale house searches at the time and the presence of so many British troops on their streets. It is heavily used in this book for that reason, and the events mentioned have been interspersed with other accounts and witness statements to get as near to the reality what happened as possible. It is also not tainted with the passing of time, as many eyewitness accounts can be. However, as always, it is up to the historian and reader to analyse and interpret the information available.

The present book also contains in-depth chapters concerning the events before, during and after the Curfew. There is one fundamental reason for this. The story of Catholic alienation in the north of Ireland, and Ireland as a whole, goes back centuries, but it was only after partition and the inclusion of half a million Catholics in the new state that this alienation began to become a burning political and social issue. Acts of discrimination, while intended to keep Catholics from power and therefore further away from a united Ireland, only served to hasten the destruction of the Stormont government. Chapters included after the Curfew are for continuity of the story, as Catholic discrimination certainly did not end at its conclusion.

Any arguments in this book are not directed against the ordinary soldiers on the ground during the Curfew. They are not directed at any individual either. The book is the story of the Curfew and its effects on the people involved, and also the story of its dubious legality. It is a story that has not had the full attention it deserves. It was a crucial aspect of the Troubles but tends only to be mentioned in passing, save for an in-depth assessment by Geoffrey Warner and a perhaps less in-depth look by Ita Connolly and Colm Campbell. That is not to say that Connolly and Campbell's work is not crucial, for it is the only work to date that has actively analysed the legal aspects of the decisions made by the General Officer Commanding (GOC) that weekend.

The Curfew was called by a GOC who had seen his army come under severe criticism for not getting tough. Unionists in the Northern Ireland government were partly to blame for this; the severe pressure they placed on the army command for tougher measures certainly played a part. The army hierarchy has to shoulder some of the blame as well, for it was they who placed troops in the area. Moreover, and perhaps more importantly, it resulted in the further alienation of Catholics in Northern Ireland, who had already for decades been subjected to severe discrimination in a state that they did not want to be in, and which did not want them.

II

While I was in Belfast researching this book, I was asked by Liam McAnoy, 'Why now?' I had no clear answer for him. Instead, I talked about how I believed that there was a story to be told, how I believed that the Curfew was a defining moment in the Troubles, and how it gave rise to the Provisional IRA and further alienated Catholics in the state of Northern Ireland. The old run-of-the-mill stuff you get from years of reading other authors' versions of events: it was the only answer I could give him, and I felt slightly embarrassed. He had probably heard it all before. After all, it was forty years ago and he has talked to many historians over that time. However, it was only when I came away from spending the day with him that I began to think about what he had said to me in that café on the Falls Road.

Liam McAnoy was there. He was present in August 1969 when Protestant mobs, backed by the sectarian 'B' Specials and members of the Royal Ulster Constabulary, invaded the district that he had lived in all his life. He saw them throw petrol bombs into Catholic homes, saw them set fire to Catholic businesses and schools on the Falls Road. He remembered Patrick Rooney, a 9-year-old boy, being killed in his bed, as did everyone else who was present. He became involved, was shot in the leg in Divis Street in the worst of the fighting in that fateful month of August 1969 and was arrested in Leeson Street on the Saturday of the Curfew. He subsequently went to prison in 1972. Listening to him, I was transfixed by his matter-of-fact telling of his story. It made me think about what I was writing and, more importantly, why.

Liam introduced me to many people that day. Women who were on the 'Bread March' down from Ballymurphy and Andersonstown to the lower Falls, women who were present inside the area subjected to curfew by the army, and ex-prisoners whom he now helped, reminiscing with them about their shared youths in a divided and dangerous society. I spent a pleasant couple of hours in that room with some very honest and proud people. I watched a film of the lower Falls in the 1960s and was offered soup and tea; I was even asked at one point if I worked for the British!

I met members of Patrick Elliman's family in their home. His death is one of the cases currently under review by the Historical Enquiries Team (HET). They talked about the Curfew as if it had occurred yesterday. They remembered the sounds of the army Saracens coming down the street, the fears that any child witnessing these events would have. I met Eamonn, nephew by marriage of Patrick, one of the nicest people I have ever met in my life; a man whom I would have loved to spend more time with, for he had a story to tell. Rita, whose hospitality was second to none, still carried a burden in her mind about her uncle Patrick and her dad James, who was devastated at his brother's death.

They all remembered the noise of nail bombs going off, the screech of bullets and the smell of burning vehicles. They remembered the anguish of their parents in trying to protect their families and homes from the battles raging around them. They remembered the closeness and the bonds that linked them all together in the lower Falls, before the developers moved in to rid the area of its slum dwellings. They remember Patrick Elliman, his shooting and subsequent death. They still ask why. The past is still with them, in their houses and refurbished streets, now one way, with old entrances and exits blocked to forestall escape routes. Above all, though, I remember the hospitality and warmth that this family showed me that day in the lower Falls.

I met many people on the Falls Road, some who were involved with the paramilitaries, others who were not. They all had time to speak to me. Many were still passionate about the events that scarred their childhood. Many also believed that the Troubles were far from over, and that it would take generations before the events would be consigned to a distant memory, and have no relevance for children growing up in peace. I met Robert 'Dinker' McClenaghan, now a Sinn Féin representative but in his youth an active member of the Provisional IRA, because of which he served time in prison. He remembered the Curfew as a child, agog at the number of soldiers on the streets that he played in. He remembered idolising soldiers before the Curfew; he remembered hating them afterwards, as was the case with many members of the Provisionals. I remember the walk he took me on, down into the lower Falls in the rain, telling me about the streets, the families that lived there and his own personal experiences. He is a very articulate and intelligent man to whom I am indebted more than he realises.

I met two rather humorous men in the Irish Republican History Museum in Conway Mill, just off the Falls Road. When I mentioned what I was researching they pointed me to a large folder with substantial amounts of information. Before I could digest this, though, I was taken out to a back room to watch a film on the history of the Troubles – the old and the new versions, 1919 and 1969, both unashamedly Republican in the telling. It was a place full of information and full of memories of the past.

Many others helped who do not wish to be named. Even forty years after the period under study, many are still fearful; as one remarked, 'The past has an awful habit of coming back and biting you on the arse!' Many of them share the same memories of chaos, fires, shootings and soldiers; memories of living in the 'no go' areas of the early 1970s, where paramilitaries, not the security forces, were the law. They are clever and remarkable people who lived through some very rough and harrowing times.

I then interviewed 'Dave', a soldier of the early days of the Troubles when everyone was unsure what was going to happen next – or what to do next, for that matter. He recalled some bad memories, and some good memories. But most of all he was extremely troubled about the poverty and deprivation that he had witnessed in Belfast upon his arrival in 1969. Even though he came from a 'slum' area in the north of England, nothing equated to what he had seen, as far as he was concerned, on the streets of a city in the United Kingdom. He spoke to me about death, destruction and fear that he had encountered at such a young age:

> What street lights there were had been either shot out, or didn't work anyway, and our Pigs headlights were being targeted regularly. We were on duty for several days … I remember sleeping in a bus shelter somewhere, and in a burnt-out bus near to Leppar Street. I was just 20 years of age at the time. The whole of that first tour changed my life. I [subsequently] watched whole rows of terraced streets burn in The Ardoyne, picked up bits of body around The Markets, was present when Gunner Laurie and Gunner Curtis were shot. I saw rivers of human blood literally flow down Belfast streets, and saw mutilated children lying in the road. Never to be forgotten.

His memories, his life, amongst soldiers, civilians and volunteers on all sides, scarred. The formative years of the Troubles, 1968–72, destroyed many lives. I spoke to many soldiers who were there; some who were keen to tell their story, and others who were not. That is understandable. The past is the past, and some want to leave it there.

Over forty years after the event, the Falls Curfew is still as fresh in these people's minds as it was then. They have witnessed many things within that forty-year period, cumulating in a certain kind of peace in Belfast, albeit still with the notorious peace walls, symbols of a society divided both physically and mentally. What many of them have not witnessed, however, is the truth. The Curfew was illegal in all eyes bar a few. Many facts of the events of that weekend were manipulated, denied or forgotten about as the years passed. It became another milestone, one of many in Northern Ireland. Four people were killed, but nobody knows why, and nobody in the establishment was held responsible. Soldiers shoot at targets, they are trained to react to particular incidents in certain ways, to react in conflict situations but, more importantly, all within the rule of law. Are they to be individually blamed? Catholic alienation after the Curfew was almost absolute. For many people, it seems that the Curfew was brushed under the carpet as other major, and more horrific, events began to take precedence. Many others believe that it was the first case of the army's subsequent alleged policy of 'Shoot to Kill'; it happened in Ballymurphy, they say, it happened in the New Lodge, it happened in Derry. Was it the first case? Did the army shoot to kill?

Something that I find amazing, and still think about a lot, is the key to their identity. They all belong to the Catholic Church. Although many do not practise their faith any more, that is where their sense of belonging lies. Catholics have had a raw deal in Ireland throughout the centuries; none more so than Northern Irish Catholics. This nurtured a sense of inferiority within the Catholic psyche that is still present today, albeit on a much reduced scale. After they were set adrift in 1922, the northern Catholics' feelings of inferiority were only added to by successive Protestant-dominated governments, which treated them like it was the seventeenth century. It took widespread education reforms in the 1940s and 1950s to breed a new generation of articulate and vocal Catholics who began to argue against this status quo, and with that challenge came a violent offspring that set out to confront the whole make-up of the British economic, political and military structure in Ireland.

The more I researched this book, the more I came to understand that the Catholics in the north of Ireland are bonded together by their history, their religion and their identity. It is because of this that they are remarkably different from their southern counterparts, who did not have to live in a state that did not want them. That is where their collective identity is strongest. Unionism attempted to take that identity away from them for fifty years. It failed in spectacular fashion in the summer of 1969. The British army was called in. The Falls Curfew is one episode in this, and there are many more. But that is why I am writing this book now.

This book is not intended to be an academic study of the events; rather, it is an attempt to tell the story of the Curfew with the people who were involved in mind. It is them, both soldiers and citizens, who suffered in differing ways and who have their own versions of the events. In-depth archival sources, while valuable, cannot tell the whole story. The book itself is part of a wider picture of Catholic alienation from the state of Northern Ireland. While the passage of time may have influenced the memories of many of the witness statements, eyewitness accounts from as little as four weeks after the event offer the researcher a rare glimpse of the Curfew and its alleged brutalities. I have also made a conscious decision in choosing not to delve into the original inquests of the four deaths of the Curfew. Inquests were held at the time and deaths of misadventure were recorded. However these cases, and many more, are with the Historical Enquiries Team, set up to investigate murders attributable to the Troubles. At the time of writing the cases are still under consideration and any conclusions they reach are likely to be the final ones.

The overriding theme throughout the book is one of Catholic alienation, which became apparent after the Curfew. It is not being written to pass judgement on how the four deaths occurred; rather, the question is why they died. It is also worth mentioning at this stage that the events talked about in the book are not a straightforward matter of one side against the other. There were, and still are, many Catholics who supported the link to the United Kingdom, and many Protestants who see a united Ireland as preferable to the Unionist-controlled government. Many soldiers also disagreed with some of the repressive measures taken against the Catholics. The Troubles in Northern Ireland were played out in three or more strands: Protestant v. Catholic, British army v. Catholic/IRA; and IRA/INLA and other paramilitary groups v. UVF/UFF/UDA and others. Therefore, the story is much more complex than a simple matter of 'black and white'.

The end of this book contains various articles, quotes and comments about the discrimination that was occurring in the state up to the beginning of the Troubles. Again, they are not put there to victimise individuals. They are there to give the reader an insight into Northern Ireland before the world's attention had been drawn to its blatant illness. They also give an insight into how Catholics felt in the state, and how alienation from the state was perhaps the best, or only, option for many.

Throughout the book, people make reference to the various groupings in Northern Ireland using a range of terms. For example, the Provisional IRA are often called 'Provos', Protestants are invariably called 'Prods' or 'Orangies', the British army are more often than not called 'Brits', Catholics are 'Taigs' and 'Fenians' and so on. Northern Ireland is also called by different names, depending on where you are situated. In the Republic it is rarely called Northern Ireland. It is generally called 'the North', or 'down the North'. Others call it the 'Six Counties'; indeed, members of Sinn Féin nearly always refer to Northern

Ireland as the Six Counties, and to the south as the '26 Counties'. Unionists mainly refer to 'Ulster' in regard to Northern Ireland.

III

I initially did not want to go down the old route of sitting down and writing out an acknowledgements list of all the people who had helped me in the research of this book, as I felt that it would be a bit pretentious of me; besides, the people who have helped me know who they are, I thought. Then an event happened to me in May 2012 that blew all that out of the water. That event was the untimely death of my brother at the age of 41.

I was aware that something was wrong; he withdrew into himself for months. Every time we spoke, he would say he was fine. He clearly was not. Nevertheless it was a shock; he was my younger brother and I naively thought he would be around for me for a long time yet. I expected to go before him, as people do who are older. This had a major effect on me, and still does. Thus, his death convinced me that I should thank all those people who willingly or unwillingly had helped me in the compilation of this book. Life is too short.

I am deeply grateful to: Danny Morrison for giving me the initial contacts with people in Belfast (from little acorns do great oak trees grow!); Robert McClenaghan, a fantastic bloke who could not do enough for me even with his busy workload; Pat in the Sinn Féin shop on the Falls Road for the interview and Lorna in the Sinn Féin office; Rita, Eamonn and their family in the lower Falls for a lovely morning of interviews and Belfast Baps, cups of tea and loads of cake – an extremely warm welcome for a stranger; Liam McAnoy for being my 'driver' for the day in Belfast and for showing me around the lower Falls, Lenadoon and Turf Lodge and for sharing his memories of 1970; the women of the lower Falls he introduced me to that day, along with the ex-prisoners and personal friends of his; the staff at the Linen Hall Library for their help; the taxi driver, of whom I know nothing except that he was a treasure trove of information – I clearly remember him saying to me, rather disappointingly, 'Don't think we are all up here singing and dancing!'; the staff at the National Archives in Kew; 'Dave' the soldier, who was a massive help after he had checked me out, and author Ken Wharton, who introduced me to him and kindly offered to put forward the British soldier's perspective at the beginning of this book; Professor Richard English for his constructive comments on my many questions to him; the *Andersonstown News* in Belfast for putting so many interviews my way; Jay Slater for having the belief; the Police Service of Northern Ireland and the army in Lisburn for giving me some details. To all the people who did not want to be identified even after so long, I am extremely grateful for your time, patience and honesty. The last words, however, have to go to my family for their support and love through many difficult periods in my life.

QUOTES ON THE CURFEW

Below is a selection of quotes from various publications and witnesses to the events. The views expressed are solely their opinions, and are used here for the purpose of context.

Anon: 'The bubble car I owned had 2 full Jerry cans of petrol as petrol was scarce. So when the Curfew was broken and all the food was brought in by the women it was used to cater for distribution to the houses as taxis and all the cars had no petrol. It was used for that so my wee bubble car came in handy. There was a post man taking pictures I think he was Polish (SHOT DEAD BY BRITISH ARMY) hope this helps.'[4]

Caroline Kennedy-Pipe, author: 'The imposition of the lower Falls Curfew had precisely the effect of allowing the Provisionals to claim that the historic British enemy was once again flexing its muscles on Irish soil.'[5]

Colm Campbell and Ita Connelly: 'The curfew was therefore probably unlawful, at least beyond its first few hours. But this was not the view taken by the Army, nor by the relevant magistrate: the only point that is absolutely clear is that there is no clarity. The legal basis for military intervention was therefore lacking in precision in respect of when the military could deploy (including the question of whose consent was needed), and what it could do after deployment.'[6]

Corporal, Kings Own Scottish Borderers: 'After the curfew it was mainly a lot of searches being done. I think the politics – looking back and understanding what I understand now – I think what the commanders were probably told was not to antagonise the situation, to try and keep the calm and have as much low profile as possible, to go in but not stir things up unnecessarily. Because the place was like a tinderbox.'[7]

Daniel M. Wilson: 'General Freeland's authority to declare such a curfew was dubious, and for that reason no one arrested for breaking the curfew was prosecuted. Ironically, General Freeland had argued against curfews on the 18th August 1969, saying, "What do you do if people disobey it? Shoot them?"'[8]

Desmond Hamill, author: 'Permission for a curfew, he [the GOC] explained, would have taken too long, which was not an underestimation, as it would certainly have been illegal.'[9]

Dr Gordon Gillespie: 'In the event the proclamation of a curfew was almost certainly illegal because it did not have the backing of the NI Minister of Home Affairs, who was the only person with the power to make such a declaration.'[10]

Gerald Kaufman, Labour MP for Manchester Ardwick: 'The noble Lord said that there was no curfew, and of course he was right. There could not have been a curfew because a curfew could have been imposed only in two circumstances: either if a state of emergency had been declared – and none had – or if the Riot Act had been read by a magistrate and nobody says the Riot Act had been read. General Freeland said there was a curfew. What is more, not only did he say it and his agents go about saying it, but it was written down. I have a copy, and I sent a copy to the Secretary of State for Defence. The Minister who is to reply to the debate told me in a letter in November that the term "curfew" was used by the Army authorities to describe the restrictions, because it is one which is widely understood. But it was far from being widely understood.'[11]

Gerry Adams, President of Sinn Féin: 'The Curfew was completely illegal, yet no one in the British army was ever charged with any offence in relation to it, and no attempt was ever made to bring any of the murderers of any of the people killed to trial.'[12]

Helena Lanigan, resident: 'The people of the lower Falls went through a hard time and I often wonder how we did it, but we never lost our sense of humour! Or maybe that's an Irish thing.'[13]

Joseph Bishop: 'There have been a few minor instances in which the military have relied on the common law. Thus, when the General Officer Commanding in Northern Ireland, acting without specific statutory authority, imposed a 35-hour curfew in the Falls Road area of Belfast on July 3, 1970, a magistrate, in an unreported decision, upheld his action as a proper exercise of the common law power to take such steps as were necessary to preserve the peace in an emergency.'[14]

Lieutenant-Colonel Michael Dewar: 'The Official IRA seized the moment to take on the army. Not surprisingly General Freeland was not prepared to let the IRA get away with it. He decided a show of force was needed and that the Falls had to be brought back under control. At 8:20pm on 3rd July the army went in. The IRA opened fire on the Black Watch and Life Guards, the latter unit having just got off the ferry from Liverpool. The army returned fire and used CS gas and, in order to avoid bloodshed, imposed a curfew at 10:00pm which was not lifted until 9:am on 5th July. While the curfew was in force the army conducted a major arms search which netted 28 rifles, two carbines, 52 pistols or revolvers, 24 shotguns, 100 incendiary devices, 28lb of gelignite and 20,750 rounds of ammunition.'[15]

Lieutenant-Colonel Jack Daw: 'There was a very marked change in attitude. We were quite aggressive as we were under orders to search every house, alleyway and drain in the area and we found a lot of weapons…But it was clear that the Catholics didn't want us there anymore. There were no more cups of tea, we were the enemy'[16]

Lord Balniel, Conservative MP for Hertford: 'No formal Curfew was called.'[17]

Martin Dillon, Author: 'Within GEN 42, a secret Cabinet meeting in 10 Downing Street, Prime Minister Edward Heath and his Home Secretary Reginald Maudling applauded the troops for what Republicans call "The Rape of the Falls" and for what others call "The Lower Falls Curfew".'[18]

Mr. Pounder MP: 'Is my hon. Friend aware that the prompt and courageous action of the Army in the Falls Road area last Friday night did much to defuse a potentially dangerous situation in other parts of Belfast, that there have been grave anxieties for a long time about substantial arms caches in the Falls Road area and that the Army was fully justified in its courageous action?'[19]

Ian Gilmour, Under Secretary for Defence: 'The hon. Gentleman made a great deal of the death of Mr Patrick Elliman, and quite rightly, because it is very sad. However, the post mortem showed that Mr Elliman was not killed by an Army bullet.'[20]

Nick Van De Bijl, author of *Operation Banner*: 'Was the incident entirely the fault of the army? Special Branch still had overall responsibility for the collection of intelligence, and was unbalanced against the Catholic community, and therefore the IRA. The army, although answerable to Westminster, was in support of Stormont, and carried out this and several other operations often against its better judgement … The Army had been under significant pressure to "sort out" the Lower Falls. "Sorting out" was taken to mean imposing law and order and enabling the RUC to patrol without assistance. The Army had relatively few options open to it other than house searches. Tactically the Balkan Street Search was a limited success. However, it was a significant reverse at the operational level. It handed a significant information operations opportunity to the IRA, and this was exploited to the full. The Government and Army media response was unsophisticated and unconvincing. The search also convinced most moderate Catholics that the Army was pro-loyalist. The majority of the Catholic population became effectively nationalist, if they were not already. The IRA gained significant support. It was ironic that, with Army assistance, there had been more police patrolling of the Falls in the period before the Search than there had been for many years. It was [also] notable that Stormont ministers had called for an end to the No Go areas but did not visit to ascertain the real situation.'[21]

Paddy Devlin MP: 'Hundreds of people, including journalists, were arrested and brought to court, but the charges were later dropped when it was declared in court that the curfew was indeed illegally imposed.'[22]

Peter Taylor, writer and journalist: 'The divorce between the army and the section of the nationalist community was complete.'[23]

Press release: 'The Director of Operations, Lt Gen Sir Ian Freeland, has declared that there to be an immediate Curfew until further notice in the area of the lower Falls …'[24]

Richard English, Author: 'The Falls Curfew … was arguably decisive in terms of worsening relations between the British Army and the Catholic working class.'[25]

Robert McClenaghan: 'I was only 12 but it had a massive impact on my life. In fact it turned a whole generation of British Army loving children into the most ruthless guerrilla fighters the world has ever seen!!'[26]

Tony Geraghty, Journalist and Author: 'Military PR added an additional twist to this macabre event. It presented triumphantly, riding high on the leading vehicle, two Unionist ministers from the hardline Stormont government … Local people had viewed the army's offensive as an invasion. The presence of Long and Brooke confirmed that they were now victims of alien occupation, not friendly protection. At Springfield Road police barracks, as press cameras clicked and whirred over captured IRA arms, Captain Brooke squeezed the arm of a young RUC constable. I stood close as Brooke murmured: "It's a grand day for us."'[27]

INTRODUCTION

As with many other aspects of its initial involvement in Northern Ireland in August 1969, the British government was at a loss as to what the best approach was to halt the spiral into civil war. The 'Irish Bog' had come back to haunt Westminster nearly fifty years after they thought Irish politics was off the agenda. Scant attention paid to the province since 1922 meant that Westminster had to start at the beginning in understanding the issues that existed there, with the result that the government believed a peacekeeping force, put in place to enable the Unionists in power to bring through reforms, was sufficient to stabilise the situation.

As the past four decades have shown, this was not a viable option for a society that by now had deep imbedded hatreds for each other, fostered by years of misrule by the majority and complete aloofness from London. By the end of the 1960s the Westminster government had lost all credibility with the ordinary Catholics of Belfast. By the time the violence became serious enough to warrant some sort of input from the government in London it was too late. The damage was done. The British government believed that putting pressure on Stormont to speed up reforms could halt the spread of the disorder, but that was not enough. The incredible ignorance of the Westminster government to conditions and events in a province of the United Kingdom – a province to which, as Peter Taylor states, questions regarding its social and economic life were assigned on average only two hours a year in parliament – reflected the ineptitude of successive British governments towards an integral part of its territory, and was to haunt relations between the two islands for decades.

Initially, upon the arrival of the British army, relations between the army and the Catholic community were cordial, and in some cases even harmonious. This was the period of well-publicised cups of tea and sandwiches at every corner along the Falls Road and a warm, if a little reserved, welcome from a populace who saw the soldiers as their defenders against the Protestant/ Loyalist mobs who had attacked the Falls Road area of Belfast in August 1969. However, as time wore on, the soldiers came to be seen by the Catholic population not as defenders, but as occupiers, there to support the faltering Unionist government at Stormont – a view bolstered by the confusing nature of the army's peacekeeping duties and Stormont's influence on decision making.

This turnaround in relations between the Catholic community of Belfast and the British army was no surprise to many people at the time. The continuance of the political structure at Stormont was a major concern, as was the slow acknowledgement of much-needed reforms. The army was seen as propping up a discredited and out-of-date administration. At the time, the intention was to have the troops there for an indefinite period while moderate politicians attempted to bring in political and social reforms that would satisfy both sides of the divide. Events, however, quickly outpaced even these limited attempts at reaching a solution.

By the beginning of 1970 opinions on both sides had hardened. The army, believing that it was there in a peacekeeping role, increasingly found itself in an unenviable position. Riots on the Protestant Shankill Road in October 1969 were a foretaste of what was to come, as a policeman lost his life to a Loyalist bullet. A warning by General Freeland, General Officer Commanding (GOC) of the army in Northern Ireland, that petrol bombers were in extreme danger of being shot after severe rioting in the Catholic Ballymurphy estate only furthered the mistrust that many Catholics now felt towards the army. The decision to allow the Orange parades for the 12 July celebrations was another crucial error, for it showed that Stormont was not serious about the grievances that Catholics had about what they saw as sectarianism from Protestants. Stormont began to see the army as a tool to enforce its law and order decisions, which were invariably aimed at the Catholic minority.

The roots of the Falls Curfew, and of the reactions on both sides, go back decades, but it was the events in the Short Strand area of Belfast the week before that provided the catalyst. Fierce rioting on 27 June after a series of Orange marches throughout the city was the moment when the newly formed Provisional IRA (PIRA) was, although slightly prematurely, in action. St Matthews, the Catholic Church for the area, was the scene for severe sectarian violence between Protestants and Catholics. This intensified as the evening wore on, and soon gunfire was heard. Debate is still ongoing about who attacked first, but what is known is that some members of PIRA, led by veteran Republican Billy McKee, decided to defend the church, returning fire as they did. Nationalists within this Catholic enclave believed that another Protestant 'pogrom' was under way. The army stood by and did not become involved, as it was severely under pressure elsewhere in the city. It is widely believed to be the first military defensive (or offensive*) action by the Provisionals, and convinced more hard-line Unionists that the IRA, in whatever guise, was now a serious threat to the stability of the state. Fallout from these events, both politically and militarily, was to have a major impact on what happened the following weekend.

As with many events in the troubled history of Northern Ireland, the controversial aspects of the Falls Curfew are based on a number of issues, each one equally important in the subsequent development of the conflict. British governmental indifference to the conditions within the state, particularly the position of Catholics, the presence of the sectarian 'B' Specials and the Royal Ulster Constabulary (RUC) on the streets of the Falls up to and including the disturbances of August 1969, and their heavy-handed approach led many within these areas to believe that only the IRA could defend them. This was especially true after the weekend of the Curfew. The army, and especially the GOC, also came under heavy criticism about the events in Short Strand the week before, and it was widely believed within army and Unionist circles that the weapons used by the Provisionals in Short Strand emanated from the lower Falls area.

While the Short Strand incident was a defining moment in the history of the rise of the Provisionals, it was also a defining moment in the army's attitudes towards the Catholic population; many in the upper echelons of government and the army now believed that areas such as the lower Falls were a haven for terrorism. It was inevitable that the army was going to react to the criticism directed at it by elements within the Stormont regime, the media and Protestants. The following weekend, acting on a piece of information handed to the police, a combined search operation between the army and the RUC was launched in Balkan Street, in the lower Falls, to recover weapons alleged to have been used the previous weekend. The Falls Curfew had begun and with it the complete deterioration of army–Catholic relations and the subsequent rise of the Provisional IRA.

The legality of many actions carried out by the army in this period has also come under some scrutiny. The issue of the legality of the Curfew, however, is one that has not been satisfactorily answered for many of the people living in the lower Falls at the time. To this day many still believe that the actions of the army on the weekend of 3–5 July 1970 were illegal. There is no doubt that a curfew was ordered, albeit to supress the movement of

---

* Professor Warner believes that it was an offensive action.

individuals and vehicles around the lower Falls. There are many reports on record that the army used this term, and a 'press release' was circulated on the night of 3–4 July stating that an 'immediate curfew' was in operation. Did General Freeland have the authority to do this? If not, who had? Was it Stormont or Westminster? Was there any legal precedent for the action? The troops were under the command of Freeland, who in turn was responsible to the Ministry of Defence in London. Was authorisation given by London? The Falls Curfew was a military operation. The conduct of the army towards the population of the area will be discussed in more detail later in the book, but suffice it to say here that there are many eyewitness accounts of the sheer scale of the destruction meted out in the area.

The Falls Curfew on the weekend of 3–5 July 1970 was a defining moment in the relationship between the Catholics of west Belfast and the British army. The army was now seen by Catholics, almost unanimously, as an oppressive and brutal occupying force, there to add support to a discredited and sectarian Unionist regime in Stormont. This simplistic view of the presence of the army on the streets of Northern Ireland, and particularly the Falls, played into the hands of the infant Provisional IRA and encouraged many young Catholics to join up to what they firmly believed to be their only true defenders.

The British army was thus the public face of what was seen as British imperialism in Ireland. It is no surprise, therefore, that the army was eventually on the receiving end of the anger that was generated by these events. For decades Republicanism had stipulated that the root cause of all of Ireland's troubles lay in the British presence, economically and militarily, and that the only answer was the complete removal of that presence. By the 1950s this was not a major issue amongst Catholics in the Province; equality and better living conditions were of paramount importance. The Republican mantra, however, was still dedicated to driving the British out. What had begun, therefore, as arguably a sectarian conflict in August 1969, quickly manifested into an issue of nationality through the incompetence of the army, Stormont and London.

This book will show that while the army's reputation amongst Catholics was ruined by the time the Curfew was at an end, aided by the aggressive house searches conducted by troops in the lower Falls, the upper echelons of the establishment, both in Northern Ireland and in Britain, allowed this alienation to happen over a period of decades, and thus encouraged the rise of a new militant Republicanism in the shape of the Provisional IRA.

To understand the events leading up to the Falls Curfew, it is necessary to go back in Irish history to understand how Catholics eventually became a minority in the state of Northern Ireland, how an inferiority complex was imbued into Catholic society, especially within the north of the country, and how the government in London, whether inadvertently or purposely, allowed the situation in Northern Ireland to develop from partition. The descent into sectarian conflict in August 1969 will also be given special consideration here; this will help the reader to understand the fears of the Catholics of the Falls Road at the time of the Curfew nearly a year later.

'THE IRISH QUESTION'

'The flame of Irish nationality is inextinguishable.'
Winston Churchill, Manchester, 1912[1]

I

On 21 June 1921 George V of England opened the new Northern Ireland parliament in Belfast. The event, marked with all the pomp and splendour associated with such royal occasions, was the climax of a protracted struggle by Protestants to remain under British rule and out of the almost homogenous Catholic state that was taking shape to the south. The king's speech on that day also reflected the aspirations and hopes of many within the British establishment, who hoped that the Government of Ireland Act of the previous December would finally rid British political life of the 'Irish Question'. In an address to the throngs of people who packed into Belfast that day, he stated:

> I appeal to all Irishmen to pause, to forgive and forget, to stretch out the hand of forbearance and conciliation, and to join in making for the land which they love a new era of peace, contentment and good will.[2]

It was a clear enough message, and one that the British parliament hoped would reach certain sections of the population of the new Northern Irish state, who at that moment were engaged in serious sectarian and inter-communal violence along the same interfaces where it had erupted on a number of occasions during the last century and would erupt again in following decades: the Falls and Shankill districts of west Belfast.

The root causes of this violence stretch back hundreds of years, and are a combination of mutual hatred, suspicion and domination of Ireland by the English, a dynamic and harrowing story which cannot be told in full here. England for the past 800 years has, and continues to be, a dominating factor in the taught history of Ireland. Most narratives of Irish history and thus of Ireland's relationship with England are full of such historical figures as Cromwell, James, William of Orange and Elizabeth I. Students of Irish history, especially in the Republic, would be taught for decades that, beginning in the twelfth century, the movement of Norman soldiers into Ireland was the start of England's long domination over the Irish. This is a wide generalisation, however. The majority of the lands of Ireland were still under Irish control for a considerable period of time after this. Irish chieftains still held sway over large tracts of land. Ireland, though, was not at peace during this period. Inter-tribal conflict and intermittent wars with the English ensured that the country was in a state of virtual anarchy for centuries. By the time of Elizabeth Tudor's reign in the sixteenth century, Ireland was still not under complete English control; their limited influence was confined to a section of the east coast known as the 'Pale'.[3] Ulster, the ancient and historic province, was at the time one of the most rebellious areas outside English domination.

In order to quell these 'unruly Irish', the English began a series of 'plantations', awarding land to various nobles and merchants who were loyal to the English crown. The immediate effect of these plantations was the removal of the native, Catholic Irish further west, confiscation of their lands and a build-up of loyal, Protestant migrants. Many of these were Scottish, and Presbyterian, which would have a major impact on future events. John Darby wrote:

> The Plantation of Ulster was unique among Irish plantations in that it set out to attract colonists of all classes from England, Scotland and Wales by generous offers of land. Essentially it sought to transplant a society to Ireland. The native Irish remained, but were initially excluded from the towns built by the Planters, and banished to the mountains and bogs on the margins of the land they had previously owned. The sum of the Plantation of Ulster was the introduction of a foreign community, which spoke a different language, and represented an alien culture and way of life …[4]

Religious persecution in Ireland also became a major issue at this time, and subsequent events have gone down in folklore on both sides of the divide. The Irish uprising of 1641 in which thousands of Protestants died was one major example; walls of public buildings back in England were covered with gruesome pictures of the butchery associated with the rising. In 1649, after seizing control in England at the execution of Charles I, Oliver Cromwell, the Lord Protector, embarked on a journey to Ireland to clear up remnants of the Royalist forces entrenched there since the end of the Civil War. His Puritan faith in God and his own memories of the 1641 massacres also ensured he nurtured a deep hatred for Catholicism. His subsequent violent and brutal sackings of the towns of Drogheda and Wexford in 1649, with many civilians allegedly amongst his victims, ensured that in Irish Catholic eyes English domination, no matter who was in charge, was brutal, sectarian and evil.

These events were thus enshrined into the collective Irish consciousness, leaving an indelible mark, and have passed down the generations, albeit with a certain amount of the usual elaboration. The very name Cromwell still evokes strong passions in Ireland, while at the same time a statue to his memory stands outside the Houses of Parliament, an example of how one man can evoke such conflicting emotions on both sides of the Irish Sea. Cromwell's time in Ireland stands for brutality; he himself wrote of the suffering he had inflicted on the town of Drogheda in a letter to parliament: 'I am persuaded that this is a righteous judgement of God upon these barbarous wretches.'

But was the campaign by Cromwell as violent as many historians make out? Cromwell himself said that he did not target civilians, although many were invariably caught up in the maelstrom. Such were the rules of war in the period. Richard Aldous and Niamh Puirsell, however, add to the debate by stating that:

Some contemporary accounts suggested his men killed every soldier, priest and civilian they came across. The level of violence was shocking even for the times. Perhaps most infamously, St Peter's church was razed and the 100 people who had sought sanctuary inside were burned alive.[5]

Other historians attest that the church was full of the remnants of the Royalist forces in the town. This is a clear example of how history can be used to form a myth about an event.

How many civilians died at Drogheda will never be known. What is known, however, is that many of the civilians were either forcibly moved to Connaught, in the west of Ireland, or shipped off to other English territories in the Caribbean.[6] Thus Cromwell left an imprint on Irish history that cemented a hatred for England that has lasted many centuries. For no matter what Cromwell's legacy is to the English, his name will forever be associated with Ireland.

By 1688 the 'Glorious Revolution' was underway in England, with the Catholic King James dethroned in favour of his Protestant son-in-law, William of Orange. Protestantism was in the ascendency in England and was also making

major inroads into Ireland, especially in the north-east. The polarisation of the
two communities in Ireland had now begun, but it would be hastened with
an event in 1690 that is still remembered amongst Protestants in the north of
Ireland as *their* victory over the 'Papists' (a derogative term for Catholics).

James decided to make a stand in Ireland, and ultimately win back his
throne. It was not to be. His armies were routed at the 'Battle of the Boyne',[7]
and William and his Protestant dynasty were now firmly in control in
England. Although this was not the last battle (James's armies did not fully
surrender until the following year), it is this battle that has gained mythi-
cal status amongst northern Protestants, who were keen to manifest their
assumed rightful superiority over the 'native' Catholics, and which has subsequently gone down as such from generation to generation.

Over the next 200 years, Catholics in Ireland suffered greatly at the hands
of the ruling English. A system of penal laws was enacted,[8] designed to per-
secute Catholics and keep them out of public life, and they did much to
breed ferment within Ireland towards English rule. The establishment in
England viewed Catholicism as dangerous; indeed, as Rafferty suggests in
Catholicism in Ulster, it was viewed as 'traitorous'.[9] Many of England's over-
seas enemies were Catholic nations; the 'unruly native Irish' were therefore
seen as a sort of 'fifth column' within their midst, ready to help England's
enemies at any given moment.

In Ireland, it is suggested that every generation has risen up against the
English. While this is clearly an exaggeration, many generations of Irish did
indeed rebel against their English masters. The Rebellion of Ulster in 1641,
in which the native Irish attempted to regain their lands after the Plantations,
the advent of the 'Whiteboys' in 1760, who destroyed Protestant landowners'
crops and livestock, followed by the 'Ribbonmen' and Wolfe Tone and his
'United Irishmen' in 1798, are but a few examples. All these events created a
sense of defiance, identity and belonging amongst the native, Catholic Irish.
Protestants in turn formed the 'Orange Order' in 1796, in order to celebrate
the memory of William of Orange and his defeat of James II. More ostensibly, though, it was an anti-Catholic organisation, dedicated to upholding the
Protestant tradition.

The Rebellion of 1798, in which both Protestants and Catholics participated, and especially the threat of invasion from France, persuaded the
English that something had to be done to pacify the country. In 1801, an
Act of Union between the parliaments of England and Ireland came into
law. Ireland was reduced, as Robert Kee states, to a component part of the
United Kingdom.[10] The collaboration between Protestant and Catholic
in 1798 was short lived, however, and mutual suspicions and animosity

returned. Protestants after the Union saw their position in Ireland as secure, their feelings of superiority over Catholics increased by the advent of the Industrial Revolution and the increase in wealth in the industrialised north-east of the country, which held the majority of Protestants. Irish members of parliament returned to London were Protestant, as Catholics were not allowed to run for election. Control over the Irish by the English establishment was virtually complete.

There were still seeds of discontent amongst Catholics, however, and it was quickly realised that a political agenda was needed if Catholics were to gain any rights within Ireland. Daniel O'Connell with his mass meetings was the first in a long line of people who attempted to awake the Irish psyche politically, and thus enable Irish people to agitate for more freedoms from the English. His grasp of the concept of peaceful mass protest and popular support enabled him through his organisation, the Catholic Association, to win emancipation for Catholics in the 1830s. This removed any legal aspects left over from the old Penal Laws, enabling Catholics to become more politically aware and take seats in parliament. Moreover through this, the Repeal of the Act of Union became a mainstay, and goal, of Irish Catholic politics for the rest of the century.

Perhaps the most enduring aspect of ill feeling between England and the Catholics of Ireland was the 'Great Famine' of the 1840s.[11] Robert Kee somewhat surprisingly suggests that this event had the same effect on the Irish national consciousness as the 'German "Final Solution"'[12] on the Jews in the 1930s – a strong statement. It certainly holds an important place in Irish history today, and is still remembered with bitterness and sadness within Irish society. It is Ireland's greatest catastrophe. The Potato Blight[13] hit the crops of the peasant farmers of Ireland for three years running. Conservative estimates say that at least a million people died from starvation in this period. At least another million more were to emigrate to America and Britain. Although the British established relief committees, these proved to be a failure. As Aldous and Puirséll suggest: 'What turned shortage into famine ... was the fiasco of inadequate relief mechanisms to deal with the effects of the crises.'[14]

The British imported cheap maize from the United States, but this in itself was not enough, as exports of cattle and other foodstuffs were still in progress from Ireland and the maize was in most cases inedible. British ignorance of the suffering of the Irish was firmly etched into Irish minds. Niall Ferguson, in *We Declare*, said: 'Not even the most jingoistic Brit could deny that in the mid-1840s the British not only failed to alleviate, but actually exacerbated, one of the great catastrophes of the 19th century.'[15]

It could hardly be classed as a Famine, though, in the strictest sense. There were plenty of foodstuffs in Ireland, from corn and maize to livestock. This, however, was not made available to the starving peasant farmers; it was exported for foreign consumption at their expense.

The population of Ireland, approaching 9 million just before the Famine, was down to just over 6 million by 1852, and continued to drop well into the next century. Forced emigration from Ireland also had the effect of exporting a hatred for the British establishment that fostered numerous organisations abroad, especially in the United States, dedicated to the removal of the British from Ireland. While the worst years of the famine were over by 1850, emigration was still a mainstay of Irish life. For those who could not afford to emigrate, the city was the only place where food and work might be found and, as in Britain at the advent of the Industrial Revolution, a great rural to urban movement began. However, according to Conor Cruise O'Brien, the Revolution 'had largely passed Ireland by ... except for the north east, where the Protestant population was developing linen and ship building industries'.[16]

This mention of the north-east, with its growing Protestant population, shows how much of this part of Ireland, although affected by the famine, avoided its most severe ravages. It also goes some way to explain how the population of the hinterland and town of Belfast dramatically increased through destitute Catholic labourers moving in search of work. These labourers moved to Belfast in their thousands. In 1757, of a population of around 8,500, the total number of Catholics in the city was just over 500, or 6 per cent of the total.[17] By 1861 the Catholics in the city numbered over 41,000, or 34 per cent. Concentrations of Catholics also appeared in the Ballymacarett area, and along the Falls Road the Catholic population increased rapidly. North of the city centre, the Catholic population rose dramatically as well; this was mainly based around York Street.[18] The fact that Catholics concentrated together into their own areas, and that future movements of population invariably followed this pattern, shows that segregation was most probably occurring at this point.

Catholics and Protestants were taking radically different courses in Ireland. Although their paths crossed many times in the history of Ireland, by the late nineteenth century their differences were virtually irreconcilable. Catholics were beginning to become enlightened, through politics, by the idea of self-determination for the Irish. Protestants, however, believed that the political awareness of the Catholics would eventually drive a wedge between them and the Union, and feared a Catholic Irish parliament in Dublin which they thought would suppress the religious beliefs and freedoms they cherished. This fear was also based on economics; the backward state of the rest of the country compared to the industrialised north-east was a critical issue for Protestants.

Thus the move towards 'Home Rule',[19] a form of limited independence, became a burning political issue in Ireland, and Britain, towards the end of the century. The idea of Home Rule as a popular movement first began to appear in the early 1870s and initially encompassed Protestants within its structure. Nevertheless, as it became a widespread political issue, it became increasingly associated with Catholics and the right of Irish self-determination.

Protestants in the north of Ireland began to react against any idea of Home Rule for Ireland. Led by Edward Carson, a Dublin lawyer, they began to campaign against any severance with the 'mother country'. Mary Harris wrote:

> Faced with the growing power of the Catholic majority [in the whole of Ireland] and the increasing influence of the Catholic Church, most Protestants sank their differences and united in opposition to Home Rule. Unionists, as those who sought to maintain their position within the United Kingdom were called, argued their case in print, in parliament and in public speeches.[20]

A 'Solemn League and Covenant',[21] in defence of their 'equal citizenship' with the United Kingdom, was signed by over 450,000 people in September 1912. A proto-paramilitary force, the Ulster Volunteer Force (UVF) was formed, with a southern counterpart, the Irish Volunteers, following soon after. Guns were illegally landed at Larne on the north-east coast in 1914 in readiness to defend their right to stay within the United Kingdom. The country was set for civil war.

Behind all the preparations for war, however, there was a gradual realisation within the British establishment that the Protestants of north-east Ireland would have to be omitted and accommodated separately from any settlement with nationalist Ireland, and the idea of the partition of the country began to be actively discussed within government circles. The first aspect of this centred on the complete severance of the province of Ulster from the rest of Ireland, but Unionists baulked at this idea, fearing that too many Catholics would be included in the new state, thus limiting their power. A four-county solution of Derry, Antrim, Armagh and Down was proposed, but this was rejected as being economically unviable.[22] By 1914 a six-county northern state, closely aligned with, and more importantly part of, the United Kingdom was actively discussed by politicians as the best and possibly the only viable solution. In this six-county state, Protestants would outnumber Catholics by a ratio of 2:1.

The advent of the First World War, however, forced the Home Rule agenda on to the back burner, and quietened Protestant fears for the moment, as British governmental duties were taken up with rearmament and transporting the British Expeditionary Force (BEF) to France. But the war did

not quieten the more militant voices of Irish nationalism; the old adage
'England's difficulty is Ireland's opportunity'[23] was certainly in the minds of
many. Nevertheless, many thousands of Irishmen enrolled in the British army
and supported the war effort, a significant number of these from the south.
Two singular events during the ensuing four-year period, however, would
have a dramatic effect on relations between the British and Irish and, more
importantly, between the Catholics and Protestants of Belfast and the rest of
Northern Ireland in subsequent decades.

II

The first of these events was an ill-timed and poorly supported nationalist
uprising in Dublin beginning on Easter Monday, 1916. A group of dedicated
and militant nationalists, led by Padraig Pearse and James Connolly, took over
the General Post Office (GPO) in Sackville Street (now O'Connell Street)
and various other strategic positions around Dublin, and proceeded to read
out a proclamation declaring an independent Irish Republic. Hopelessly
outnumbered by reinforcements from Britain, however, with British gun-
boats sailing up the Liffey to shell the rebel bases, the rebels surrendered a
week later, leaving the centre of Dublin in ruins. Local people, seeing the
destruction of their city, openly abused and taunted the rebels as they were
marched away. The cause of Irish self-determination seemed all but lost
within the ruins of the centre of Dublin.

It was the subsequent trials and executions of the main leaders however
that enshrined the rising in Irish folklore. Execution followed execution as
the British attempted to make examples of the nationalist leaders, whom they
considered traitors, especially at a time of danger to the mother country. James
Connolly, who was well known throughout Ireland, was executed in a chair
after he was injured in the fighting. Thus the events of Easter 1916 and the
subsequent deaths of the leaders of the rebellion at the hands of the British
became synonymous with Irish attempts to gain nationhood and cemented a
deep hatred for the English presence in Ireland in many southern Irish minds.

On 1 July 1916 the Battle of the Somme began in France, a desperate
attempt by the Western Allies to break the two-year deadlock on the Western
Front. The UVF, initially discouraged from leaving Ireland in the period of
high tension at the beginning of the war, eventually left for France. The first
day of the battle proved to be deadly for many divisions, and the 36th Ulster
Division (including the UVF) was no different. On that first day they suffered
more than 5,000 casualties; over the duration of the war the division had over

33,000 casualties. In Protestant and Unionist minds, this sacrifice confirmed their status as loyal British citizens and they assumed, correctly as it turned out, that Britain would not abandon them to a disloyal Catholic Ireland.

At the conclusion of the war in 1918 the political strife and violence that had engulfed Ireland before the war now returned with a vengeance. At the British general election in 1918 the old Irish Nationalist Party, a bastion of moderate Irish Catholic opinion, was wiped off the Irish electoral map by a radical new force, Sinn Féin (we ourselves), established in the early 1900s, which won the majority of Irish seats.[24] However, instead of taking their seats at Westminster they set up an illegal 'Dáil' (parliament) in Dublin. On the same day the Irish Republican Army (IRA), the newly formed militant wing of republicanism led by Michael Collins, and the successor to the Irish Republican Brotherhood (IRB), began to attack British security personnel throughout Ireland.

The country descended into chaos. IRA attacks in the south against members of the security forces ran parallel with sectarian attacks on Catholics in Belfast and other areas; the Falls Road in Belfast and the roads leading to the Shankill district were particularly violent at this point. The British recruited ex-soldiers to bolster the security within the country; these were collectively called the 'Black and Tans'.[25] This force became synonymous with violent attacks on belligerents and civilians alike, further feeding the separatist movement and hatred of the British security forces.[26] During this period Home Rule, with partition and two parliaments, became law but was completely ignored in the south where a full-scale insurrection was now under way.

This 'Anglo-Irish War' was bloody, indiscriminate and ferocious, but it could not continue indefinitely. The IRA was close to exhaustion after months of guerrilla warfare, and atrocities committed by both sides were alienating large sections of Irish and British society. A truce between the two belligerents was declared and after protracted negotiations between the British, led by Lloyd George, and the Irish, led by Michael Collins, a treaty was signed giving the Irish slightly more than Home Rule but not the united Ireland many had fought for. Irish Catholics had their state, now named the 'Irish Free State', and Protestants had theirs; but, held up in enclaves in Belfast, Derry and around the border areas of the new states, was a sizeable minority who, as time went on, would be judged as inferior to their Protestant neighbours, and would have fewer rights and employment opportunities. Protestants were in control, and they now made sure that it remained that way.

By the time peace returned to the country, Catholics and Protestants were more polarised than ever. Sporadic IRA attacks still occurred throughout the north and along the border, instilling a sense of siege and defence amongst

Protestants. Many Catholics in the north did not recognise the political structures of the new state; for instance, many councils in nationalist areas of the north pledged their allegiance to the southern parliament (Michael Collins, the Minister of Finance in the new state, was secretly funding these councils along with IRA border units in an attempt to undermine the Northern Irish state). The ceasefire and subsequent British treaty with the south also created initial difficulties; amongst these were a Council of Ireland which drew immense anger from the Protestant community, and a Border Commission designed finally to demarcate the border between north and south on demographic grounds.

The border itself ran along the boundaries of counties, rather than around major centres of population. Thus, it ran through farms, splitting them between north and south, down the centres of streets in the towns and villages that dotted the old county borders, and even through people's houses. The Border Commission intended to look at these discrepancies, but Protestant public opinion was angered. (The ensuing civil war in the new Irish Free State in the south, as bloody as the War of Independence, alienated many Catholics in the north as well. However, it was also powerful in convincing Protestants that the IRA was still a major threat to them.)[27] As far as the ruling Unionist government of Northern Ireland was concerned, the six-county entity was their territory, and they were adamant that a transfer of territory to the south was out of the question.

After much deliberation, and an alleged leak to the press of sensitive information,[28] the boundary was left as it was, including substantial nationalist areas with no allegiance to the northern parliament whatsoever. Protestants were not budging from their position. To have transferred tracts of land to the south, even those with a Catholic majority, would have looked like surrender, and would most probably have made the new state economically unviable, due to the amount of land that was inhabited by nationalists. Thus, the fear of being absorbed into a united Ireland was ever present in Unionist dealings with the Boundary Commission.

Protestant fears of the minority left in Northern Ireland were huge, and formed the bedrock of their subsequent governance of the state. They knew the IRA was still active, was still present in the Falls district of Belfast and in the fields and rural towns. They also knew it was present in the southern state. The Protestants were in a majority in the north, yet still feared a resurgence of violence through the minority in the north and the majority in the south. Peter Bull wrote:

> In the North, the Catholics were a minority, but in the context of Ireland as a whole, the Protestant majority in the North were also a minority.

This resulted in a siege mentality, in which both communities felt beleaguered, and deeply threatened by the other.[29]

The late A.C. Hepburn also summed up Protestant feelings towards the minority during the period between the two world wars when he said:

The underlying problem in the new six-county province of Northern Ireland was the sharp divide between the Protestant majority and the reluctant and resentful Catholic minority amounting to more than one-third of its population. In parts of western Northern Ireland, Catholics formed a majority. Furthermore, neither the British government nor the new Northern Irish government made any effort to achieve reconciliation between Protestants and Catholics. The political structure established in Northern Ireland by the British government emphasized majority rule and offered no encouragement to the governing party to seek out the middle ground. The Unionist government in turn made little perceptible effort to do so. Thinly veiled government rhetoric equated patriotic opposition to nationalism with anti-Catholicism and Catholicism with disloyalty. The bias was reflected in civil service hiring patterns. This Northern Irish Protestant point of view was only reinforced by the increasingly hard-line rhetoric of the province's southern neighbour. In 1937 the Irish Free State (under the new name of Eire or, in English, simply 'Ireland') adopted a new constitution that claimed jurisdiction over the entire island of Ireland, 'pending reintegration of the national territory,' and declared the Roman Catholic religion to have a special position in the state.[30]

The Irish Free State to the south was on a path of disentanglement with Britain, and as such was deliberately or non-deliberately distancing itself from the Catholic minority in the north. As Rafferty states:

The results of the civil war in the Irish Free State to some extent began a sense of alienation and despair amongst northern Catholics in their dealings with both parts of Ireland. While many northerners actually fought on the Free State side, it quickly became clear that the Cosgrave government, despite the presence in it of northerners such as Ernest Blythe, did not – understandably – intend to give northern Catholic affairs a high priority in Free state policy.[31]

III

As time went on the issue of partition became embedded in the collective psyche of Irish Catholics both north and south. But the majority of these either could not or would not act on it. Political parties in the south, while claiming unification with the north as part of the overall answer to their problems, did not follow this through with more aggressive anti-partition policies. Only the politician DeValera and his Fianna Fáil party retained an ideological link to the issue of partition (DeValera would tour many countries where the Irish diaspora lived in the 1950s, trying to gather support for unification). Also, the handling of the one million Protestants in the north posed a major issue in any discussion on partition in the south. Thus, unification became an unattainable dream for many. The IRA was still there, proclaiming the Republican dream of a united Ireland without British interference, but it was a weak and divided organisation since the treaty with Britain, partition and the ensuing civil war in the south. All of this ensured that Protestants were constantly on the alert for any signs of dissention from Catholics in their community:

> Many Protestants perceived Northern Catholics as the enemy within. The Catholic Church's outspoken criticisms of the government's failure to protect Catholics from attack reinforced anti-Catholic feeling. The Irish Free State's intense hostility towards the Belfast government exacerbated Protestants of siege.[32]

Shortly after the establishment of the new state in the north, the government enacted the Special Powers Act, initially in response to on-going friction over partition. Even in its milder aspects, however, the Act could only be seen as draconian. It gave far-reaching powers to police in dealing with disorder within the state, allowed the banning of parades and marches, and gave the government wide powers in the control of the populace. Nationalists have always believed that this Act was designed to minimise any unrest amongst the Catholic minority; indeed, statistics show that in the majority of cases it was Catholics who bore the subsequent brunt of the provisions of the Act.[33]

In the meantime Unionists began to take over control of the instruments of power in the new state. No Catholics were appointed to any of the influential posts in government. The civil war in the south between supporters and opponents of the Anglo-Irish Treaty ensured that Northern Ireland would stay on a permanent war footing. The Special Powers Act, initially enacted as a temporary measure in the emergency, was renewed annually and subsequently became permanent.[34] Craig, as we have seen, destroyed any northern input in the Boundary Commission and returned to Belfast with the Protestant state more secure than ever. The setting up of the Royal Ulster Constabulary (RUC) and the auxiliary forces of 'A', 'B' and 'C' Specials, who were predominantly Protestant, was another aspect of a society that was increasingly moving towards a one-party state, with the minority in perpetual opposition. The RUC was also predominantly Protestant; Catholics either did not wish to join or were unable to because of peer pressure or community loyalties. Anders Boserup summed up the methodology behind the new state:

> After Partition a peculiar social and political system developed in Northern Ireland. It was based on two main elements; on the one hand the continued threat to the state posed by militant Republicanism in the South and Catholic disloyalty in the North, and, on the other, the perpetuation of the 'Orange' coalition and its sectarian policies.[35]

While the state consolidated around a Unionist-dominated structure, from the fixing of council wards to ensure Unionist majority in council, both local and national, to the absence of a universal one person, one vote structure in local elections, the Catholics retreated into their own areas. A polarised society was now firmly in existence in Northern Ireland.

Catholics tended to socialise amongst themselves, and went to different areas to shop, work and attend church. Working-class Protestant areas were similar. Education in the state was segregated, although this was a product of the polarisation of the two communities and not a move sponsored by the government. Catholic children were educated by their church while Protestants chose the established state schools.[36] Protestants saw this type of segregation within the Catholic community as an example of the authoritarian nature of Catholicism, as many Catholic schools, on orders from the Catholic hierarchy, refused to recognise the established Ministry of Education.[37]

Those nationalist political parties that were in existence consistently refused to participate in political life, as the abolition of proportional representation (PR)[38] gave Unionists control over many areas, even with nationalist majorities. Politics in Northern Ireland thus did not follow the traditional paths of left, middle or right wing; they were conducted along lines of religious faith. The ideological and political paradox of working-class Protestants voting for right-wing Unionists was a confusing feature of political life in Northern Ireland, but Catholics always voted, when they did, for the nationalist parties. Decades of research by historians have shown that the advent of a Unionist-controlled devolved government in Northern Ireland in 1922 did indeed usher in a period of discrimination towards the Catholic minority.[39] The old fears of the war years, of IRA insurrection and of the enemy within, all added to the siege mentality of Protestants, and increased the need for dominance over their Catholic neighbours. As Gerry Adams stated in *Before the Dawn*:

> The north remained under a permanent state of emergency. Republicans were imprisoned in every decade. The Unionist instinct was to rise to any hint of threat and to ban parades by Catholics. They also experienced a geographical and constitutional insecurity, fearing that they would be gobbled up by nationalist Ireland.[40]

Apart from the few examples mentioned above, there were many more cases of sectarianism and discrimination on a state-wide scale. The continuation of the Special Powers Act after the return of peace in the mid-1920s and the continuation of the notorious 'B' Specials, the exclusively Protestant Special Constabulary, are but two examples. Internment without trial, whereby suspects could be imprisoned indefinitely, was another, and was used on a number of occasions throughout the fifty-year Stormont regime, at one point lasting for eight years.[41] Although these measures were designed to curb any form of dissention, the majority of those interned were Catholics.

Catholics within the Northern Irish state always cited employment as a main area of discrimination, in that a working-class Catholic would find it almost impossible to secure employment while his Protestant counterpart with the same skills was more likely to be in work. This is an area that is undergoing major study, however, as many historians are re-evaluating just how much discrimination occurred. As Christopher Hewitt suggested:

> It is generally argued not only that Catholics were denied political rights and their 'fair share' of government goods and services, but that they suffered from economic discrimination. The Stormont government concentrated funds for economic development in the heavily Protestant areas east of the Bann [river] while ignoring the more Catholic west.[42]

While these allegations are debated by historians, it is worth mentioning here that in 1961 during local elections in Belfast the three candidates for the St George's Unionist Association 'employ[ed] over 70 people and [have] never employed a Roman Catholic'.[43] There are many more examples of Protestant employers taking pride in not hiring Catholics, and they were openly encouraged by bellicose statements from leaders and men in high positions of power. Sir Basil Brooke, prime minister from 1943 to 1963, appealed in a speech to Loyalists in July 1933 that they should, 'whenever possible ... employ good

Protestant lads and lassies'.[44] James Craig (later Lord Craigavon), first prime minister in 1921, also boasted of a 'Protestant Parliament for a Protestant people' in 1934, clearly an ominous sign to Catholics.[45]

The Second World War also polarised the two communities in the state. Britain's declaration of war on Germany on 3 September 1939 meant that Northern Ireland became involved. However, the Irish Free State immediately followed a policy of neutrality, due in part to a lack of a sufficient defence force but more to an assertion of complete independence.[46] Unionists in Northern Ireland were aghast at this decision, considering it as disloyal to the empire at a time of need. Northern Ireland, however, played a vital role in the war, its strategic ports and shipbuilding industry adding to the overall war effort. Belfast was heavily bombed during the war, on account of its heavy industries. United States troops were stationed there in their thousands in preparation for the assault on occupied Europe, much to the anger of the Irish government.[47] Britain's overtures to the Irish government concerning support for a united Ireland if the country entered the war on the Allied side also angered Unionists, and galvanised the 'siege' mentality of many Protestants.

By the end of the war, the two communities in Ireland were further apart than ever. Irish neutrality, while asserting its sovereignty, alienated the state from other countries, especially Britain. Unionists in the north had shown loyalty to the British, and were rewarded in the Ireland Act of 1949. This was enacted in response to Eire declaring itself a republic, reaffirming its territorial claim to the 'six counties' in the north and leaving the Commonwealth in 1948. The Ireland Act was intended to reassure Unionists that their position within the United Kingdom was assured. Chapter 41 of the Act states:

> It is hereby declared that Northern Ireland remains part of His Majesty's dominions and of the United Kingdom and it is hereby affirmed that in no event will Northern Ireland or any part thereof cease to be part of His Majesty's dominions and of the United Kingdom without the consent of the Parliament of Northern Ireland.[48]

This provision, whereby Northern Ireland would remain part of the UK with the consent of the parliament of Northern Ireland, rather than the people, enshrined Unionist domination over the state. With a constant majority within parliament, Protestants were assured of their place within the UK and, with the fixing of electoral boundaries in their favour, this was to remain so. Rousing statements in parliament about the new republic to the south also helped in building the siege mentality of Protestants: 'What the Free State want is the rape of Ulster; it is not marriage. It is the rape of Ulster, and when they have done that dreadful deed they will throw that wretched girl on one side and rob her of means.'[49]

The minority Catholic population in Northern Ireland were now in a position where it was difficult to reap any social or economic benefits. As Richard English suggests:

> ... against the insecure background of a hostile southern Ireland and a large disaffected minority within its own territory, Ulster Unionists had built a Northern Ireland which prized and rewarded loyalty, and within which many Catholics experienced discrimination in areas such as employment, housing and electoral practice.[50]

Governed by a Unionist-dominated government that was dedicated to keeping them as second-class citizens, with few rights and opportunities, they were destined to remain in that position for as long as they were in the minority. The new republic to the south, almost homogenously Catholic, was drifting away from the decades-old issue of partition, and becoming more concerned with its own economic and social issues.[51] The IRA, long the 'protector' of the Republic declared from the steps of the GPO in Dublin in 1916, was now, after the fiasco of its 1956–62 campaign, on a course that would consign it to insignificant, socialist protests about fishing rights on rivers and proposals that elections should now be contested and seats taken – anathema to Republicans. When Northern Irish society finally exploded in the late 1960s, it was the radical, militant element of the IRA that came to the surface, and consigned Cathal Goulding's socialist-leaning IRA to the sidelines.

British governmental involvement in the affairs of the state remained indifferent right into the 1960s. No politicians showed any eagerness to look any deeper into Northern Ireland. Even up to the general election in 1964, when Harold Wilson took office, there was no change in policy. John Conroy, who spent many years in the Clonard district of Belfast in the 1980s, talked about his opinion of the role that Britain played in Northern Ireland before the Troubles:

> As the decades passed, the British paid little attention to the province; the Treasury wrote checks [cheques], the Northern Ireland government passed laws and spent money. In London no senior civil servant worked full time on the north. Until October 1968, the General Department of the Home Office held responsibility for Northern Irish affairs; the office also regulated London taxi cabs, liquor licencing, the protection of animals, and the British version of Daylight Savings time.[52]

However, there were a few MPs who were beginning to show a keen interest in the affairs of the state. Paul Rose was one of these, and he actively tried to counter the rules in parliament about questioning the Stormont government of Northern Ireland. He found his interest in Northern Irish affairs after attending a meeting in Manchester in 1962 about civil liberties. There was an Irish contingent present.[53] He subsequently went on to found the Campaign for Democracy in Ulster, eventually bolstered by a few other MPs. His intention, as he said, was to 'penetrate the blank wall of incomprehension and ignorance about Ulster'.[54]

He also found a similar impenetrable wall at Westminster when he tried to question the system of discrimination he found in Northern Ireland. There follows an appendix discussing how the Westminster parliament was finally made aware of what was happening in an integral part of the United Kingdom:

> During the 14th, 15th and 16th April, 1967 three Labour Members of Parliament, Dr Maurice Miller, (Glasgow Kelvingrove), Mr Stanley Orme, (Salford West) and Mr Paul Rose, (Mlc. Blackley), visited Northern Ireland at the personal invitation of Mr Gerard Fitt, MP. Their objectives were to investigate the position in Northern Ireland with regard to discrimination, electoral law and practice, and the general economic situation. A further objective was to inform a wide spectrum of citizens of Northern Ireland of the activities at Westminster of Labour Members interested in Northern Ireland affairs.[55]

This group of MPs visited various places in Northern Ireland, from Belfast to Derry, and Dungannon, Strabane and Coalisland. They were met with warm greetings from many nationalists. They gave many TV and radio interviews and appeared at many public meetings. The issues of discrimination and gerrymandering in local councils and housing were all discussed. They also met politicians from opposition parties such as the Labour Party, and met many independents and nationalists.[56]

The group's conclusions were that there was overwhelming evidence of the accusations made to them on their visit about discrimination in housing, gerrymandering of boroughs and discrimination in public life, where Catholics were hardly represented in the civil service of Northern Ireland. They left their views of the Unionists to the last paragraph:

> Unionist reaction to the visit was hostile and provocative. The party was described as 'anti-Ulster', and 'interfering and unwelcome'. The Unionists refused to meet the members of the party, although invited to meet them

on both the Saturday and Sunday. The pretext that they could not meet on
a Sunday was a political manoeuvre intended to raise the sectarian issue and
discredit the party in the eyes of devout Protestants. It ignored the fact that
they could have met the party on the Saturday, and that all but the Unionists
attended the meeting in Derry.[57]

As late as June 1968 the Westminster government was still holding back from
any interference in the instruments of government in Northern Ireland. In
the *Tribune Magazine* issue dated 14 June 1968, Andrew Boyd gives a candid
and frank analysis of the effects of the Campaign for Democracy in Ulster on
the Labour government:

> Lord Stoneham is Minister of State at the Home Office, with, it is said,
> 'special responsibility for Northern Ireland.' If that is so then I'm afraid this
> Minister-Peer is not facing up to his responsibilities. He came to Belfast
> last week with words of comfort for nobody but the Tories who control
> Stormont … 'Her Majesty's Government,' he assured the Unionists, is not
> going to interfere in matters which are domestic to Northern Ireland …
> And that is as much as telling Paul Rose, Gerry Fitt and Stanley Orme that
> they had better try their 'Campaign for Democracy' tactics on some other
> country and leave Ulster alone.[58]

No politician in government in Westminster wanted to get their hands dirty
in the 'Irish Bog'.[59] Martin Dillon, in *Trigger Man*, sums up his opinion of
Westminster indifference:

> For some political observers in London, it was the old Irish problem ema-
> nating from a Protestant majority's siege mentality and Catholic resentment
> of the partition of Ireland. The analysis ignored the origins of the ongoing
> conflict – the abdication of responsibility by successive British governments
> in London. For decades, British political leaders viewed Northern Ireland
> as a seemingly intractable problem and preferred a hands off policy. The
> most dangerous consequence of Britain's failure to accept responsibility for
> an integral part of the United Kingdom was that sovereign British gov-
> ernments allowed subordinate Unionist administrations to act as though
> they were sovereign administrations. British political leaders cared little
> that Protestant majority rule was maintained through repressive legisla-
> tion, resulting in the denial of British civil rights to Catholics. Therefore no
> one in Westminster saw the writing on the wall when Catholic civil rights
> marchers took to the streets in the mid-1960s. There was no recognition

that all those historical variables in both communities were the sparks that would light a bonfire and a long war.[60]

Terence O'Neill, educated at Eton College, born in England, prime minister of Northern Ireland since 1963 and considered 'moderate' by Northern Irish standards, was the man who was expected to bring in much-needed reforms and hopefully keep Northern Ireland in the political wilderness.

IV

Catholics in Northern Ireland in the 1960s were still no better off than their parents or grandparents were in the state. The ghettos of the Falls Road and other inner-city areas were still acutely poor and housing was inadequate for the needs of the community. By the late 1960s, however, an active and burgeoning civil rights movement within Northern Ireland, the Northern Ireland Civil Rights Association (NICRA), was gaining ground. Influenced by the civil rights movement in the southern states of America and the rising worldwide tide of protest against the Vietnam War, the movement rapidly gained support from a whole generation of Catholics brought up on free education and enlightened by the university experience. The civil rights movement organised marches and demonstrations, demanding an end to the discriminative system of voting in local elections, the abolition of the Special Powers Act and equality within the society they shared with the majority.[61] This type of active protest, however, ultimately attracted a more militant backlash from many Protestant Loyalists, who saw the movement as a front for extreme Republicanism.

On 5 October 1968, a civil rights march in Derry was the catalyst for violent demonstrations across the state in subsequent months. William Craig, Stormont's Minister of Home Affairs, had banned the march from going ahead. Ignoring this, NICRA went ahead. The march descended into chaos. RUC officers baton-charged the crowds; many people were injured in the melee, including Gerry Fitt MP. The Republic's state TV broadcaster, RTE, was there on the day to film the march. The pictures it filmed were broadcast around the world and did much to undermine Stormont's status.

The government, however, was going ahead with its limited reforms. Below is a selection of them taken from Stormont's accompanying statement to the Cameron Report.

The Reforms of November 1968

The violence and civil disturbances which the Cameron Commission were asked to examine started on 5th October 1968. On 22nd November 1968, the Government of Northern Ireland announced a series of reforms as follows:

(1) Allocation of Houses
The Government undertook to ensure that all housing authorities placed need in the forefront in the allocation of houses, and that future housing allocations would be carried out on the basis of a readily-understood and published scheme.

(2) Investigations of Citizens' Grievances
The Government agreed to consider the need for effective machinery to investigate grievances in an objective way and in the area of Central Government activity to introduce legislation to appoint a Parliamentary Commissioner for Administration.

(3) Implementation of Londonderry Area Plan
The Government announced that it would take all possible steps to ensure that prompt and effective action would be taken to implement a Plan, designed to transform the economic and social life of the City and to assist this objective by the appointment of a strong, well-qualified and objective Development Commission.

(4) Reform of Local Government including the Franchise
The Government indicated its firm intention to complete a comprehensive reform and modernisation of the local government structure within a period of three years – that is, by the end of 1971 – to review the franchise in the context of the organisation, financing and structure of the new local government bodies, and to abolish the company vote in local government.

(5) Special Powers
The Government announced that after discussions it had agreed with the United Kingdom Government that –
(i) as soon as the Northern Ireland Government considered this could be done without undue hazard, such of the Special Powers as are in conflict with international obligations would, as in the past, be withdrawn from current use; but

(ii) in the event of the Northern Ireland Government considering it essential to re-activate such powers, the United Kingdom Government would enter the necessary derogation.[62]

The Special Powers Act was to remain on the statute books, however, and reform of the local government franchise was going to take three years. These reforms were clearly not enough as the civil rights movement moved from strength to strength. To add fuel to an already smouldering fire, another organisation dedicated to reform was born out of a group of students at Queens University in Belfast. Adopting the name People's Democracy (PD), it included future household names in Ireland such as Bernadette Devlin,[63] Eamonn McCann and Michael Farrell. They would end up being at the forefront of socialist agitation in Northern Ireland in the turbulent months leading up to August 1969 and the descent into political and social anarchy.

Further afield, the civil rights movement did succeed in highlighting the inequality within Northern Ireland, despite the growing violence associated with it. O'Neill was acutely aware of the need to placate the rising tide of Catholic anger at their situation. However, meetings with his southern counterpart, Sean Lemass, and public visits to Catholic schools, while making little impact on the Catholic population as a whole, only inflamed hard-line Protestants who saw O'Neill as becoming too liberal in the face of Catholic agitation. Many in the Catholic community now believed after the march on 5 October that only radical and far-reaching changes to the very fabric of Northern Irish society and political life would bring about an equal and peaceful society, whether it was a united Ireland, an equal partnership with the United Kingdom and all the benefits this entailed, or more rights within the governance of the state. However, O'Neill believed, naively as it turned out, that Catholics could be placated by better living conditions, new cars and more employment opportunities. In this way, he believed, the minority Catholic population would happily live under an authoritative Protestant regime.

An example of O'Neill's ignorance of and naïve assumptions about Catholics in the state is highlighted in a speech he gave in 1969, not long after his resignation.

It is frightfully hard to explain to Protestants that if you give Roman Catholics a good job and a good house, they will live like Protestants, because they will see neighbours with cars and television sets. They will refuse to have eighteen children, but if a Roman Catholic is jobless and lives in a most ghastly hovel, he will rear eighteen children on National Assistance … If you treat Roman Catholics with due consideration and kindness, they will live like Protestants and in spite of the authoritative nature of their church.[64]

O'Neill's tenure as prime minister is summed up in this quote from *'We Shall Overcome':The History of the Struggle for Civil Rights in Northern Ireland 1968–1978*:

> He seemed to successfully bring Northern Ireland from the crude sectarianism of the Brookeborough era into the more fashionable sectarianism of the sixties. But his success was nothing more than a media illusion because what O'Neill had achieved was a partial change in attitudes to a 50 year old problem, but he had made no effort to tackle that problem. There was no attempt to change the local government voting system so that one man had one vote and no more than one. He made no reference to the arbitrary powers of arrest and internment under which citizens of the state could be arrested and detained indefinitely without charge or trial. He failed to tackle the serious problem of the unacceptability of the forces of law and order. In short he changed the facade of life in Northern Ireland and left the reality untouched. His true politics emerged when he was asked to implement basic legislative reforms which would have protected the civil rights of the people to whom he waved at his civic weeks. He hung back.
>
> O'Neill failed the first test of liberalism when he neglected the opportunity to implement basic democratic reforms in Northern Ireland. When the civil rights campaign presented him publicly with a set of demands for reform he turned them down. It has been suggested that O'Neill was a prisoner of his own right wing and that the granting of civil rights demands would have forced him out of office, but he came to power in 1963 and the first civil rights demands were not made on a large scale until 1968. His five years in the convent parlour was no substitute for democratic reform.[65]

O'Neill hung back because the limited reforms he did begin were heavily attacked by the right wing of his party. From the outset, O'Neill was in trouble. The hawks within his party were waiting to attack. This ignorance of Catholics within the state was widespread among those in power at Stormont. However, other Protestant radicals saw the upsurge in Catholic agitation as a threat to the whole fabric of the state and feared that a resurgent IRA was about to be unleashed on the Protestant population. Ian Paisley, a radical anti-Catholic Presbyterian, was one of these, and became the voice of extreme Loyalism in the early days leading up to the 'Troubles'.[66] In 1964 two days of rioting occurred in Divis Street, Belfast after Paisley demanded the removal of the Irish Tricolour from the office of Sinn Féin.[67] He was also a vehement critic of the reforms that O'Neill was trying to introduce in the wake of the civil rights agitation, and was imprisoned in 1969 for an illegal demonstration in Armagh, against a civil rights march.

A confidential document highlighting how the Unionist government viewed the Catholic minority within the state was written by a Mr Slinger, in the Ministry of Community Affairs. In it he states:

> A sizable number of people do not accept the validity of the state. How large the number is [is] uncertain but the important point is that the majority believe it to be large. This attitude is seen as provocative and threatening by even moderate Unionists. Unionist fears are in turn heightened by acts of violence against the state, by the facts of the population trends and by the often hostile and bitter attitude of the Republic. The second difficulty is that large numbers of Roman Catholics positively distrust Unionist government and this applies not only to central but, and perhaps even more forcibly, to local administration.[68]

The Unionist government structure, for so long a discriminatory one, was now seeing the fruits of its work.

The PD organised a protest march, beginning on 1 January 1969, from Belfast to Derry in order to highlight the slow pace of reform in Northern Ireland. Their influence for this was the famous civil rights march from Montgomery to Selma in the United States, which highlighted the inequalities of the black community within one of the richest nations on earth. Sectarianism reared its ugly head three days into the march, however, when the marchers were attacked by a combination of Loyalists and off-duty 'B' Specials. The general consensus is that the marchers walked into a carefully prepared ambush, which the RUC was completely aware was going to occur; stones were gathered the previous evening and put in concealed piles at the site. Also, people had been congregating from early morning in readiness.[69]

The march was heavily criticised in the Cameron Commission[70] and by O'Neill, who blamed the marchers themselves for the violence along the route, especially at Burntollet:

> Provided the marchers acted within the law and provided others respected, as law abiding citizens should do, the right of peaceful demonstration there was no reason for physical violence of any sort on the route of the march to Londonderry … Some of the marchers and those who supported them in Londonderry itself have shown themselves to be mere hooligans ready

to attack the police and others ... had this march been treated with silent contempt and allowed to proceed peaceably, the entire affair would have made little mark and no further damage of any sort would have been done to the good name of Ulster.[71]

O'Neill also criticised the Loyalists who attacked the march, but reiterated that the blame for the violence rested firmly on the shoulders of the marchers and those who organised the march. The point was now made, however. Northern Ireland was a state built on sectarianism. By 1969 the situation within the state was at breaking point. Civil rights marches were met with counter-demonstrations by Paisley and his followers, O'Neill was facing a vote of no confidence in Stormont, and Westminster was finally shaking off decades of inaction in Northern Ireland by informing Stormont that any deviation from the reforms set in motion would not be tolerated. Mary Harris commented:

> Following the outbreak of disturbances in 1968 the British government abandoned its long term policy of leaving internal Northern Ireland affairs to the Belfast government. Northern Ireland came under scrutiny in the British parliament and the British press, and Catholic demands for civil rights resonated in an ideological climate ...[72]

Thus Northern Ireland was coming back in from the cold, much to the annoyance of the British establishment. However, coming in it was, and the slow, mild reforms that O'Neill was attempting to put in place were grasped by Harold Wilson, British prime minister, in London, who saw them as the only way to remove the province from British politics again.[73] Wilson put extreme pressure on O'Neill at this point, but O'Neill had his own demons within the Unionist Party to deal with first. Paul Rose, in his book *How the Troubles Came to Northern Ireland*, mentions that Harold Wilson, clearly desperate at this juncture, threatened to withhold increased financial payments to Northern Ireland if the reforms instigated by O'Neill were deviated from in any way; however, this is not mentioned by O'Neill in his version of events.[74]

O'Neill called an election on 3 February 1969 in an attempt to shore up his party and quieten his opponents. He failed. Although he was returned to power, he was to resign the premiership of Northern Ireland in April 1969 after the resignations of Brian Faulkner and many of his backbench MPs proved too much. In November 1970 an article about O'Neill appeared in the *Irish News*:

Why, during his six years of Premiership at Stormont, did he do so little to ensure that Catholics could get houses and jobs, in his anxiety to have them live like Protestants? When houses and jobs were going, even then, Lord O'Neill's[75] henchmen saw to it that, if possible, they were denied to Catholics. Unionists frankly advocated discrimination (and many still do) in pursuit of the preservation of their Protestant privilege. Did their view conflict with that of Prime Minister O'Neill?[76]

O'Neill was succeeded by his cousin James Chichester-Clark.

In August 1969 an Apprentice Boys march took place in Derry, one of hundreds of marches that take place across the state in the summer months. The Apprentice Boys fraternity march every year to commemorate the Siege of Derry in 1689 when King James's siege of the city was defeated by King William's navy. However, the simmering tensions between Catholics and Protestants finally came to an explosive head on this day. Stones were thrown by both sides; the RUC became embroiled with Catholic stone throwers on the outskirts of the Bogside and intense rioting ensued. The 'Battle of the Bogside' lasted for three days, brought the RUC to the point of defeat and brought the British army on to the streets of Belfast and Derry for the first time in fifty years. It would be nearly forty years before they left 'the Irish Bog'.

2

THE FALLS ROAD, REPUBLICANISM, POGROMS AND THE BRITISH

'However much the streetscape has altered, at times for the better and at times not, resilience remains today. The local geography may have changed. The people have not. Part of a political statelet from which it is excluded; the Falls remains a place apart, a state of mind and even, at times, a political statement. But more than all this the Falls is its people.'

Gerry Adams, 1993 [1]

'In view of the continued worsening of the situation in Londonderry City on this date as outlined in the attached copy of a warning message sent to the Home Office, London, and the fact that this situation has deteriorated further since the timing of the message to the Home Office, I now request the assistance of forces under your command in Londonderry City.'

A letter from the Inspector General, Royal Ulster Constabulary to the General Officer Commanding, August 1996, Northern Ireland [2]

I

The Falls Road is a main arterial route out of Belfast city centre that winds its way up to the sprawling housing estates of Turf Lodge and Andersonstown. In Irish, *Bothar na bhFail*, translated as 'the road of the high hedges', [3] was transformed from a winding country lane to a bustling thoroughfare with the advent of the Industrial Revolution, when the increase in demand for linen created working opportunities for rural labourers forced from the land due to lack of employment and the general rural to urban demographic movement. These workers, invariably poor Catholics, settled within the Falls area and the newly constructed side streets, creating a sizable Catholic community in the process.

Similar shifts in population were happening further north and west, with the Shankill Road becoming populated by working-class Protestants.

This working-class community, members of which were extremely loyal to each other and their religion, was, and still is, a deeply committed centre of nationalism and Republicanism. Its proximity to other, more affluent Protestant neighbourhoods near the city centre and its use as a source of cheap unskilled labour for prosperous Protestant mill owners ensured there would always be a sense of 'them and us' about the area. It was also an extremely poor area of Belfast. Paddy Devlin, a prominent Labour (and former IRA) figure within the community in the 1960s and 1970s, touches on this in his auto-biography, *Straight Left*, reminiscing about the hardships of the 'Depression' years in the 1930s and the daily struggles of his parents in keeping food on the table. Gerry Adams also talks about the sheer deprivation of many people in the area, including his own family: 'We were poor, but it didn't matter, at least not to us children. We didn't know any different, and we were too busy to notice.'[4]

Much of this hardship ultimately came from the lack of a skills base for the majority of the people in the community, overcrowding and large families only adding to the deprivation. Moreover, many also attest to the policies of the Unionist-controlled 'Poor Law Guardians' in their dealings with the needy, not only of the Falls area, but also of the Protestant Shankill district as well. Devlin clearly remembers: 'Portly men with gold watch chains stretched across their ample bellies [that] spread terror in the district when they arrived.' This fear was palpable to the mothers and fathers on both sides of the divide as they worried about the visit. The Board of Guardians existed in Northern Ireland up to the late 1940s.

Republicanism in the Falls stems from close-knit family units, networks of friends and roots that were put down decades ago. Generations of families have grown up, lived and died in the Falls, each one imbued with the ideals and aspirations of their parents and their parents before them. Gerry Adams comes from a long line of Republican activists; his uncles Dominic and Paddy Adams and his father were all activists long before 1969.[5] Adams' father was subsequently imprisoned during the Second World War. Adams is also related to another prominent Republican family from the Falls, the Hannaways. Paddy Devlin, whose own parents were very politically aware, stated that he inherited his own political awakening from his parents actively debating politics in the family home.[6]

Not far away were the Protestant streets and roads of the Shankill district. However, to many children growing up on the Falls it was a world away. The closeness of their community enabled many to ignore the more discriminatory aspects of the state, but sectarianism still showed its ugly face even to these children:

> We got a house 'cause we had just returned from living in England and my da had just finished the army. I remember going in and the windows were all whitened out, and on one of them somebody had scrawled 'Fuck the Pope' with his finger. At the time I didn't know why they did that, 'cause in England nobody minded us being Catholics, and they had no problem with seeing us as Irish – yet here, it seemed there was a part of Ireland where you weren't supposed to be Irish, and you weren't even wanted if you were Catholic. It was while attending the Christian Brothers School that I realised there was such a thing as an Irish language or an Irish culture. There were Gaelic games played – the ban was in force at that time and you weren't allowed to play soccer. You said your prayers in Irish, you answered the roll in Irish. Now that might still be considered tokenism, but it was highlighting the fact that we were Irish. I think my identity was crystallised not here but when I went to England. Even staunch Prods are treated like 'Paddies' when they go to England. Maybe it would do them the world of good – send them off to live in 'mother' England for a few years!'[7]

Although the Falls was a deprived area, perhaps more so than many other areas of Belfast, the state as a whole was dependent on large subsidies from Britain.[8] This was due in part to the radical changes in the welfare system in Britain, and these policies were introduced into Northern Ireland at a huge cost to the British Exchequer.[9] Also, as Belfast and its hinterland had the major industries, infrastructure and a large pool of labour, new economic investments went there, to the detriment of the west of the state, which was largely rural and Catholic. Protestants in Belfast were invariably 'looked after'[10] when new employment was created in the area.[11]

Republicanism in the Falls was thus enhanced by the closeness of the community in the face of intimidation from both Protestants and the RUC, but it also stemmed from decades of Belfast being a divided city mentally, physically and religiously. As Devlin suggests: 'Its rigid sectarian barriers, mental as well as physical, have blighted the lives and hopes of successive generations.'[12] These 'mental' sectarian barriers traversed streets and workplaces and underscored the polarisation of the two communities. Successive Unionist governments fostered the belief amongst working-class Protestants that Catholics were not to be trusted.[13] However, many children growing up in the 1960s remember having Protestant and Catholic friends. There were no sectarian mental barriers in these children's minds while they played football together and played on swings tied to lamp posts. Those 'mental' barriers were put up by the generation before them, and the society around them.

Housing in the Falls area was a constant source of distress and anxiety for Catholics; indeed, the country as a whole had a chronic social housing shortage. Many of the streets had been laid out at the time of massive growth in the linen manufacturing industry and as such were generally two up, two down types with no indoor toilets or bathrooms. Many had been built in Victorian times, and were ill equipped for the families who occupied them. Narrow alleyways separated the houses from each other and some of the streets were only 6 to 8 feet wide. This instilled in many a sense of claustrophobia.

Many of these streets bore the names of past wars fought by the British Empire in its heyday. Sevastopol Street, Odessa Street, Balaclava Street and many more are associated with the Crimean War. Others, such as Balkan Street, Bosnia Street, Belgrade Street and Cyprus Street, are associated with the Balkans. India, as the most prized asset of British colonialism, is represented by Kashmir Road, Bombay Street, Cawnpore Street and others.[14]

There were no gardens at the front, children played on the streets. Overcrowding was the norm, and often more than two families shared the same dwelling. Limited attempts were put in place by the Unionist governments over the years, such as the Divis Street complex, a monolith structure of flats to alleviate the overcrowding.[15]

Not only Catholics, but many Protestants were disenfranchised by the voting system in place. Many who were tenants (or sub-letting) or at home with parents were unable to vote. Owners of businesses were also entitled to more than one vote. As more businesses were owned by Protestants, invariably Catholics lost out. The 'one man, one vote' rallying cry of the NICRA was not only for Catholics though, but also for working-class Protestants, many of whom were in the exact same position as their Catholic 'enemies'. This archaic voting system did not really have any impact on day to day life, however. Living in poverty, with no way out, was the main worry for many.

It was the newly educated Catholic youth who subsequently began fighting for universal suffrage in the 1960s. But years of domination and coercion by the state had turned the Catholic areas of west Belfast into a combustible, tinder-dry place. When Derry exploded in August 1969 it was only a matter of time before the simmering tensions from that city would reach the Falls.

II

While Derry was in turmoil, Belfast, and particularly the Falls Road area, was at a crisis point. Sporadic violence was occurring all around the district for most of the year, but it was in August that the situation worsened significantly. Nationalists in Derry called on other nationalists across the state to 'relieve' pressure on the Bogside by organising marches and demonstrations in an attempt to draw any RUC reinforcements away from Derry. Nationalists in Belfast responded to this plea by attacking RUC stations and rioting.[16] This mobilisation of nationalists and republicans in the Falls district was organised in part by Billy McMillan, Belfast commander of the IRA.[17] In Derry, the 'B' Specials were mobilised in support of the RUC, further stoking the tension.

On the evening of 13 August, Jack Lynch, Taoiseach of the Republic, acted under pressure from hawks within his cabinet and gave a television broadcast regarding the deteriorating situation. His comments about the government of the Republic 'not standing by'[18] and his subsequent decision to send field hospitals and troops to border areas adjacent to the most sensitive areas only served to worsen an already volatile situation.[19] The people of the Falls, watching these events unfold, were also full of trepidation. Because sporadic trouble had been ongoing for much of August, many believed that it was only a matter of time before wide-scale and extreme violence returned. On 13 August it did. Ronnie Munck, in 'The Making of the Troubles', gives a vivid account of the scale of the violence on the streets of the Falls, and of its effects on the population, from a young woman's perspective:

> In August 1969 there had been a lot of rioting in Derry and Belfast and we had boarded up the front windows. My father was out working and we were waiting for him to come home. We could hear the rioting getting bad up the street. He came in earlier than expected and he told us he had seen a man around the corner with a gun who told him to go round a different way to go home. He was only in when we heard five single shots which was quite shocking as the only time we had heard shots was on TV in cowboy films! Later we heard what can only be described as somebody trying to put the door in with a pneumatic drill and we knew it was a machine-gun ... That night somebody else tried to break our door in and he shouted 'There's no Fenians [Catholics] here', probably because the house next door was empty.[20]

One can only imagine the abject fear that many living in the streets of the Falls who were now under attack felt. It was a time of anarchy and disorder. Devlin recalls:

In Belfast, where British troops had not yet gone in, it was a terrible night. The Police thought that a full-scale IRA-inspired uprising was under way and they put Shoreland armoured cars, equipped with Browning heavy machine-guns, on to the streets. They fired hundreds of rounds throughout the night ...[21]

Protestants had seen the NICRA attempt to dilute the power they held, seen rioting in Derry and other towns, seen the RUC come under severe attack and were inflamed when Lynch made his provocative television speech on the 13th. At the moment the fighting was between Catholics and the RUC, but it would not be long before the sparks from the Falls would reach across to the Shankill. Anger was at a critical point on the Shankill Road. A Protestant who participated in the violence gave his opinion on the feelings that were prevalent in his community at the time:

I [didn't] disagree with the actions [the Protestant incursions] because it was the only thing we could do in those days, there was nothing else we could do, other than just sit back and let the civil rights trample us down. I for one was not going to do that.[22]

Fired up by years of rhetoric about the 'enemy' in their midst and by Ian Paisley warning of impending doom, Protestants were ready. It was also no surprise that there was going to be a reaction. Fierce fighting between the RUC and nationalists was at its height when Protestant gangs, following the RUC and the 'B' Specials, invaded the Clonard and the Falls, burning houses and businesses as they went. Devlin again describes the scene as Protestants launched a full-scale attack on the Falls: 'Local [Protestant] people who knew the streets daubed whitewash marks on the doors or windows of Catholic homes. These homes were then emptied of people and burned.'[23] Serious disorder and fighting now engulfed west Belfast. Protestants and Catholics were once again facing each other in scenes that had appeared in the past on many occasions. This time, however, the forces of the government were facing the Catholics as well. Catholic opinion was hardening again all forms of security of the state.

The next day was worse. After 'false' information was passed around the Protestant districts about IRA men in and around Clonard Monastery, gangs of Protestants again invaded the Clonard district in an attempt to gain access to the monastery. The army had arrived in Belfast, but not in the Clonard. Sean Murray, in *An Phoblacht*, remembers the scene:

A large mob advanced from Cupar Street at its juncture with Kashmir Road, armed with sticks, stones and petrol bombs. As many of the local men were still at work, the initial defence of the area was left to a handful of teenagers and young men, who bravely held the mob at bay. Around this time, a local priest phoned the RUC at Springfield Road Barracks, requesting their assistance, but no help came … Fr. McLaughlin decided, given the gravity of the situation, to go directly to Springfield Road RUC Barracks. He observed RUC men sitting around, drinking tea, but was informed that they were under orders not to leave their barracks, fearing an imminent IRA attack! Fearing a massacre, Fr. Egan attempted to contact the British Army's GOC in Lisburn to request the presence of troops to deter the murderous onslaught that was now underway. As residents desperately tried to defend their homes, without any assistance from the 'forces of law and order', in spite of earlier guarantees, fires began to take hold in many homes as the petrol bombs rained down relentlessly. This was obviously not a spontaneous attack given the ferocity, confidence and size of the mob and the number of petrol bombs in continuous use. It was well-organised and well-resourced with deadly intent: a brutal, murderous plan to completely destroy the Clonard community. The Falls was in the firing line the night before; it was Clonard's turn today.[24]

The above account shows that, while a lot of the violence ended up as spontaneous, there was an element of initial planning involved. The following account from a Catholic worker amongst Protestant workmates confirms this, but also shows how not all people from the two communities regarded each other with hatred and suspicion:

In '69 I was working as a plasterer with a Protestant firm, I was the only Catholic in it. And we were coming up from Cookstown after finishing a job, and they normally dropped me off in Wilton Street on the Shankill Road and I'd walk down onto the Falls and get a bus home. But this day as we were coming in towards Royal Avenue they said I'd better get off there. And I said: 'sure just drop me off on the Shankill.' And the driver says, 'no, no, you'd better get off here.' So I got out of the car and walked up Castle Street and then I noticed all the places burning and the smoke coming out of everywhere. And further up the road I met a friend of mine who told me: 'The Orangies have attacked.' I realised then that the guys that was dropping me off must've knew that that attack was coming and knew not to bring me up the Shankill Road but to drop me off before.[25]

The Protestant mobs attacked Catholic homes in the adjacent streets, petrol bombing most of the houses in Bombay Street, Kashmir Road and Clonard Gardens. Fire engines were powerless in the face of the rioting; local people were left to fight the fires and thus commandeered a fire engine that had been abandoned by its occupants. The army, unaware of the geographical aspects of the area, was in the Falls Road at the time and belatedly arrived on the scene, attempting to push back the Protestants towards the Shankill. Devlin disputed this account, however, saying that the military actually stood by, 'not lifting a finger'.[26]

It is commonly assumed that the IRA was a spent force by 1969, and thus was mainly inactive during the riots, but this is a misconception. IRA units were active in Belfast during the unrest; however, they *were* limited in what impact they could have. Their last major operation, between 1956 and 1962, ended with the IRA 'dumping arms', claiming lack of support from northern nationalists. After that point the leadership in Dublin, headed by Cathal Goulding, concentrated on a Marxist-inspired socialist programme, organising pickets and engaging in social agitation. Rearmament was not high on the agenda of the leadership; neither was shooting at Protestants. Thus, in August 1969 there was a severe lack of weaponry and ammunition at hand to defend Catholics. There was also a fear amongst the leadership that the limited defence that they could muster would only exacerbate the situation. As McMillan stated:

> We realised that the meagre armaments at our disposal were hopelessly inadequate to meet the requirements of the situation and that the use of firearms by us would only serve to justify the use of greater force against the people by the forces of the Establishment and increase the danger of sectarian pogroms.[27]

McMillan himself was arrested by the RUC on 15 August and detained for a short period.

As the Protestant gangs descended on the Falls, backed up by elements of the RUC and the 'B' Specials, the IRA became involved in shooting incidents, firing back at both the RUC and Protestant mobs along the streets that run between the Falls and Shankill roads, and also at the end of Divis Street, killing a Protestant and injuring scores more. Protestants were also involved in shootings, returning fire on a number of occasions.[28] Amidst all of this chaos, more casualties of the rioting on the Falls occurred when the RUC, using machine guns attached to the roofs of armoured cars, shot dead a 9-year-old boy, Patrick Rooney, in his bed in Divis flats.[29] It was later discovered that the bullet passed through a number of walls in his house before hitting him.[30] An off-duty soldier was also killed in the Divis flats; he was on a balcony watching the rioting when a bullet hit him.[31]

By dawn on 15 August, the British army were in some sort of control on the Falls Road, and calm gradually returned to the area. Hundreds of families had moved out of the district[32] and over 180 houses were damaged beyond repair. Such was the scale of destruction that many of these houses were left to burn themselves out, there being no way to save them. At least seven people were killed in the violence and many hundreds injured. The army now stood between the two factions in a formal peacekeeping role. Devlin initially welcomed the decision to use the army in Belfast:

> With troops on the streets in Derry, and Belfast in turmoil with no effective police presence, we decided to call for the military to step in. [Paddy and] I went into a house opposite the Falls Park, where we telephoned Home Secretary James Callaghan to give him a first-hand account of the dreadful situation that had developed and to plead with him for soldiers.[33]

For Devlin, with an IRA past and a history of socialist agitation, personally to call the British home secretary and request British troops on the Falls Road shows just how serious the situation on the ground was. People were in real fear for their lives, their homes were destroyed and the discredited police force was nowhere to be seen. It is no wonder that troops were welcomed with open arms on the Falls.

The British army in Northern Ireland was led by a 57-year-old distinguished general, Ian Freeland. Educated at Wellington College and Sandhurst, he saw action in Europe in the push into Germany in 1944. He spent some years in the 1960s in Africa where he was GOC of British Land Forces Kenya. He was awarded numerous promotions before being appointed General Officer Commanding of British forces in Northern Ireland, in July 1969. At the time the army in Northern Ireland stood at 1,000 troops, as it was not believed that any more would be needed. By the end of August, just two months after he started, there was serious rioting and troop levels had reached at least 7,000, many of whom were now on the streets of Belfast separating the two communities.

John Kelly, an ex-IRA staff member, also greeted the troops initially, feeling sorry for what the community was going through:

> Well, I didn't like it but I couldn't blame them. They were only ordinary folk and they were going through a state of shock. There were some elderly

people who lived through the 1920 trouble when people were burned out of their houses. They'd thought that was the last they seen of it. But they were wrong. There was one woman who said that this was the third time she'd been burned out of Cupar Street – 1920, 1935 and 1969. You couldn't blame those people if they took anybody in and gave them a cup of tea.[34]

Others were not happy to see the British army, however. Veteran Republicans such as Joe Cahill and Billy McKee were apprehensive about what it meant for the future. Gerry Adams was 'outraged'. He later said:

In our view the British government had been using the RUC and the Unionists to uphold and disguise the nature of their rule in this part of our country. We experienced a sense of victory in having exhausted and defeated their first line of defence – the RUC. Although the Unionists were still in charge, it was now the British soldiers who were holding the line for the British government ...[35]

Thus a more militant and aggressive Republicanism, dedicated to the complete removal of the British presence from Ireland once and for all, was born out of the arrival of British troops in Catholic areas of Belfast that August.[36]

III

Conor Cruise O'Brien describes the arrival of the British army on the streets of Belfast as 'freezing the film' of the descent into civil war.[37] Looking back, it seemed as if civil war between Protestants and Catholics was a real possibility. August 1969 changed everything. There had been sectarian strife in the past between the two communities, but this time was markedly different. Barricades were now erected between the Falls and Shankill roads, sometimes halfway down a street. Whole areas around the Falls were either completely destroyed or in urgent need of repair. The late author Andrew Boyd described the scene:

On Sunday morning, 17th August, the streets around Millfield, the Pound, Shankill Road and Falls Road were in a state of utter desolation ... everywhere pavements torn up. In some streets barricades had been erected and shops boarded up against attack. In every street which bordered on the Catholic and Protestant districts, pickets of armed police and soldiers stood guard.[38]

Jack Lynch, himself not happy at the introduction of troops into Northern Ireland,[39] gave a speech at Tralee, in County Kerry, in September 1969 to 'set out the basis of our thinking and policy' on the situation in the north. He hoped that the speech, entitled *A Review of the Situation in the Six Counties*, would 'reduce those tensions in the north which arise from misunderstandings or apprehensions about our attitudes or intentions'.[40] Undoubtedly he was thinking about the speech he had given on television in August which had inflamed Protestant fears and given false hope to Catholics about southern intervention.

> I want to make it clear, once more, that we have no intention of using force to realise this [end of partition] desire ... The unity we seek is not something forced but a free and genuine union of those living in Ireland based on mutual respect and tolerance and guaranteed by a form or forms of government authority in Ireland providing for progressive improvement of social, economic and cultural life in a just and peaceful environment.[41]

Protestants for decades had seen the Republic as a conservative, backward and economically poor state run by, as far as they were concerned, the Catholic Church. There was no hope that they would now join up with the very people whom they were fighting in Belfast. Lynch then went on to talk about the recognition of the state of Northern Ireland:

> It is quite unreasonable for any Unionist to expect my government, or any future government, to abandon the belief and hope that Ireland should be reunited. It is unnecessary to repeat that we seek reunification by peaceful means. We are not seeking to overthrow by violence the Stormont parliament or government but rather to win the agreement of a sufficient number of people in the north to an acceptable form of reunification. In any case the Stormont government, being the executive instrument of a subordinate parliament, cannot receive formal international recognition.[42]

Speeches like these, and Lynch made a few, only served to harden Protestant attitudes in the north. They also encouraged Protestants to believe that the violence now engulfing the state was an IRA insurrection, supported by Catholics with the secret connivance of the Republic.

Republican folklore remembers this period of time in Belfast as the 'Pogroms', linking it with similar outbreaks of communal violence in the 1920s and the creation of the Northern Irish state. In this way the blame for the communal violence in August 1969 is firmly laid at the doors of the

Protestant community, the RUC and the 'B' Specials. But it is not as clear cut as this. Events on 13 August had seen Catholic gangs attack RUC stations, ostensibly in an attempt to take the pressure off nationalists in Derry. Protestants watched the unfolding drama on the Falls Road with some trepidation, believing that an IRA-inspired insurrection was under way. The TV broadcast by Lynch on 13 August also added fuel to the situation; indeed, many Protestants on the Shankill believed that the Irish army was on the point of invading the state. Malachi O'Doherty, a witness to some of the events, goes into more detail concerning these differing interpretations in his work *The Pogrom Myth*:

> The flaw in this [Pogrom] version of August 1969 is that it takes no account of the plain fact that it was rioters in Ardoyne and the Falls Road – Catholics – who started the Trouble in Belfast that week, and it was very big trouble they started. Of course, violence had been building since October 68 when a Civil Rights march in Derry was broken up by the police wielding clubs and a succession of marches had turned into major riots since, particularly in Newry, Armagh and Derry. The rioting in August was part of a plan to overstretch the police who had been drawn into a huge riot in Derry after the Apprentice Boys parade on August 12th. No shots had been fired in Derry. I watched the Falls Road part of the operation on the second night of rioting, August 14th.[43]

In regard to the diversionary tactics used by Catholics in Belfast, O'Doherty is correct – as he mentions, McMillan organised trouble in Belfast to divert the RUC away from Derry. O'Doherty then discusses the original confrontation between Catholics and the RUC, although there are many who would disagree strongly with his analysis of the trouble in Ardoyne. He describes the violence in the Falls area as follows:

> The plan there was, apparently, to burn down a redbrick police station at Hastings Street, situated just where the Westlink now comes off Divis Street. The rioters would chuck stones and petrol bombs. The police fought with a combination of baton charges and 'whippets', Shoreland light armoured cars with mounted Browning machine guns, designed for use against an open field cross border attack. As the rioters inched closer, the whippets would prance out of side streets to scatter them and then the baton charge would go forward and try to grab a couple of them. The other part of the rioters' plan was a squad at the top of Divis Flats with petrol bombs. I saw them drop a milk crate of unlit bombs onto the road and when the police

ran after the rioters, someone dashed a proper petrol bomb on to this to set
the whole lot alight.

This was entirely a Catholic attack on the police. It was clever and it was
dangerous. The Minister of Home Affairs later shed tears on television for
not having been able to cope with this without the use of guns. There was
an audience of about a dozen of us watching this. I had joined this group
after leaving my girlfriend to the bus station at Smithfield so that she could
get the last bus home to Rathcoole. I watched the B Specials arrive in a
civilian commercial van and make their way along the wall of the station
with their rifles.[44]

There was rioting that night, and it *was* started by Catholics. The scale of
their involvement, however, has not been discussed where the 'Pogrom' thesis
is concerned. O'Doherty, as an eye witness, gives a compelling account of
the violence on the Falls Road on the 14th but was not present on the 13th;
therefore his analysis of what happened on that night is his own interpretation
of the events. He finishes with a return to the contemporary account of the
events on 15 August:

> That afternoon, Protestants rioters burnt Bombay Street, and that attack
> became the symbolic moment of the whole period, according as it did
> with the easy myth that innocent Catholics were swooped on by Protestant
> bigots and barbarians. Indeed, for many who had stayed at home that night,
> that is exactly what their experience was.[45]

Myths were created on both sides in the initial days of the conflict, as they
were throughout the next three decades of violence. Republicanism has made
good use of them, creating a seamless picture of these days. Prince and Warner
go into more detail about the use of the word 'Pogrom' in their book. They
agree with O'Doherty that, while Protestant gangs did indeed invade the Falls
and inflicted heavy damage on the districts adjacent to the Shankill, there was
also damage inflicted by Catholics in Protestant areas, and on Protestants.[46] The
communal violence affected both sides, although Catholics were, in regard to
damage to property, affected more. For example, at the beginning of August
Catholics were throwing petrol bombs into Protestant streets, while expulsions
of families from mixed areas on both sides were happening at the same time.[47]
Far from being a 'Pogrom', it was a case of extreme violent behaviour inflicted
by both sides of the community and thus should really be seen in that context.

The conclusions of the 'Scarman Tribunal' released in April 1972, more of
which are contained in the appendix to this book, describes in detail the

events of August 1969, particularly how it was feared that there might be a serious challenge to the state.

There was serious rioting by Protestants on the Shankill Road near Unity Flats in the early days of August. In the course of these riots, the Protestant mobs made a determined attempt to invade Unity Flats, and also appeared in force on the Crumlin Road. They were successfully resisted by the sustained efforts of the police, who incurred the anger of some sections of Protestant opinion by their baton charges up the Shankill Road. It is significant that during these Protestant riots of early August two senior policemen, the Commissioner and Deputy Commissioner for Belfast, concluded that the police were unable any longer to control serious disturbances in the City of Belfast. Both these officers felt the time had come to call the Army to the aid of the civil power.

It was clear therefore that serious failings were found in the RUC even before the situation degenerated into full-scale inter-communal fighting. The reaction of the RUC to the situation was also noted:

On the night of the 14th, the worst violence of the 1969 disturbances occurred in Belfast, notably in the Ardoyne and on the Falls Road. The police, who believed by now that they were facing an armed uprising, used guns, including Browning machine-guns mounted on Shorland armoured vehicles. Four Catholics were shot dead by police fire: one Protestant was killed by a shot fired by a rioter in Divis Street. Catholic houses were burnt by Protestants, especially in the Conway Street area. The only clear evidence of direct IRA participation in these riots occurred at the St Comgall's School in Divis Street, where automatic fire was directed against the police. On the same night there was a riot in Armagh, as a result of which a Catholic man was killed by USC fire.

By the morning of 15 August the police were exhausted. They failed to control the violence which broke out that day on the Crumlin Road and in the Clonard area of the city. Nor did they prevent the burning of factories by Catholics and public houses by Protestants. It has to be admitted that the police were no longer in control of the city. On the evening of the 15th, the Army entered the Falls Road, but not the Crumlin Road, which was the scene of a serious confrontation between Protestants and Catholics. Two people – one Protestant and one Catholic – died by civilian shooting in Belfast on 15 August. Catholic houses were burnt that night by Protestants at Bombay Street (Falls Road area) and Brookfield

Street (Crumlin Road). On the evening of 16 August, the Army entered the Crumlin Road and thereafter the disturbances died away. In some riot areas barricades remained. Defence committees began to exercise de facto authority in several Catholic areas. So far as the Falls Road district is concerned we are satisfied that the disturbances produced the committees rather than the committees the disturbances.[48]

IV

The Belfast that the troops were sent into was markedly different from the Belfast of today. Whole areas of houses in the lower Falls, and the Falls area in general, were in need of substantial repairs, even though the occupants did what they could to alleviate the more serious ones. Now many more were damaged, some beyond repair. Many Protestant areas were in a similar condition, especially in the Shankill district. Soldiers talked about the similarity between the streets of Belfast and streets in industrial cities in the Midlands and north of England. However, there was one major difference, as an ex-soldier I shall call 'Dave' recalled:

> As soldiers, many like me brought up in slum areas of England, we were horrified by the abject poverty that the Catholic community were living in. Their houses, mostly rented I think from Protestant landlords, were hovels of the lowest order. Their children were mostly barefoot, and I remember marvelling at how the kids could run around with no shoes, seemingly impervious to any pain or discomfort. We truly felt sorry for them, and of course at that time, we were welcomed into the Falls, its side streets, and the homes of the residents, because they saw the soldiers as saviours from the Prod [Protestant] intimidation (mainly the 'B' Specials and the RUC).[49]

Poverty was rife in some of the Catholic neighbourhoods and many soldiers reported families with no food, limited clothing and unsafe accommodation. August 1969 only increased this poverty and desolation for many of these families. 'Dave' remembered his first posting in Belfast in 1969.

> Belfast stank, and was almost permanently shrouded in the filth from coal fires and industry, being in a bowl between the sea and the hills of The Black Mountain. Only when a breeze came in from the sea did conditions improve. It was like the smogs I remember as a child in England.[50]

Many of the soldiers, recently arrived from other colonial warzones, were unaware of the religious geography of west Belfast where, in the mixed areas close to the interface between the two communities, one house could have a Catholic family and next door could be Protestant. This was to cause major problems when the army decided to man the so-called 'peace lines' between the factions, initially made of strips of corrugated iron and barbed wire. Soldiers also found the situation a strange experience, as this statement from *Operation Banner* attests:

> The soldiers found patrolling the streets, that in England would be regarded as slums, and standing on street corners with a loaded rifle, steel helmet and gas mask, watching people go about their daily business, to be surreal. Many [soldiers] sympathised with Catholics, when told over cups of tea, cakes and biscuits, about the discrimination and were confused about the politics; but at least learning a foreign language was not necessary, although they soon became schooled in distinguishing dialects.[51]

'Dave' often held conversations over a cup of tea and a biscuit with the Catholics of the Falls when he arrived in Belfast. He also had many conversations with members of the RUC and the 'B' Specials. Although listening to Catholic complaints about the security forces was getting a bit repetitive, he quickly formed his own conclusions about the 'B' Specials:

> The men of the 'B' Specials I met were nothing but animals. [When the 'Specials' were disbanded] these same men joined the newly formed UDR in droves, just so that they could keep their rifles. The 'B's openly bragged to us of raping Catholic women and girls, in exchange for 'protection', running all sorts of money making scams, and protection rackets amongst the few Catholic shop owners and tradesmen.[52]

Dave was outraged by the matter-of-fact way in which sectarianism was openly displayed by the 'B' Specials, and was disgusted at the abject poverty and desperate living conditions he encountered.[53] He was not on his own. Many soldiers told similar stories about the conditions they encountered. Speaking to the RUC and the 'B' Specials ultimately left him with a very low opinion of them, and afterwards he tended to avoid contact with the Security Forces of Northern Ireland whenever he could.

As the areas settled down into a quiet but tense autumn, discussions between the army and the various defence committees, set up in the wake of earlier violence, led to the removal of most of the barricades. The army still patrolled the streets, still received cups of tea and a reserved welcome. There was a general feeling of hope that maybe the excesses of August were the pinnacle of the disturbances, and that the arrival of the army had subdued the more extreme elements on both sides. Things seemed to be happening. The 'B' Specials, the hated, exclusively Protestant, militia, were to be phased out. The RUC was to be disarmed. A visit by the British home secretary, James Callaghan, was greeted with anticipation and hope by Catholics. As J. Boyer Bell states about this period: 'There were no barricades, no civil rights confrontations ... no sign of the IRA, in fact.'[54]

Callaghan returned to London and in a debate in parliament in October spoke about what he had seen and his perspective on the situation. He initially described the conditions in Northern Ireland prior to the outbreak of violence. He then went on to say:

In August, this led to a confrontation in which in Northern Ireland 572 houses were damaged, 174 of them totally destroyed, and many of the remainder suffering from very severe damage. Probably over 5,000 people lost their homes in the riots of August, and of those rather less than a half have been able to reoccupy their repaired houses.

It was at that stage that the Northern Ireland Government, on 14th August, decided that it was not possible for them with their resources to restore order, and troops were ordered in at that time to separate the communities. Our objectives were clearly stated then and still hold good today: first, to keep the peace between the communities; second, to ensure that there is in Northern Ireland, as in the rest of the United Kingdom, a common standard of citizenship; third, that the forces which sustained the State and which for a number of reasons had been unable at that time to maintain law and order should have their role examined in order that the reasons for the breakdown could be made clear and remedies proposed; fourth, that the Government of Northern Ireland should be given every help by Her Majesty's Government to make the necessary changes themselves and to carry on the task themselves.

It is to those objectives that policy has been directed during the last two months. Some of these things are being achieved, while others have been achieved. Let me make it clear, in relation to law and order, that what underlay the very strong conviction of both Governments that a committee should be set up under the chairmanship of Lord Hunt to review the role and structure of those forces was the belief that law and order cannot be maintained in isolation. It is part of the totality of social, economic and political policies. In a democracy it must rest upon the consent of the general body of citizens, neither outraging the majority, not inflaming the minority. To those who suggested at one time that Westminster might confine itself to the problem of law and order and allow others, the elected Government, to carry on with the social, economic and political policies that they thought appropriate, I say that it seemed to Her Majesty's Government that it was not possible, in a democratic State, to do this. The whole context must be considered together.

It is not my intention, Mr Speaker, especially in the light of your request for short speeches, to take the House through the events since 14th August; they are well known to hon. Members and are on the record. But there has been, continuing, small-scale violence, sometimes growing larger, and at others dying away. Many areas have been unpoliced since that date in August, notably in Belfast and Londonderry. Some have said that the troops should have gone in and ensured that those areas were policed forthwith.

It is not a policy that I recommended to the General Officer Commanding and I would not recommend it to this House. It neglects the whole back-ground of the situation. I must point out to some of those rather more militant gentlemen who are now anxious for British troops to go quickly into these areas, and who have been pressing for that since August, that the two major areas were unpoliced, in an effective sense, before 12th August. It was, alas, the case that, in the months preceding, as we have heard from the many experts who went over there, in parts of what became known as 'No Go-Land' in Belfast, the police went only in response to the most urgent 999 call. They did not patrol at all during the night and, when they went, never less than two cars attended, with one to cover the other.

I am speaking, I want to emphasise, of the period prior to the time when the troops were asked to take over this situation. In my view, it would have been extremely irresponsible, in the face of, at that time, the unreformed political situation, with tensions as they were, to have expected the troops to have immediately gone in and restored order in a situation where the civilian forces, with their natural links with the population, had been unable to do so. Areas of the Bogside have been unpoliced for even longer, because the police were unacceptable. This was the situation in which the Army had to do a most difficult and thankless task and it has done that with exemplary courage, patience and diplomacy.[55]

Callaghan was worried about the situation that he witnessed in Northern Ireland. He clearly saw that there were fundamental flaws in the make-up of its society, that law and order had virtually ceased to exist in certain areas and that confidence in the government of the state was diminishing rapidly.

However, as with previous British governments, he failed to grasp that it was the existence of the Stormont government that had created most of the issues that he had witnessed. The troops were there to 'aid the civil power', and the London government would support the Stormont government is its aim of restoring its authority. It would support the latter's efforts at reform. However, for the minority Catholic population, Callaghan missed a vital point. Stormont had to go.

While all this was happening, however, the IRA was in meltdown. The Dublin leadership was heavily criticised for its failure to defend the northern nationalists. The feelings within the rank and file that Goulding and the rest of the leadership had taken the IRA on a course that was completely alien to the real situation in Northern Ireland were now coming to a head. The arrival of the army, and the welcome it had been given by nationalists, also caused some discomfort amongst the more militant of the Belfast IRA, who felt that the tradition of physical force in removing the British presence was being diluted. These 'militants' met at the end of August to formulate a plan to get rid of the Belfast command and replace it with themselves. According to Tim Pat Coogan the men were Gerry Adams, Billy McKee, Billy Kelly, Joe Cahill, John Kelly, Leo Martin, Jimmy Drumm, Seamus Twomey, Dáithí O'Conaíll (David O'Connell) and Jimmy Steele.[56] The plan would be put into effect at the next available opportunity.

The crisis in Belfast came to a head on 22 September. The militants stormed a meeting that McMillan had arranged for his volunteers after his release from jail, and demanded, at the point of a gun, that the Belfast leadership cut all association with the leadership in Dublin. McMillan subsequently consented to their demands under duress, but had no intention of carrying them through. Nevertheless, the veteran IRA men went ahead with their plans, setting up their own Belfast Brigade. By mid-December, however, the tensions within the movement were reaching crisis point, and would ultimately end up creating the 'Provisional' IRA.

In the IRA Army Convention of December 1969, a vote on ending abstentionism was put to the delegates, but even the idea of such a move, coupled with the events in the north the previous August, was enough for the more militant within the hall – a sizeable contingent walked out. The decision to walk was influenced by the absence of any representatives from the Belfast leadership, and was also the result of the influence of Seán MacStíofáin, IRA director of intelligence from 1966, a vocal critic of Goulding's moves towards the left, and Ruairí Ó Brádaigh, the ex-chief of staff of the IRA and an influential member of Sinn Féin. Another reason was that the walkout was pre-planned; MacStíofáin had seen to that. He thus went to Belfast and immediately set up a Provisional IRA Council.[57] The new grouping had no time for the abandonment of the armed struggle, as envisioned by Goulding and his contemporaries; the only way to remove the British presence from Ireland, they believed, was through armed violence. It worked in the rest of the empire; the British would 'soon get fed up and go home'.[58]

While the arrival of British troops on the streets of the Falls was welcomed by most, there were clear indications even before the Falls Curfew that the welcome was to be short lived. Many Catholics during the autumn of 1969 began to see the troops as puppets of Stormont, there to prop up a faltering government. This view was in part due to Stormont being left intact after the near communal breakdown in August. The RUC, distrusted for decades by the majority of Catholics, was now seen as a sectarian force, incapable of policing the interfaces with impartiality. The army's role in Belfast at this point, however, is confusing. The army was initially sent 'in aid of the civil power', but it was clear to many Catholics that the 'civil power' was the problem. The GOC very early on stated that the army was 'under military command', and was not subordinate to the RUC.[59] Trained in warfare, not in policing, the army was subsequently going to come under fire from all sides in the conflict. The confusing nature of its initial deployment is summed up in the following statement from one Stormont official at the time, quoted in *Pig in the Middle* by Desmond Hamill:

> The army was not built to act in a political role. It is the mailed fist of a failed government. At the very least the army should have had firm political control, but it did not. Although Sir Ian Freeland repeatedly asked for a statement of aims, he was never given one. He was made Director of Operations, which allowed him to take the chair at army/police meetings, but he had no other powers.[60]

To any observer, this implies that, although the army was sent in initially to act as a peacekeeper, it was ultimately under political influence, and in the process was heavily influenced by Stormont.[61] On 20 August 1969 Downing Street issued a statement after a protracted meeting between the two prime ministers and members of their cabinets. At this meeting the RUC was placed under the direct control of the GOC for 'security operations', and the GOC was responsible to the Ministry of Defence in London.[62] In effect, all security procedures were now theoretically under the control of the government at Westminster, over two years before the suspension of Stormont and the advent of direct rule. The GOC, however, had to liaise with Stormont and the inspector general of the RUC on a regular basis, thus limiting his influence and impartiality on the ground. To confuse matters further, any 'normal police duties outside the field of security' were to remain under the direction of the inspector general.[63]

The confusing nature of the army's role on the streets of Belfast was evident, and did little to make Freeland's job any easier. It was also compounded by pressure from Stormont about the existence of the 'no go' areas. These were now being 'policed' by local 'Citizens' Defence' committees. They were clearly an embarrassment to the government at Stormont, who viewed them as safe havens for terrorists, especially the IRA, to operate from and use to create havoc in the city centre. Even with most of the original ramshackle barricades gone, the areas were still dangerous and tense. The army was in the front line in these areas, sometimes on its own without any support from the RUC or the Special Branch,[64] thus intelligence gathering was mainly left to the army, was often amateurish and clumsy, and was beginning to harden attitudes within the Catholic community.

3

BRITISH IGNORANCE AND THE RISE OF THE 'PROVOS'

Come all you young rebels and list while I sing
For love of ones land is a terrible thing
It banishes fear with the spread of a flame
And makes us all part of the patriot game
'The Patriot Game' [1]

I

After the violence of the previous summer, 1970 began relatively quietly. The government in London had finally acted, vigorously urging Stormont to implement its reform agenda. A commission, instigated by O'Neill while he was in power, was set up to investigate the slide into inter-communal violence.[2] The commission, headed by Lord Cameron, confirmed what many already believed, that the Unionist state set up in 1922 had deliberately embarked on a policy of discrimination towards the Catholic minority. Part of its conclusion stated:

A rising sense of continuing injustice and grievance among large sections of the Catholic population in Northern Ireland, in particular in Londonderry and Dungannon, in respect of (i) inadequacy of housing provision by certain local authorities (ii) unfair methods of allocation of houses built and let by such authorities, in particular; refusals and omissions to adopt a 'points' system in determining priorities and making allocations (iii) misuse in certain cases of discretionary powers of allocation of houses in order to perpetuate Unionist control of the local authority ... (2) Complaints, now well documented in fact, of discrimination in the making of local government appointments, at all levels but especially in senior posts, to the prejudice of non-Unionists and especially Catholic members of the community, in some Unionist controlled authorities ... (3) Complaints, again well documented, in some cases of deliberate manipulation of local government electoral boundaries and in others a refusal to apply for their necessary extension, in order to achieve and maintain Unionist control of local authorities and so to deny to Catholics influence in local government proportionate to their numbers.[3]

The RUC also came under extreme criticism in the report for its behaviour at civil rights marches, especially in the banned march in Derry on 5 October 1968 when, as mentioned previously, marchers were baton-charged by the police in full view of the media:

> The police handling of the demonstration in Londonderry on 5 October 1968 was in certain material respects ill co-ordinated and inept. There was use of unnecessary and ill controlled force in the dispersal of the demonstrators, only a minority of whom acted in a disorderly and violent manner. The wide publicity given by press, radio and television to particular episodes inflamed and exacerbated feelings of resentment against the police which had been already aroused by their enforcement of the ministerial ban.[4]

This criticism of the RUC was justified. Long seen as a sectarian force, it was a main aspect of the grievances that the Catholics had against the structure of the state. The Hunt Report, led by Sir John Hunt and published in October 1969, also recognised this, and also recommended that the force be disarmed and a new inspector general put in place.[5] In this way, it was hoped that a greater percentage of Catholics would join the RUC and a new reserve force, which was to replace the hated 'B' Specials, thus making it as impartial and as balanced as possible. Hunt emphasised this in his conclusion:

> We particularly hope that in these new conditions more Roman Catholics will wish to join the ranks of the Royal Ulster Constabulary and will offer themselves for service in the new part-time forces, the setting up of which we also envisage.[6]

While these aspirations were commendable, it was too little too late for many Catholics, who had seen the actions of the RUC and the 'B' Specials at first hand, whether it was in the Bogside of Derry or on the streets of the Falls.

II

Belated British involvement in the Northern Irish state, apart from sending in the army, also included putting in place a permanent United Kingdom representative. Attached to the office of the prime minister, James Chichester-Clark, Oliver Wright was the eyes and ears of the London government in Northern Ireland. In this way, London hoped that it could immediately address grievances amongst the warring factions before they spiralled out of control. Wright himself, however, was aware that the Foreign Office in London was at a loss about how to handle the deteriorating situation in the state, stating that it was 'lacking in ideas … for handling the current situation'.[7]

This analysis could be due, in part, to suggestions that the British initially viewed the developing conflict in Northern Ireland in 'colonial terms': that is, that the use of repressive measures against the population by the army could, in effect, strangle the conflict at birth. Many nationalists and Republicans at the time and for a considerable period afterwards viewed Northern Ireland in the context of a 'colony', and this was part of their overall view of the 'artificial' statelet carved out of Ireland in 1922. As John McGarry states:

> This [has] helped to underline the Republican position that Ireland, unlike Scotland and Wales, has never been a candidate for integration into the British nation. It has further suggested that the conflict is unfinished business left over from the imperial era, and that the appropriate prescription is British withdrawal.[8]

Henry Patterson, however, disagrees:

> Northern Ireland's status as part of the UK with MPs at Westminster, its proximity to the 'mainland', ease of access and, despite the onset of street violence, its lack of any significant discomfort or threats to visiting journalists and TV crews meant that its daily reality was that of a contested and disturbed fringe of two modern European states, not that of a colonial or neo-colonial dependency.[9]

McGarry nevertheless gives a convincing argument that the Westminster government did, and still does, treat Northern Ireland as a 'colony'. The *Prevention of Terrorism Act* allows the government to bar people from Northern Ireland entering Britain, and British political parties are not active there.[10] Perhaps his most compelling evidence is the idea that the people of Ireland, north and south, can unite under self-determination if they so wish. As he states, it is very rare for sovereign nations to 'grant such rights' to 'integral parts of their territory'.[11]

Decades of indifference to the social conditions within Northern Ireland, however, lend testimony to the fact that the government in Westminster completely ignored the way that the state was governed. Ever since the Government of Ireland Act in 1920, Westminster had made every attempt to deviate from any interest in the political workings of the new state, even when questions were raised in the Cabinet about the establishment of the 'Special Forces', the electoral gerrymandering of wards and the early signs of discriminatory practices.[12]

Did Britain want to remain involved in Northern Ireland? What was the motivation? The end of the Second World War brought many changes to Britain. The country was broke, and guarding far-flung territories was simply not on the agenda. India went in 1947, followed by a disastrous campaign in Egypt over the Suez Canal in 1956. Territories in Africa soon became independent. Northern Ireland, however, strengthened her link with Britain. A few believe that it was the loyalty shown to the Crown by Protestants who were descendants of the original settlers from England and Scotland that enabled Northern Ireland to remain part of the United Kingdom. Many in government in the 1960s, however, had a different view, as Peter R. Neumann suggests in *Britain's Long War*.

> Below the surface ... Westminster's attitude towards Northern Ireland has been more ambiguous. To Westminster, the Unionist idea of being British was alien, and at times, it seemed to contradict what it believed to be the very essence of Britishness. London's concept of Britishness entailed the presumed virtues of British political culture, such as fairness, tolerance, moderation and the rule of law. Unionists, on the other hand, appeared only to appreciate the symbols of Britishness (the Queen, the Union Jack), but not what they stood for. They were regarded as backward bigots who abused their supposed Britishness for selfish reasons, to establish a false sense of superiority over their Nationalist neighbours, and to extract political and financial support from the government at Westminster.'[13]

This could be an important reason for their lack of interest in the affairs of Northern Ireland. Neumann goes on to say:

> There was therefore little emotional attachment that would have resulted from the 'Britishness' of the Unionists, and the pledge to maintain the constitutional status of Northern Ireland as part of the United Kingdom

was upheld for reasons that had little to do with a shared sense of national identity. In fact, in the course of more than 30 interviews for this study, not a single NIO [Northern Ireland Office] minister or senior civil servant expressed any enthusiasm about Northern Ireland's continued membership in the United Kingdom.[14]

To Westminster, Northern Ireland was part of the 'Irish Question' and during the years of self-government the government in London saw no reason to reignite the question. Ireland as a whole had dominated British politics for so long that the indifference shown to Northern Ireland, which allowed it to become a 'Protestant' state, built on a sense of their own superiority by the majority, was understandable but inexcusable. These 'Protestants' were different. They were intense in their beliefs. They were bordering on xenophobia. They were nothing like the British. They should solve their own problems. Neumann suggests:

> Westminster had convinced itself that the people and the culture of the province were foreign to what it believed to be the British way, and that – if not for a rather unfortunate accident of history – Northern Ireland really belonged to the rest of the island of Ireland. The British government believed itself to be an outsider in what was an Irish conflict, and the best it could do was to assist the Irish in bringing about a solution themselves.[15]

Questions about the competence and performance of the Northern Ireland government asked in the Westminster parliament were subsequently forbidden under a convention in 1923 despite concerns from members;[16] thus the autonomy of the 'Protestant' state was assured in the establishment's eyes. It seems that London did not want to hold on to her first and last colony. However, the 'Irish Question' was to come screaming back into British politics with a vengeance.

III

By March 1970 the army had been on the streets of Belfast for some six months, and a relative but tense peace prevailed. Sporadic trouble was occurring, but was nothing on the scale of August 1969. However, mindsets on all sides were changing. While Catholics, as we have seen, initially welcomed the army, old hatreds and suspicions were coming to the fore. Many soldiers did not feel this way towards the Catholics, however, in the early days of the conflict. A considerable number felt a certain sense of sorrow for what they were witnessing, but as they were 'there in aid of the civil power', they obeyed orders: 'Most soldiers were very sympathetic towards the Catholics, their plight, and their aim of civil rights, but the Army was greatly manipulated by Stormont.'[17]

Nevertheless, there was change in the air. Most Catholics began to view the British uniform in historical terms. It was the enemy. Nothing that the army could do was going to change this view. The GOC recognised this at the time, suggesting that the 'honeymoon' would not last forever. All that could be done was to adopt a neutral stance, and then hopefully the politicians would have solved the situation. As O'Brien states: 'From the summer of 1969 to 1970 the British army had maintained a position of something like impartiality, through a balance of unpopularities. Catholics tended to object to its presence in principle, but felt the need for it in practice.'[18]

Unionist attitudes also began to harden fast in the north when, at the beginning of May 1970, two of the Republic's most senior politicians, Neil Blaney and Charles Haughey, were sacked from Lynch's inner cabinet after a considerable amount of arms were discovered at Dublin Airport. It was widely believed at the time that the arms were destined for Provisional IRA units in the North. After their arrest and subsequent trial they were acquitted of all charges brought against them.[19] Nevertheless, the mud stuck, and Lynch's government was dogged with controversy about its financial support of the emerging PIRA.[20]

Army searches were now beginning to harden Catholic attitudes towards the army. Inevitably it was the Stormont government that was putting pressure on the army to conduct these searches. Knowledge of the various groups 'defending' vulnerable Catholic and Protestant enclaves on the interfaces was of paramount importance to the army if the level of violence seen in the previous summer was not to be repeated, and the fledgling Provisional IRA was to be subdued. Tim Ripley and Mike Chappell state: 'From the first days of the army's deployment in Northern Ireland it has had an insatiable appetite for intelligence information on terrorist groups. The army's experience in colonial counter insurgency campaigns had convinced it that only through good intelligence would the terrorists be defeated.'[21]

The PIRA, formed in the wake of the August violence and its fallout, was now organising new recruits on all levels. While the 'honeymoon' between Catholics and the British army was slowly deteriorating due to an increasingly aggressive attitude from the troops, those within the PIRA were now concentrating on making sure that the Catholic community knew who the real enemy were: the British establishment and its army. This was helped, in part, by the behaviour of the army. Peter Merkl has suggested that 'the most influential factor behind the deterioration was the army's own actions in trying to establish its control over Catholic areas where it was in effect responsible for law and order'.[22] Thus Catholics were beginning to see house searches, information gathering and weapons seizures as being directed at them and their communities. As one subsequent member of the PIRA said:

> Despite what I had witnessed on the Falls in '69 I didn't join up at that stage. I went and looked for another job; I worked in the docks for a while, alongside my father and a couple of uncles. And we used to go up to my Aunt [name withheld] for our lunch every day, which was handy. And one day we were walking up the New Lodge Road and this Welsh patrol pulled us. They were all big, hefty guys, and they started giving us lackery an' all, and we started giving a bit of lackery back. The next thing we knew we were all rifled up against the wall, spread-eagled, kicked, generally roughed up, and searched. And I think that was the first time I really said: 'Fuck these bastards!' So it was more of a reaction to that sort of thing. There was no real staunch Republican history in my family, it was more a reaction to the Brits and their attitudes – here were these people from a foreign country pushing me up against a wall with their rifles. And within a few weeks I had joined the IRA, for it was easy to join at that time.[23]

The propaganda that the PIRA needed to convince the Catholic population that the British presence was the root cause of all their problems was given a massive boost in March 1970. An Orange parade that passed the predominantly Catholic areas of Ballymurphy and the Clonard districts of west Belfast resulted in serious rioting between Catholics and the British army in Ballymurphy, a sprawling housing development to the west of the city centre. The OIRA were involved in instigating trouble in the Clonard. Michael Farrell states that this was the first significant confrontation between Catholics and the British army in the current phase of the Troubles.[24] The army went in and used CS gas to quell the rioting. Warner and Prince attest that Billy McKee, one of the group who attempted to oust McMillan as Belfast commander the previous autumn, attempted to get the PIRA to 'open fire on the troops', thus provoking a reaction from the army that would show them to be the oppressors.[25]

Catholics, however, now saw the British army as the defender of the Protestants' right to march through sensitive Catholic areas, thus showing that they were indeed there to prop up the Unionist/Protestant/Orange regime in Stormont.[26] To further antagonise the situation on 6th April the GOC announced that persons throwing petrol bombs would be liable to long terms of imprisonment, or might [even] be shot. Although it was aimed at both communities, indeed anyone who was throwing petrol bombs, this statement was further proof to Catholics that the army was one of 'occupation'.

However, Stormont was not happy with the performance of the army in Ballymurphy, and the criticism levelled at the army was to gain momentum within the next few months. The following transcript is from notes taken at a meeting in Stormont on 22 April which were to be taken up with the GOC the same day. They give a clear insight into the mindset of the Unionist cabinet at a time of immense pressure for solutions to the problems facing them:

> This [law and order] can only be improved on the basis of quick and firm action (especially in terms of numbers of arrests) against troublemakers. It is to be hoped that never again will the army have to submit to such treatment as they received on the first Ballymurphy night, without taking counter-action. It is also hoped that there will be no further reports (though one accepts that most are untrue) of refusals by soldiers to enter certain streets in Belfast to investigate alleged crimes. This, I accept, is the RUC's job and they have orders to do it but it is often alleged that the army says in reply to a complaint 'we can't go there' which gives a disastrous impression.[27]

The Stormont cabinet was clearly out of touch with what was happening on the ground. It was indeed the job of the RUC to handle alleged crimes. But the subsequent meeting with the GOC showed the early pressure placed on him to get results. These 'results' would have to come, according to Stormont, from army actions in Catholic areas:

> He knew the GOC would like him to speak plainly and indeed circumstances demanded that he should do so. He had been concerned that the Army had not taken firm counter-measures when first attacked in the [Catholic] Ballymurphy area; at reports, no doubt in the main untrue, that soldiers had refused to investigate alleged crimes in certain areas and as recently as Monday when the BBC and the Belfast Newsletter had reported that a joint foot patrol had been taken out of [Catholic] Rossville Street [in Derry] in an Army vehicle having been stoned by a gang of youths. He wondered if the GOC felt in any way inhibited in taking decisions because of policy decisions or orders emanating from London?[28]

The GOC replied that he did not, but it is interesting to note that Chichester-Clark seemed keen on knowing whether London had any input in the operational management of the army, considering that it was London that was in charge of it. The rift developing between the RUC and the army was also mentioned at this meeting, with the GOC stating that 'The...whole problem is the RUC.'[29]

In his notes for his meeting with the GOC, Chichester-Clark mentions various names of applicants to the new Ulster Defence Regiment (UDR), set up to replace the discredited 'B' Specials. It is a testament to the mentality of the man and his cabinet at the time that he intended to complain to the GOC that 'allegedly well-known Republicans' were being accepted into the new regiment but that a 'prominent' member of the Orange Order was 'not acceptable': 'If people like [name withheld] who [along with the prominent member of the Orange Order] both served in the British Army in war,[30] are to be suspect, there is bound to be a lack of confidence.'[31] He then went on to say:

> This is a list of minor allegations, but they are symptomatic of the general unease, particularly of those who live in country districts. Until they are convinced that the UDR is as effective as the USC [Ulster Special Constabulary, the 'B' Specials], there will continue to be agitation and trouble.[32]

In London, the Labour government under Harold Wilson was still acutely unaware of how the situation on the streets of Belfast concerning the army was changing. Although it recognised the provocative nature of the Orange marches, the tendency seemed to be to immediately blame Republican elements within the crowds of rioters for the disorder.

Stormont, not surprisingly, agreed. The Unionist government had long been of the opinion that the civil rights movement, the rioting of 1969 and the need for troops to bolster the forces of law and order in the state were a Republican-inspired attempt to destabilise the existing regime.[33] Unionists now laid the blame for every incident at the door of militant Catholics. This was especially true of the weekend of 27–28 June 1970, the next phase in the long and tragic history of the conflict.

Before this event, however, there were major political changes in Britain. On 18 June 1970 the Conservatives were returned to power in a British general election. This was greeted with a certain amount of joy in the Unionist community. As Peter Taylor stated, 'Protestants were elated ... the Conservatives were after all the Conservative and Unionist Party'.[34] Protestants now believed that firm action would be taken against the militants within the Catholic minority. As Michael Murphy, in *Gerry Fitt: A Political Chameleon*, suggests: 'The Conservative Party and the Unionist Party had, of course, strong and close historical links. Unionist demands for a military solution would have found sympathetic ears in certain "law and order Tory" circles.'[35]

Under the new prime minister, Edward Heath, Reginald Maudling became the new home secretary, with Lord Carrington defence secretary. The new government at once declared that there would be no change in London's policy towards Northern Ireland. Nevertheless, there is an ongoing debate about the true nature of the Conservatives' policies towards Northern Ireland in their first few weeks in power. Michael Cunningham suggests that the policy of reforms forced on Stormont by Labour in 1969 and the security policies they originally implemented were not likely to change; as the Conservatives had supported these policies in opposition, they would continue to implement them now in power.[36] Maudling, in his first visit to Belfast as home secretary, said: 'First of all I think there is an impression in some quarters that a change of government in Westminster would mean a change in policy towards Northern Ireland. This I may assure you is not so.'[37]

Sabine Wichert suggests, however, that the army gained more freedom of action at this juncture.[38] The GOC, in a meeting of the British Cabinet on 26 June, asked for an increase in troop numbers before the election, citing foreseeable trouble in the traditional marching season, and was given an extra 'five additional battalions' by the new government.[39] The traditional support that the Conservatives had given to the Unionists in Northern Ireland in the past, and also the 'hands off' approach of successive Conservative governments in London, may also have played a role in the subsequent handling of the Stormont government. Ronald Weitzer has suggested that Heath initially had little or no interest in the situation in Northern Ireland, and that Maudling constantly advised against any form of interference in the situation at all.[40] Taylor suggests that Heath's new government, unaware of the complexities of the situation, regarded it as a 'law and order' problem, and thus acted accordingly.[41] Whether this is a correct portrayal of the initial months of Heath's government is open to debate. Nevertheless, Heath's ignorance of the complexities of the situation was compounded in the Cabinet meeting on 26 June when he suggested that 'the security problem might be eased if some way could be found of ending the traditional and provocative practice of routing marches and demonstrations by one contending party through the territory of the other'.[42] If this could have been achieved, the conflict would indeed have been stifled at birth and the warring communities would have retreated into their own territories and lived a peaceful, if segregated, existence. However, the Protestant assumption that they could march anywhere on the 'Queen's Highway' and Catholic anger towards these denigrating symbols of superiority were always going to exist. Centuries of tradition and suspicion had ensured that, and would continue to do so.

IV

The Short Strand area of east Belfast is a Catholic enclave surrounded almost exclusively by Protestant districts. It escaped the worst of the severe violence that engulfed the Falls district the previous summer but was still a tense area. Inter-communal tension naturally existed here, as in other parts of Belfast where the two communities lived in close proximity to each other. All eyes though were on the impending marching season, and anticipation within Belfast was high that it could turn out to be another summer of violence and mayhem. Discussions were held in Downing Street about the possibility of banning all marches that summer, but the conclusion was that this might inflame the situation even further.[43]

On 26 June sporadic rioting broke out after an Orange march on the Crumlin Road and lasted well into the early hours of the next morning. However, Saturday 27 June saw some of the worst rioting in Belfast since the summer of 1969. Another Orange parade was determined to march down some of the most sensitive routes in Belfast, passing the Clonard area and Cupar Street. Prince and Warner suggest that there was a certain amount of organisation in the ensuing violence; members of the military present were aware that members of the OIRA were ready to attack the marchers.[44] Taylor found it 'an astonishing error of judgement' that the parade was not banned, considering the tense atmosphere in Belfast in the preceding weeks.[45]

Nevertheless, both sides were ready for violence that day. Orange marchers were seen carrying bricks and bottles,[46] although it could be argued, and was suggested, that these were for 'defensive' purposes. As the rioting intensified, with three Protestants losing their lives, violence spread to the Short Strand area.[47] Once again differing opinions exist as to who started the violence in the Short Strand. Prince and Warner offer the following explanation, quoting from Raymond Quinn:

> Passing the notorious Catholic Seaforde Street, close to the [St Matthew's] chapel ... it [the parade] launched into its usual zest of 'Kick the Pope' tunes. Stones began to fly in each direction as the Irish Flag was waved from Seaforde Street. As in Ardoyne earlier, shots rang out and fire was returned without injury.[48]

Another young witness described the scene at the time the march reached Seaforde Street:

> A Loyalist band stopped at the bottom of Seaforde Street to play sectarian tunes and taunt nationalists. Later, an Orange mob looted and destroyed

Catholic owned premises along the Newtownards Road before launching a full scale attack on the area ... the Strand must have seemed like an easy target for Orangemen seeking revenge for being prevented from marching through nationalist west Belfast.[49]

While the above statement could have come straight from the annals of the PIRA, there is a certain element of truth in it. Protestant mobs *were* attempting to set fire to St Matthew's church. Billy McKee, who was in the Clonard area at the time, had gone to the Short Strand with others to see what was happening. They ended up in the grounds of the church. McKee procured weapons from a dump in the Falls and began to fire at the Protestant mobs, who returned fire towards the church. In the ensuing gun battle McKee himself was shot in the back and one of his 'comrades' was shot in the throat.[50] McKee later spoke of the encounter to Peter Taylor, in *Provos*:

> I told Henry to get behind a tree as a couple of men came forward. I told him fire and he did but I don't think he hit anybody. All I heard was a clomp like a wet log hitting the ground. It was like a big tree falling. I knew he was hit when he went down. He never said a word. He was hit in the throat. He was taken to hospital but died that night ... As I turned round to give Henry another order, I was shot in the back and the bullet came up through my neck. There was a lot of blood. So I spun round and got the wall. As I held it, two men came up to me. They thought I was gone but they fired a shot and hit me in the arm. I just clomped down and there was all blood everywhere. I think they thought I was shot in the chest and dead. I survived, Henry didn't.[51]

Warner disagrees that Henry McIlhone was a 'comrade' of McKee's, however. In '*Belfast and Derry in Revolt*' he attests that he was a bystander, and that the conclusions of the HET investigation into his death not only confirm this, but state that it was also Republicans that shot him.[52] Two more Protestants were also killed that evening, bringing the day's death toll to six.

Soldiers were alleged to have stood by, 'like statues', and watched the ensuing gun battle develop.[53] Adams states that when the army was asked to intervene in the area, soldiers refused to get involved.[54] However, the consensus is that the army was seriously overstretched that night in Belfast and, considering their numbers, possibly felt unable to intervene. This is the more likely scenario. Rioting was still intense in other parts of the city. Contrary to what Adams has said, when the army was asked to intervene, it said that 'troops would be deployed at 1.05am', but these soon withdrew from the scene as they came under sustained attack.[55] The GOC could only deploy one platoon to the area and, as Taylor says, this was forced back by a Protestant mob.[56] By early the next morning, however, the rioting and shooting had stopped. The Short Strand was like a war zone. British troops, freed from other areas of Belfast, moved into the area.[57] Now, on the morning of Sunday, 28 June 1970, the recriminations and accusations would start in earnest.

V

The fact that the PIRA was in offensive action on the night of 27 June convinced many within the authorities, citing the relative calm in the area that preceded the violence, that the rioting in the Short Strand was pre-planned.[58] However, this can be disputed. An Orange parade was allowed to march through the area, as a gesture for cancelling other smaller parades. Considering the extreme tension within the city as a whole, and in Catholic areas in particular, random provocation was inevitable. Ronald Burroughs, the new UK representative in Northern Ireland, tried in vain to have the Orange marches re-routed away from Catholic areas, correctly foreseeing trouble.[59] After the violence had subsided, Burroughs then reported to London that 'the Catholics started the rioting', and also claimed that the Catholics fired the first shots.[60] Protestant witnesses also described abuse being shouted at the marchers as they went by the Catholic Seaforde Street. Catholics threw stones and other missiles, which were returned by the marchers.[61]

It is hard to see how the rioting in the Short Strand was pre-planned. Burroughs uses the fact that the Catholic Church had stopped 'bombard-ing me with accusations or pleas'[62] as some sort of admission of guilt that Catholics had started it. The PIRA claim they were acting in defence of the area when they started shooting, although as Patterson states: 'The [P]IRA action made its own contribution to inflaming an already dire situation, but one where the main threat was to church property, not Catholic lives.'[63]

Billy McKee was in the Clonard that evening, well away from the trouble spot.[64] It was only when word was given to him about the violence in the area that he went there. There was shooting on both sides, but it cannot be proven conclusively who fired the first shots. One factor did emerge from the Short Strand rioting, however. The PIRA, not the army, were now seen as the natu-ral defenders of the vulnerable Catholic communities in the eyes of many.[65]

Tensions were at boiling point in Belfast after the rioting of 27–28 June. General Freeland was under severe pressure for the inaction of the army in the Short Strand and the lack of a coherent plan for the defence of vulnerable areas.

Protestants were aghast that the army had not done more in the rioting in the
Short Strand; indeed, in Stormont, during a debate on the Criminal Justice
Bill, the performance of the army in the Short Strand came under severe criti-
cism, resulting in the Unionist MP for the district stating that he could:

> ... ask without fear and I do so courageously for the removal of General
> Freeland as head of the Army in this part of the Province. I think once he
> is removed we will get back to a reasonable understanding with the Army
> and then perhaps the Army will be able to do its duty in the manner it is
> supposed to do.[66]

He then went on to discuss with the house the complete inadequacy of the
army at that juncture:

> I again call for the arming of the police in times of riot and in riotous
> areas even if only as a temporary measure. If the police had been armed on
> Saturday night perhaps the deaths which have taken place would have been
> avoided. I criticise the Army for standing like statues on the Newtownards
> Road. When the shooting was coming from the direction of St Matthew's
> Chapel they did not even return the fire. They did not even make an attempt
> to get the sniper or snipers but stood there like statues.[67]

Devlin, however, disagreed with this analysis, and told him so:

> A number of people were shot outside and inside St Matthew's Chapel. No
> one has referred to the fact that there were people inside the chapel who
> were shot. How were they shot? Did they shoot themselves? Of course not.
> The sexton's house went on fire first and the people of the area went in
> to defend the chapel. The people outside who were shot came from other
> areas further up the Newtownards Road. They came there not to see what
> was going on but to join in the attacks on the chapel and set it alight. It is as
> simple as all that.[68]

The limitations on the accuracy of information received about the weekend's
events is evident in a lot of speeches made at the time in Stormont, and did little
to quell the rising anger that was now being directed towards the British army
from Protestants, and General Freeland in particular. Protestants had seen their
police force disarmed and the 'B' Specials disbanded. The army was the army,
not policemen, however, and this was becoming more evident as the summer
months of 1970 wore on. Freeland had only two battalions at his disposal in

the city that weekend, and the seriousness of the rioting meant that these were stretched to the limit. Taylor, in *Brits: The War against the IRA*, states:

> To Unionists, the weekend had been a disaster because the army had not been tough enough. The Provisional IRA had flexed its muscles, killed five Protestants, and got away with it. At St Matthew's Church, the unionist nightmare had come true and there had been no 'B' Specials to banish it.[69]

Reginald Maudling, who was paying a flying visit to Northern Ireland during this critical week, was also at a loss as to how to handle the developing situation. The PIRA had suddenly shown that it could defend Catholic areas. The 'defence' of St Matthew's church is widely viewed as being the PIRA's first real action in the Troubles and has gone down in Republican folklore as such. McKee and his compatriots were now heroes, ready, in the eyes of many Catholics, to defend them against British and Loyalist forces. In a speech to parliament on 3 July, Maudling, recognising that the previous weekend's violence had as much to do with confusion and a lack of communication between army and police as the actions of the rioters, said:

> There is need to improve even further the liaison between the police and the Army. Much has been done, and much is being done at the present moment. I discussed this with the GOC and the Inspector-General; they know the need for it, and they are urgently determined to improve liaison and make absolutely clear what are the relative functions of the two arms, as it were, of the security forces at this time. This is an urgent task, and I know that it is being tackled.[70]

However, he also gave an ominous warning to the purveyors of violent disorder: 'But let us be clear on the use of firearms. Firearms will be used by the Army against people who use firearms themselves. This is right for the protection of the public and the GOC has made that quite clear.'[71]

Much has been said, and written, about Reginald Maudling and his apparent aloofness concerning Northern Ireland. As home secretary in the new Conservative government, he was new to the job, with other areas of concern to worry about. He is, however, alleged to have been distant from the real issues facing the army and government in Northern Ireland, to the degree that he was often accused of 'sluggishness' and having a 'sense of detachment' from the people of the province.[72] He is probably most remembered, as many historians attest, for his quote on leaving Northern Ireland that week: 'For God's sake get me a Scotch, what a bloody awful country.'[73]

Notwithstanding Maudling's disinterest in Northern Ireland and its issues, the government in London was from the start under extreme pressure in the province, and without any coherent plans for a solution to the mounting problems. This was to be a fatal error. Not only Maudling, but Heath himself did not understand the complex religious and political issues at work in Northern Ireland. This is not surprising, since Northern Ireland had not been on the radar of Westminster for decades. Chichester-Clark, the Northern Ireland premier, under extreme pressure himself from Unionists, was now pushing for tougher security measures to be directed at the Catholic 'no go' areas and the army was becoming more alienated by both sides of the communities. The rioting in the Short Strand had also shown that the Provisional IRA was armed and ready, unlike the IRA of August 1969. The army now had to be seen to be in control, to get tough on the perpetrators of the violence. At the next opportunity it would indeed show the terrorists just how tough it could get, and in the process completely alienate generations of Catholics.

Criticism of the army and its inability to counter the rising level of violence was a common occurrence after the rioting in the Short Strand. The freedom of movement that Republicans had in Belfast, as the passage of IRA weapons into St Matthew's church had proved, showed many Unionists in Stormont that the army was not in control of the situation. RUC morale was at an all-time low. It was at this time that London reinforced its military presence in Northern Ireland. This consisted of 'six major units, a squadron of armoured cars and a brigade headquarters'.[74] Clearly Westminster felt that the immediate solution to the situation was more troops, especially as the main Orange parade of 12 July was fast approaching and more trouble was expected.

On 30 June the Criminal Justice (Temporary Provisions) Bill was pushed through the Northern Irish parliament. This Act carried provisions for a minimum sentence of six months for riotous behaviour and up to twelve months for public order offences. The period of time that the 'Temporary Provisions' of the Act were to last was to be dictated by the length of the 'state of emergency', thus they were for an indefinite period.[75] It was another example of Stormont panicking in the face of mounting violence.

Belfast was now was on a knife edge. Catholic areas of the city were on high alert for more trouble following the increase in violence the previous weekend. This was especially true of the Falls area, and the streets and alleyways of the lower Falls. Traditionally, this area was the 'largest, most active, and most influential area within the Republican Movement in Belfast'.[76] Much of the inter-communal violence of August 1969 happened around its narrow streets, and the Official IRA had entrenched itself deeply within the district. By the summer of 1970 the two IRAs, Provisional and Official, were operating within the area. The PIRA in the lower Falls were heavily outnumbered by the Officials, and thus were not as active in the area. The Officials, seeing the Provisionals on the ascent, began to stockpile weapons in the lower Falls area.[77] In this way, the Officials were preparing for reprisal attacks on the British army after the dire warnings from the GOC that petrol bombers were liable to be shot. Moreover, they were also preparing for another 'Doomsday' situation, similar to August 1969.[78]

The Officials regarded themselves as anti-sectarian; while they would defend Catholic areas against further Protestant incursions, their units were under strict orders to refrain from attacking Protestants and also to prevent Catholics partaking in sectarianism.[79] They believed that the Provisionals' actions the previous weekend only served to alienate working-class Protestants and Catholics from each other. The army was now on full alert. The Protestant marching season was entering its busiest phase and Belfast was combustible.

4

CURFEW?

'In a hundred years from now, when the last of the 'Operation Banner'
soldiers are long dead, then historians will be able to get a taste of what
really took place.'
Soldier, Northern Ireland, 1970 [1]

I

On Friday, 3 July 1970, the RUC had a tip-off that there were weapons in a
house in Balkan Street, off the Falls Road. Searches for weapons had been
carried out in other areas of Belfast, but the lower Falls area had yet to experience a search. The RUC had not been in the district since August of the
previous year, and an RUC search in conjunction with the British army was
always going to look provocative to the people of the Falls.[2] The timing of
the raid on the house is still under some debate; however, an eye witness states
that between 4 and 5 p.m. a joint army/RUC patrol of six vehicles entered
Balkan Street and cordoned off both ends.[3] The housewife at no. 24 later
spoke about the moment the patrol turned up:

> It was a quiet day, and I was in the house, making the children their dinner.
> I sent the eldest lad down the chippy for chips. In the meantime the door
> was rapped and the army and the RUC came in. The soldiers went straight
> into the scullery [kitchen] and knocked all the delf [plates] down. The RUC
> turned the TV off ... they asked where he [the husband] was and I said
> I didn't know and then they went upstairs and found stuff [weapons]. They
> asked about it and I said I knew nothing about it. In the process ... they
> were going to arrest me; they were just going mad and shouting. At one

stage a neighbour managed to get into the house and explained that I was only out of hospital. They sort of took her word for that. They were in the house for a couple of hours and then after they left … there were a whole lot of people about. There was shouting and things, and then next thing the CS gas started and everybody was scared … the defence committee came in and took me and the children out of the house.[4]

The total amount of 'stuff' found in the house consisted of 'one rifle, one Schemeisser sub-machine gun, fifteen pistols and a quantity of explosives and ammunition.'[5]

The following statement is from Mr Maguire, resident of 24 Balkan Street:

Well I was coming home on 3 July; it would have been after 6 p.m. It was a Friday night. I was with the boss in the car and we were coming up wee McDonnell Street and you could see right up, there was rioting going on and the boss stopped the car on the corner of Leeson Street. I asked this fella, 'what's going on?' He said 'your house is raided'. I said to the boss, 'get me out of here quick'. But I said 'hold on I want to see how my wife and kids is'. So we drove up another wee bit and a certain person said, 'look don't worry your wife and kids are taken care of, we need to get you out of this area'. But unfortunately I couldn't and I spent the whole night in the Curfew in a certain person's house.[6]

It is interesting to note here that Maguire was, according to the *Sunday Times Insight Team*, an 'auxiliary' for the Official IRA. This meant that although he was not a full member of the organisation he did offer his services. Subsequently, according to the *Insight Team*, '… a small group of men approached the occupant of 24 Balkan Street… They were from the Official wing of the IRA… The officials now asked the man to store a load of arms.'[7] He agreed, on condition that they were taken away in 24 hours. At this point it seems that they were not collected at that time, and his wife then went to the Officials to ask for them to be removed. By that evening however the raid on the house was underway.[8]

By this time people were gathering on the street, curious as to what was happening. As the search continued, the tension amongst the people on seeing the RUC back in the lower Falls began to build. A priest was asked to liaise between the people and the army in order to avoid trouble. The priest and local defence volunteers went around the area in order to calm people's fears about the raid, and also asked the army officer in charge to 'hurry up', considering the amount of anger that was now building up on the street.[9]

The joint army/RUC patrol, their search finished, proceeded to pull away. They turned up Osman Street and left into Raglan Street. It was here that two youths, clearly annoyed with their presence, threw stones at the column of trucks. This is also the moment when the army was alleged to have come under attack, with 'heavy organised rioting'.[10] Many witnesses, however, attest that the army overreacted at this point, returning CS gas at the stone throwers.[11] The Central Citizens Defence Committee's (CCDC) report from the time backs up the overreaction analysis, saying that the army had not learned the lessons of the Ballymurphy riots in the spring, and allowed a minor bit of stone throwing to escalate into a riot.[12] Lieutenant-Colonel Michael Dewar gave his version of events in his book:

> After the find one Platoon was effectively besieged in the middle of the Falls. Elsewhere in the same area one Company was stranded. Two more Companies were despatched to the rescue and they were forced to fire CS [gas]. By 5.40pm that afternoon the Falls was in chaos. More troops went to rescue the rescuers. Residents took this for an invasion.[13]

Whatever the case was, and there are still wildly differing opinions, the whole area erupted. More people came on to the streets, incensed with what they saw as army brutality. As the situation developed, more troops were called. Barricades were being hastily erected in an effort to keep the reinforcements out of the area. At 6.55 p.m. the first use of explosives was recorded, a couple of home-made nail bombs which were thrown at the troops.[14] There is every reason to believe that it was the Provisionals. The Officials, worried that the arms they had stored in dumps would be found if the army launched a full-scale search, began hastily to move their weapons from the area.[15] It was at this point, about 8 p.m., that shots were fired at the army.

Taylor suggests that Billy McKee telephoned the Officials commander in the lower Falls to offer 'comradely assistance' from the Provisionals, but this was declined.[16] The lower Falls was the domain of the Official IRA and if any defending was to occur, they were to do it. They had the weaponry, the volunteers and the motives. The request could have also been turned down because of the show of strength by the Provisionals the week before at the Short Strand. The Officials did not want to be upstaged in the lower Falls. However, the Provisionals did participate that night, although in limited form. Brendan Hughes, later Officer Commanding of the PIRA Belfast Brigade, was a volunteer in the Provisionals 'D' Company, which covered the lower Falls. Radicalised and seasoned during the August riots of the previous year, he was already a rising star within the PIRA. He recalled later: 'During that whole day there was a continuous gun battle, [with] blast bombs being thrown at the British.'[17]

It was at this point that the first fatality of the weekend occurred. Charles O'Neill was a 36-year-old ex-RAF man who lived with his mother, niece, her husband and baby. Invalid with a chronic asthmatic problem, he was well known in the area and as such many people still remember today the circumstances surrounding his death.[18] Taylor, in *Provos*, states that it was in the confusing atmosphere that he was accidentally crushed by an army Humber one-tonner on railings.[19] Warner suggests that he was deliberately run down, but says that there was no independent evidence to prove it.[20] Eye witnesses have, however, stated that he was killed by an army truck, travelling at speed, while he attempted to warn them of the agitation they were causing amongst the people of the area.[21] Many witnesses also attest that the vehicle accelerated when O'Neill walked out on to the road.[22] Liam McAnoy states that he was killed around 6.45 p.m.[23] O'Neill's body was taken away in an army ambulance.[24]

At around 7 p.m. the Provisional IRA decided to attack the army with what limited ammunition they had. Billy McKee is said to have ordered the unit to attack the army anyway, then immediately leave the area.[25] This they did, with what amounted to between five and twelve minutes of shooting. As mentioned, the Provisionals probably also threw the first nail bombs. This was, in effect, the only Provisional action of the Curfew. Hughes and a number of other Provisionals hid in various houses waiting for the situation to settle before they could make their escape. General Dyball, in charge of the operation under the GOC, decided around 7.15 p.m. to seal off the lower Falls area to prevent movement of people and weapons.[26] It was at this point, however, as McAnoy says, that 'Dyball decided to mount a large scale search operation involving four battalions.'[27] More reinforcements were arriving hourly, some of whom had only arrived in Northern Ireland recently. 'Dave' was one of these who were immediately rushed to the lower Falls. This is what he initially witnessed:

Things were heating up. Houses around the lower Falls were being searched, and the Catholics suddenly changed their attitude towards us. No more cups of tea, just hard stares from the women, then stones being thrown by the kids. We were ordered to reply with CS, in grenade and cartridge, which filled the small streets with thick clouds of the stuff. Half our respirators didn't work too well, and those that did soon filled up with sweat, so that we had to lift the bottom up, letting the sweat out, and the gas in! Our equipment had been designed for a war with Russia, and not with civilians.[28]

CS gas was now saturating the area. The army, allegedly, was launching canisters indiscriminately into the lower Falls. These canisters landed on the roofs and in the back yards of the terraced houses, forcing people to take cover wherever they could. One witness described canisters of gas going directly into people's houses through windows and doors; such was the ferocity of the barrage.[29] Another man, a local Republican activist, remembers the fears that many people had as the barrage continued: 'They fired all sorts of CS gas, obviously the people panicked. It came from everywhere … the army went up Raglan Street … they were firing [CS gas cartridges] randomly.'[30]

The Officials by this point were manning the barricades and distributing weapons amongst members. Roughly seventy men were now involved in shooting incidents with the army, with heavy firing in Plevna Street being reported.[31] Sniping continued throughout the evening, and vehicles were commandeered to help secure the barricades at Albert Street.

Meanwhile, on the Falls Road, the situation seemed to be calming down. Pat, who lived at the bottom of Sevastopol Street where it joins the Falls Road, recalled that the army was now in control and that things seemed to be easing off.[32] She had two young children with no food in the house. Talking to a neighbour over the back wall, whom she was asking for milk and cigarettes, she was informed that nobody was to leave their homes on pain of being shot.[33] Just around the corner, however, William Burns, a 54-year-old local maintenance man, was standing at his front door talking to a local shopkeeper who was shutting up his shop. As the CCDC later reported:

> At the other side of the road near the corner of Panton Street an army patrol was approaching … the derelict Clonard Cinema. At about 8.20 p.m. …there was a burst of fire. The neighbour for the moment had no idea that his friend was hit, but William Burns took a few steps through the doorway and collapsed across the living room couch.[34]

William Burns died on the way to the hospital. The bullet that killed him hit him 'in the right breast only a few inches below the shoulder'.[35] It was also reported that the army said to his sister that he had 'no right standing at his door'.[36] This allegation was subsequently brought up in the London parliament; however, it is not verified elsewhere.

Upwards of a thousand people were taken out of the area as the situation was deteriorating. These included the elderly, the infirm, sick residents and young children. They were evacuated by members of the Knights of Malta and the Legion of Mary, first-aid volunteers within the area. Many types of vehicle were commandeered to carry the people out of the area and away from the effects of the violence.[37] At this point the main issue with the residents, however, was not the number of troops or the gunfire; it was the amount of CS gas that was being launched into the area. All of the witnesses whom the author spoke to remember the gas and the effect that it was having on the people. 'Lorna' was one and, although a young age at the time, she clearly remembers being worried about her mother who was heavily pregnant and suffering with the effects of exposure to so much gas.[38] A soldier who was in the thick of it in the lower Falls that evening recalled: 'CS was everywhere, and even today I get the smell of that muck coming back to me, it makes me retch.'[39]

A local priest, Fr. Padraig Murphy, attempted to stop the army firing so much gas into the area and phoned army headquarters in Lisburn. He was put through to General Freeland. There follows a transcript of the telephone conversation that was reported by the CCDC at the time. There was a witness to the conversation, Paddy Devlin, Stormont MP for the area:

> **Freeland**: Fr. Murphy, you are now under my orders.
>
> **Fr. Murphy**: I dispute that – I am not under your orders. I am under the moral law. I myself and also my vigilantes have been repeatedly gassed while attempting to persuade the people to disperse. This is an entirely new situation. Can you not give some order that would allow us to go about our work of persuasion without this hindrance?
>
> **Freeland**: You will get out on those streets and tell those people of yours to get in or they will be shot.
>
> **Fr. Murphy**: This is the point I am ringing about. How can I do this without vigilantes?
>
> **Freeland**: I don't recognise your vigilantes.
>
> **Fr. Murphy**: I am only one man, and there are about thirty thousand people in the whole area. How can I go around and contact them all individually?
>
> **Freeland**: Very good then. Use your men.
>
> **Fr. Murphy**: Can I tell my men they will not be gassed?
>
> **Freeland**: No! They are better gassed than shot.[40]

This conversation with Freeland suggests that he was under extreme pressure to deliver on the Unionist demands in sorting out the Catholic no-go areas. It also suggests that the GOC ultimately saw the whole area as a hotbed of Republican militancy, whether of the Official IRA or the Provisionals. There seemed to be no difference between the two at that point in the GOC's mind.

The GOC might also have been embarrassed by comments made by Jim Sullivan, an Official IRA leader, and might thus have employed a certain amount of pre-planning in his subsequent search operation. According to

Devlin, Sullivan had 'recently criticised army policy and Lieutenant-General Sir Ian Freeland in particular.'[41] This is unlikely on its own to have influenced the GOC to plan for the searches,[42] but the idea that there was pre-planning for the Falls Curfew *has* got its adherents. The search happened at tea time on a Friday, just as many people in the area were returning from work or the local pubs.[43] Devlin mentions 'hundreds' of soldiers in Durham and Divis Streets with armoured cars and lorries, parked up and waiting to go.[44] This story is given more credence by McClenaghan, who is convinced that the whole operation was a pre-planned one; he personally saw rows of armoured vehicles lined up as well.[45]

At about 10 p.m. a helicopter flew overhead and announced to the lower Falls that the whole area was to be placed under curfew. The helicopter had been out all evening, observing the worsening situation. *Operation Banner*, the army's assessment of its period in Northern Ireland, suggests that the helicopter may have been hit by gunfire coming from the lower Falls. It later made an emergency landing.[46] Although *Operation Banner* has now been withdrawn because of inaccuracies, this detail is also reported elsewhere.[47] This point is interesting. It is known that the brigade commander who was in the helicopter was in constant touch with the GOC during the time he was over the lower Falls. He had another conversation with the GOC soon after the helicopter made an emergency landing.[48] It is quite possible that his conversation with the GOC tipped the balance towards sending in four battalions of troops and ordering a large-scale search of the area, which ultimately increased the violence.

'Gill', then an 18-year-old girl living in Theodore Street, described how she and her family heard the helicopter overhead stating that there was to be a curfew and that everyone had to get indoors. The soldiers who were by now on her street were also telling people. She witnessed soldier brutality at first hand; many of them were going around literally throwing people into their homes. At the best of times, people were forcibly put in. She remembers the feeling of being hemmed in, and that everyone in the house was scared. She also wondered about the old people who lived on her street, and wondered if they were all right. She remembered the blast bombs thrown by the IRA, and remarked how they reminded her of cigarette butts in the dark.

She also stated that soldiers wrecked houses that nobody was living in, pulled ceilings down in the ones that were occupied and took what they wanted from the homes that they raided. She alleged witnessing soldiers looting a pub, filling up a lorry with the goods and taking it away.[49]

The stipulations of the Curfew were that people were to get indoors immediately or face arrest. It was also announced by loudhailer on the ground and published as a press release.[50] This had the desired effect of dispersing many of the people, but the Officials were still out, exchanging gunfire with the troops. By now the whole area was sealed off and troops were stationed at the entrances to the lower Falls. The area the Curfew encompassed was initially up the Falls Road from the Albert Street junction to the Springfield Road, down the Grosvenor Road to Cullingtree Road and from there to the junction with Albert Street. Later, on the Saturday, the Curfew area was extended to include streets on the other side of the Falls Road, namely streets off the Springfield Road and the district of Clonard, although there was some confusion as to exactly where the Curfew was in force. The whole area encompassed about sixty streets. Nobody was allowed in or out of the area. Pat McCotter, then a 16-year-old boy, recalls:

> I was sitting on our street at Westrock bungalows that over looked Beechmount and the Royal [Hospital]. We could see the helicopter hovering over the curfew area; never saw it so far up, maybe it was out of shooting range, but we could hear them very clearly announcing that there was now a curfew in progress and every one in that area had to get indoors by a certain time and I think everyone else was told to stay out of the area. We could hear the gun fire and nail bombs going off.[51]

Another witness described leaving work in the centre of Belfast at about 11 p.m. and smelling CS gas. He knew that something was seriously wrong, considering the distance he was from the lower Falls. As the evening wore on, sporadic gunfire was still being exchanged between the Officials and the army. Three soldiers were injured by a sniper in Omar Street as the army began to move into the narrow streets to conduct a major search operation. Hanley and Millar described the shootings of the soldiers: 'It was purely coincidental, they [The Officials] were in the right streets at the right time, they knew the streets; the backyard walls came in very handy.'[52] 'Dave' also remembers the shootings: 'I was manning a dannet wire street block at the bottom of Omar Street, when we came under heavy fire ... Bullets were whistling down the street, and one soldier I remember was hit in both legs. All hell let loose.'[53]

The following account of the events of that harrowing first evening of the Curfew was kindly given to the author by Danny Morrison, former Sinn Féin director of publicity and now an author and writer. The account is from Thomas Quigley, who was subsequently jailed for his activities in the PIRA.

> By the time it was getting dark the shooting was really starting. A crowd of us were standing at a place called The Gap when a Saladin Tank wheeled around the corner. We couldn't believe it, when it turned its cannon on us.

We started running like lunatics and it fired [the soldiers had fired from the tank's 76mm main gun]. The roar was deafening and the houses shook but later we realised that they had fired a blank shell ... A ferret car pulled up outside the [Raglan Street] school [which was set up as a makeshift first aid centre] and opened fire on the building with a machine gun. The people were shouting out the windows, 'This is a first aid station! This is a first aid station! There are people wounded in here!' The Brits got out and put an explosive device against the metal doors which had been locked behind us and blew them open. They stood pointing their rifles and shouted that if we came out and got searched they would let us go home. People started filing out but when they got us outside they beat us up.

We were put in the back of lorries and taken first to Springfield Road barracks, but it was packed with prisoners. [We were] then [taken] to Andersonstown Barracks, but there was no room there, either. Finally, they took us over to Castlereagh Barracks in East Belfast.[54]

Many witnesses also attest that they were unaware that a curfew had been ordered by the GOC.[55] It was only when the army physically handled many of these indoors that they became aware. As people began to get indoors, the streets began to quieten down. One of those who were probably unaware of any restrictions on the streets was a 63-year-old man called Patrick Elliman, who lived at No. 12 Marchioness Street with his sister Kathleen. At about 11 p.m. he decided to take a walk down Marchioness Street to the corner of Cullingtree Road. His nephew by marriage, Eamonn, gave the following account to the author.

Residents were told to stay indoors, but Eamonn's wife's uncle, Patrick Elliman, most probably did not hear the order of Curfew. Mr Elliman decided to go for a walk to the end of Marchioness Street, to its junction with Cullingtree Road. As he was doing this, Eamonn got word to his brother, James, that Patrick was outside. As the brother went to get Patrick in, there was firing from, as Eamonn attests, the British soldiers. Eamonn did not say where from, but was adamant that it was British fire. A bullet went into the side of Patrick's head, Eamonn put a cloth on the wound and Eamonn and his father-in-law (Patrick's brother) carried the dying man back to No. 22 Marchioness Street, James's home.

Eamonn said that when he went to take off the cloth that covered the wound, bits of brain and fragments of skull came off with it. He then decided to go and seek medical assistance, and began to run towards Sultan Street. It was at this point, according to Eamonn, that he was fired upon by British soldiers 'from about 50 yards away'. He also added that it was 'daylight'.

He managed to get to Sultan Street, 'dodging bullets all the way', and gained the assistance of an Order of Malta person. Eamonn said that he had a hold of the person 'by the back of his white coat', and was hiding behind him all the way back to No. 22 Marchioness Street. When they got there, the Order of Malta person took a look at Patrick and told Eamonn and Patrick's brother that there was nothing that he could do for him.

According to Eamonn, when an ambulance was requested, it took a 'long time' for it to arrive. Eamonn said that Patrick Elliman was in his slippers when he went out, and had rolled up shirt sleeves, so why would he go out like this if he was 'going to shoot' at somebody?[56]

Patrick Elliman never regained consciousness after the shooting and died in hospital nine days later. His brother James was also on the receiving end of the army's violence, being whacked over the head by a baton and having his head grazed with a bullet. He carried the scar as a reminder of that weekend for the rest of his life. James's daughter Rita remembers her father's emotional turmoil on the day of Mr Elliman's funeral: 'On the morning of the funeral my father was upstairs sitting on his bed. He was crying, sobbing. All he kept saying was "They murdered my brother, they murdered my brother".'[57]

A subsequent inquest was held into the death of Patrick Elliman. According to Eamonn, who was present, it 'was a whitewash'. Eamonn was threatened with contempt of court for saying that his uncle by marriage was 'murdered', and states that the court took the word of the 'squaddies', whose identities were protected, rather than the general public, some of whom witnessed the event. The conclusion of the inquest, according to Eamonn, was that Patrick Elliman died as a result of 'misadventure'.[58]

A request for information on the death of Patrick Elliman was sent to the Police Service of Northern Ireland under the Freedom of Information Act. Information was denied because there is an ongoing enquiry by the Historical Enquiries Team into one or more of the deaths that weekend, and any information given could jeopardise the investigation.

In a debate in the Westminster parliament in January 1971, Ian Gilmour MP, the under-secretary of state for defence, stated that Mr Elliman was not killed by an army bullet.[59] The witnesses who saw Patrick Elliman shot disagree. 'Gill' stated to the author that it was the 'Welsh Guards' who shot Mr Elliman,[60] although there is no independent evidence to support this.[61]

Many press reporters and journalists were in the area covering the evening's events, and were just as liable to arrest as the public. The following is an extract from an article by the *Irish Times* reporter Henry Kelly, who was in the Curfew area:

Shortly before midnight I was walking up Divis Street. The limit of the Curfew area was not clearly defined, and some people, principally press-men, were still trying to make their way up to a concentration of troops at Albert Street traffic lights. With a colleague from the Press Association [name withheld], I made my way from shop door to shop door towards the troops. Without warning a soldier in front of us, not more than 100 yards, spun round and several soldiers shouted. We both roared 'Press' and tried to show our press cards by waving them. One of the soldiers however dropped to one knee and fired a single round which hit the wall several feet above our heads. Again we called who we were and this time we got a sharp com-mand. 'Come out into the middle of the street with your hands up.' As firing was continuing in the area there was a moment when neither of us knew what to do, but as the order was repeated we had little alternative.[62]

Clearly the troops were dealing with some sort of trouble at the intersec-tion of Albert Street and the Falls Road, judging by their response to the appearance of the two pressmen. Kelly then said:

For almost a minute we stood, hands high, in the middle of the road, under cover from several soldiers. Then we were ordered to run towards them, stop again a few feet from them, and then, with our credentials checked, we were ordered to run, heads down, a distance of about thirty yards across the open junction of Albert Street and the Falls Road to the shelter of some army vehicles.[63]

Kelly and his fellow pressman were subsequently taken to Hastings Street police station and arrested for breaking the Curfew, even though, by walking up Divis Street towards the Albert Street junction, they were, in fact, outside the Curfew area. By this time the whole area was subdued, there were no people on the streets and the shooting had stopped, save for an odd rattle from a gun. One resident, a first aider who ran out and attended Patrick Elliman, described the scene: 'The area was completely dead at the time; it was the most eerie feeling. It was like walking through a ghost town. You could hear noises in the distance but the immediate area was just like a blank silence.'[64]

The third death on the night, and the fourth in total, occurred not long after the shooting of Patrick Elliman. Zbigniew Uglik was a British-born London postman of Polish extraction. The circumstances surrounding his death are still sketchy, and are unlikely to be any clearer for a number of years due to HET investigations. The CCDC, however, suggested at the time that he was an amateur photographer taking pictures of the night's events. Others suggest, although it must be stressed that this has not been verified, that he was working for British Intelligence. Holed up in a house during the worst of the fighting, he decided to leave by the back entrance. The police version of his death at the time was that he was shot on the roof of an abandoned house in Albert Street.[65]

Tony Geraghty, in *The Irish War*, describes how the army recovered a body during the heavy sniping. As they got the body back to where they were based, they began to swear and kick out at the body. They then threw it into the back of a truck parked in front of the one that Geraghty was in – he had been arrested for allegedly 'impeding the military'. Geraghty states that the body was 'almost certainly' Uglik.[66] A subsequent request for information held by the police on the four deaths that occurred, including Uglik's, was refused by the Police Service of Northern Ireland (PSNI). An investigation into one of the deaths (unnamed) is, at the time of writing, still in progress, and the author was informed that any information given could jeopardise this investigation.[67]

An interesting addendum to this is another event described in Thomas Hennessey's *The Evolution of The Troubles* whilst talking about an exchange of fire between a soldier and a sniper, who opened up on the troops 'from the chimney stack of a house at the junction of Ross Place and Albert Street'.[68]

> After a game of cat and mouse with the sniper, who was moving around, a Corporal, shouted that a Private thought that he had hit him. This was about 2.30 or 3 a.m. About an hour and a half later an investigation troop went with a section and carried out a search for the body. The body of an unidentified male was recovered.[69]

Was Uglik the sniper? Or was it a case of mistaken identity?

It is worthy of note here that the army later claimed to have shot dead two members of the IRA, although both the Officials and the Provisionals claimed they had no deaths among their members.[70] Many within the Officials later claimed that this was a ploy by the army to justify the deaths of civilians within the area:

> The British claimed at the time to have killed two IRA members, and continued to do so despite the fact that there were no bodies. The media, Irish as well as British, reported this claim as accurate. This set a dangerous precedent, with the British army seeking to justify civilian deaths by claiming the deaths of non-existent snipers and bombers.[71]

The *Irish Times* subsequently reported on Monday 6 July a quote from army headquarters in Lisburn: 'The one definite thing is that the army killed two snipers, one at the junction of Albert Street and the other ... Marchioness Street.'[72] Zbigniew Uglik was shot in Albert Street that night; Patrick Elliman was shot in Marchioness Street. Fifty-seven people were also injured on the Friday night, although, as many would not have gone to hospital for fear of arrest, the actual figure is almost certainly much higher. Dave recalled seeing the injured on the ground in the lower Falls, and was extremely surprised that there were not more, considering the scale of the violence.

II

A widespread search operation was now under way for arms and explosives in the lower Falls, and mass arrests were occurring within the area, with the arrested mainly taken to Springfield Barracks. Liam McAnoy was one of those arrested, at midday on the Saturday. It was at this point, however, that *certain elements* within the ranks of troops positioned in the area under curfew are claimed to have acted aggressively and maliciously. Devlin recalls: 'They axed doors down that could have easily been opened, ripped up floorboards, broke furniture unnecessary and tipped the contents of drawers and cupboards all over the place.'[73] Other residents spoke of widespread stealing by the soldiers. Many were allegedly drunk on the proceeds of looting local pubs. Residents also spoke of the effects of the gas on their families and the damage caused by the soldiers to their properties.[74] Sectarianism was rife; the army units within the area included the Black Watch from Scotland, the King's Own Scottish Borderers (KOSB) and the Life Guards from England. The Black Watch was especially aggressive, using sectarian names and slogans against the women of the area.[75] In Eamonn's opinion, however, it was the KOSB that inflicted the most harm in the lower Falls: 'The King's Own Scottish Borderers were the worst, the most ruthless.'[76]

Along with sectarianism, many instances of religious bigotry were also reported by witnesses. Religious statues were broken and trampled on by many of the troops in the houses they entered. Pictures of religious figures on walls and cupboards were also smashed. Religious pendants were flushed down toilets. Devlin even suggests that symbols of Glasgow Celtic football club were smashed and destroyed by the Scottish troops, such was the petty nature of the violence.[77] 'Gill' remembers religious statues being broken in her house; it was done, she said, by the Black Watch.[78]

The radicalisation of the people living in the lower Falls, especially the youth of the area, was now in progress. Many witnesses who spoke about their subsequent lives as members of either the Provisionals or the Officials gave the Curfew as their reason for joining. It was a miscalculation of enormous consequence by the Stormont and London governments who allowed it to happen, and convinced generations of young people that the establishments both in Northern Ireland and in London were working against them. McClenaghan remembers the impact of what he witnessed on him and other young people:

> I was only 12 but it had a massive impact on my life. In fact [in my opinion] it turned a whole generation of British Army loving children into the most ruthless guerrilla fighters the world has ever seen.[79]

'Lisa' was another witness to the events unfolding in the lower Falls, and they dramatically changed her life. As a child growing up in the Falls area she was not aware of the religious tensions present in the city, although she was often told to take off her school uniform before she ventured anywhere other than her locality. Once the Troubles began, however, she became acutely aware of the sectarianism and religious bigotry between the two communities. The Curfew, in her mind, changed everything. The brutality of the soldiers and the CS gas are firmly etched in her memory, as was the fear of not knowing what was going to happen next. The Curfew split families apart, she said; husbands and sons went on to join either the Official or Provisional wings of the IRA. 'Lisa' herself subsequently got married and had six children. For most of their youth the father of the children was not present, having been given ten years in prison for concealing weapons and bomb-making materials, and for other offences.[80]

Hennessey also mentions many more episodes of maltreatment of people in the lower Falls; obscene language being used, valuable articles being stolen from houses and troops occupying homes and stealing food from them.[81] He also mentions a claim made by Gerry Fitt to ministers in Westminster that some women were 'molested' by soldiers.[82]

There follows an interview with a prominent Republican who witnessed the events unfolding on the streets of the lower Falls:

Interviewee: Well the British army seemed to have a free hand until the people decided to show a bit of resistance, because they were doing that much damage the people couldn't stick it anymore.

Interviewer: Well we know from media reports at the time that there were a number of British regiments taking part in this destruction. Are there any regiments that stick out that you can recall?

Interviewee: One of the regiments that sticks out were the Black Watch, and obviously the reason that they were sent in was because they were a Loyalist mob, a Loyalist mob with British uniforms on.

Interviewer: The Black Watch at that particular time and today of course had a very sectarian background. So what you are suggesting is that they were deliberately sent in a Catholic area to instil terror?

Interviewee: Instil terror and provoke some sort of reaction. You have to think this happened ten months after the pogroms in the Falls Road in 1969 when the RUC, 'B' Specials and Loyalist mobs attacked this area. So they sent the Black Watch in, and the majority of them would be Loyalist; as people know the Loyalists, be it Scottish or English, don't like the nationalist people.[83]

Beyond the witness statements of the people who lived in the lower Falls, photographs taken of the damage give a clear and concise picture of the destruction caused by the army to people's homes. There is no doubt that widespread damage was done. Soldiers went in by kicking doors down, put rifle butts through TV screens, pulled down ceilings, wrecked outside lavatories, ripped up floorboards and staircases, and tore fireplaces from walls. All of this was photographed and documented. They also broke plates and cups in the little kitchens, ripped open settees and damaged doors and windows. One witness told of troops stealing food from local shops and handing it out of the windows and doors to each other. That the army went into the lower Falls heavily there is no doubt. That some of these troops behaved with courtesy and respect for the people whose houses were being searched there is also no doubt. But the lasting memories of the population of the lower Falls at the time are of army brutality, degradation and coercion.

Amongst all the carnage that was taking place, however, there were many light-hearted stories, including children's interpretation of what was happening around them. Helena Lanigan, 7 years of age at the time, remembers one such moment:

We lived in McDonnell Street between Lady Street and Marchioness Street, with Lyle and Kinnegans brewery and minerals behind us. One Friday afternoon my mum sent me to Fusco's to buy fish and chips, and by the time I got back they had put a curfew on our block! Anyway, they wouldn't let me back in! So my mum asked the lady in the first house for a chair ... 'Sit down there and eat your dinner!' she told me. I was so embarrassed and told her I wasn't hungry ... but my mum's eyebrows lowered, and when this happened you DIDN'T argue!! She opened the paper, put on salt and vinegar, and in front of a very angry crowd ... she ORDERED me to eat! I was humiliated!

It was the first time I didn't have to share with my older sister, and I couldn't even enjoy them! But the poor soldiers blocking my path got the worst of it! They must have been starving, and the smell must have been too much, because they all looked at each other and let me through.

Another time [under curfew] my brother asked a soldier would he like a cup of tea. 'Yes please!' he said. My brother said, 'OK, just one problem … we have no teabags left. If you go to no. 29 over there, he'll give you some!' When the soldier came back, my brother said, 'Thanks, now if you go to no. 33 she'll give you some milk!' When the soldier came back the second time he said, 'There you are, I don't take any sugar!' … My brother said, 'Thanks very much, mate!' and closed the door in his face![84]

Stories like these emphasise that, while the area was under curfew, having aggressive house-to-house searches and serious rioting and shooting, some residents could still see the humorous side of life. But it also shows the disregard that many now had for the forces of law and order. There was also a sense of 'normality' amongst the people that was not crushed by the events taking place around them. This was solely down to the sense of community and togetherness that the area had nurtured for generations. Their religion, their sense of alienation from a state that did not want them in their Protestant midst, and years of ignorance to their plight from the government in London, not to mention Stormont, also added to the strong bond that people had with each other.

III

But what did the ordinary soldier on the streets of the lower Falls that July think about the events? It is believed, as mentioned, that the GOC was under extreme pressure that weekend to be seen to be getting tough in Catholic areas. Devlin, in describing the GOC after the phone call with Fr. Murphy, described him as 'quite hysterical'.[85] Fr. Murphy said that he believed that he had somewhat 'lost control of himself'. Did this pressure on the GOC feed down to the ordinary troops on the ground?

A corporal of the King's Own Scottish Borderers gave his account to Max Arthur about the beginnings of the Curfew:

When the Curfew was imposed on 3rd July we were split up into small detachments of three men and put out at various road junctions. We were told to stay there and keep the Curfew. The rules were given that if

anybody was out, we were not, obviously, to open fire indiscriminately but
to challenge them and to find out why they were on the street. If they were
unaware of the Curfew, we were to make them aware of the situation and
then urge them to go indoors under cover and stay there until such time as
they were allowed out.[86]

While this is probably a correct assumption of the role the army was to play in
the Curfew, events quickly overtook this. The statement seems to follow the
army command line of what to do in a riot situation. In direct contrast to this
is another statement from a private in 1 Para:

> The Curfew stemmed from the time the Scottish regiment did those
> searches, and that was probably when the real trouble started – not from
> '69, with all the civil rights and the focus of attention on the plight of the
> Catholics, but 1970. That's when the IRA first emerged. They'd say 'Look
> what the soldiers are doing to you. Look how they treat you. We want to
> protect you'. And the people would think, 'Ah, we need some protection
> here'. The IRA could have lain dormant for years, but they were looking for
> an excuse and they found it then, during the time when that Scotch regi-
> ment did those searches.[87]

It is clear to see from the above statement that not all the soldiers either agreed
with the way the house searches were conducted or were involved in the
wanton destruction of properties. Sending Scottish troops into an exclusively
Catholic neighbourhood to search for weapons was a huge error, given the
historical enmities between Catholics and Protestants. Many of the Scottish
soldiers were Protestants, a fact that was probably lost on the GOC and army
command at the time due to the complex nature and immediate pressure
of the operation. The corporal of the KOSB gave more of his account of
the Curfew:

> The Curfew area was the Falls, lower Shankill, Unity Flats, Turf Lodge,
> Ardoyne, all that part. The actual city centre didn't have a Curfew. You
> could draw a line right along Royal Avenue and dog-leg it down Churchill
> Street, and anything above that line was in the Curfew. If I remember right
> there wasn't much movement in the city centre at all. I was at the Unity
> Flats junction, and the only traffic I remember was a milk lorry and some
> bread vans, which were allowed to travel round. The streets were dead, very
> dead, deserted, in a major city. The traffic lights were still going as if there
> were people there, still going in sequence, but no traffic.[88]

Aside from the corporal's obvious lack of knowledge about the geographical aspects of the Curfew, which throws some doubt on his testimony, fear of the unknown and the knowledge that the area was well known as an IRA stronghold could have been another factor in the behaviour of some of the soldiers. Many were newly arrived in Belfast and were rushed straight into a major gun battle. Many were still under the age of 20 and were put up against formidable opponents, seasoned by over a year of rioting and confrontation. It is no wonder that 'errors' occurred.

'Dave' remembers the abject fear that he and many other troops on the ground felt at the time, but he also talks about the part that the police, the traditional law keepers, played in the Curfew. The RUC was by now a discredited force within Catholic areas of Belfast. The rioting of August 1969, as 'Dave' remembers, had seen to that, and this was the opinion of many within the rank and file of the army. The RUC was very good at stoking the fires of hatred in the working-class areas of west Belfast, but when the fire became out of control they ran behind the army, a witness told the author.[89] Desmond Hamill describes how, by September of 1970, the GOC and RUC chiefs were 'barely on speaking terms'.[90] The view on the ground of the animosity between the army and RUC, witnessed by many soldiers since the original deployment is summed up by 'Dave'.

> The RUC were no better [than the 'B' Specials]. They had several Shoreland Armoured Cars at the time [August 1969], and delighted in running them up and down The Falls at night, shooting up the shops and houses with the .30 Browning machine guns.[91]

In the following statement he described his feelings and fears during the initial stages of the Curfew, just as the Officials took the fight to the army, and further furnishes his own personal feelings towards the RUC:

> We took cover as best we could, and returned fire at any muzzle flash we saw. I fired about eighteen rounds that night, out of the thirty issued. All was confusion, on our side at least. We had no ambulances, and the civilian ones refused to attend. Hardly any soldiers had flak jackets, and I can tell you that we were bloody scared. When the shooting started, the RUC officers ran off. We didn't see them again for almost a week.[92]

Many of these soldiers would havehad little or no experience in urban fighting.

There were plenty of situations before the Curfew that instilled fear into the troops deployed in Belfast. The Ballymurphy riots in the spring were one example. Soldiers felt exposed in the urban environment, while their adversaries knew the area well. Soldiers were ill prepared for this type of violence and riot control. For example, one soldier during the Ballymurphy disturbances asked for permission for them to replace their 'Glengarries' (their soft hats) with steel helmets, such was the ferocity of the firing. The answer was a firm 'no'.[93] It was clear that many of these troops therefore approached the Curfew with a certain amount of trepidation; the fear of an unseen enemy made everyone a suspect. Ignorance of the enemy also affected this judgement; the IRA was the IRA, no matter in what guise it presented itself.

III

Saturday 4 July was a strange day in the lower Falls. The streets were silent, save for the roar of an army truck or a shout from a soldier. The weather was hot and humid. People were still barred from leaving their houses. Army searches continued; as the CCDC stated, much of the damage to homes in the area was allegedly done on the Saturday night. People were also not allowed into the area; subsequently, many people who could not get back to their houses on Friday evening were also not allowed in the next day. These included mothers who had left their children alone at home and fathers late home from work. Gerry Fitt, the Westminster MP for the area, was repeatedly refused permission to enter the lower Falls over the Curfew period. Devlin himself was arrested and held at gunpoint whilst taking complaints from residents in Osman and Sultan streets and was told by a soldier that he would 'blow his brains out' if he did not stop resisting. The GOC had no intention of calling off the Curfew; significant amounts of weaponry were still being found in the searches.

Hughes, who was holed up in a house in Servia Street all through Friday night, waiting for the inevitable, heard movement and shouting outside. 'Then we heard the doors getting kicked in. [Unnamed] was in the house directly facing me and his door was kicked in ... a few other doors were kicked in and I was just sitting waiting my turn. Fortunately it didn't come.'[94]

The people, however, were beginning to suffer. Many had no food, medicine or milk for their children. Many were also suffering from the effects of CS gas. Everyone was still told to stay indoors. There was no mention of the hardships imposed on the people of the lower Falls when General Freeland attended a meeting of the Joint Security Committee (JSC) at Stormont on 4 July. The GOC described the events of the previous night as a 'battle', and informed the committee that 'Occupants of the area were ordered into their homes for their own safety.'[95] This is the first mention of a restriction on the movement of people in out of the area. Later in his report the GOC was to rephrase this as a 'tight clampdown on the area'.[96] But perhaps the most important aspect of this meeting was the discussion about the legalities of the 'clampdown'. It was beginning to dawn on those present that there might not be a precedent in law for the GOC's actions the previous night: 'The advisability of legalising the "curfew" in the Falls Road area by an order under the Special Powers Act and the ancillary problem of a permit system was considered. Decision deferred for consideration by legal experts.'[97] In other words, was the Curfew legal?

At some point on Saturday afternoon it was decided to allow residents out of their homes for a period of two hours to gather much-needed supplies; however, people were still not allowed into or out of the area. This agenda was also discussed and agreed at the JSC meeting that morning. The CCDC stated that literally thousands began to queue at designated shops that were permitted to open.[98] The GOC had stated in his report to the security committee that he would authorise bread and milk to be delivered to the area between the hours of 3 and 4 p.m., and shops could open between 5 and 7 p.m.[99] Film footage of the Curfew clearly shows the people of the lower Falls queuing outside shops for a considerable time in order to gain supplies, watched by troops.

General Freeland's report to the JSC also contained information that was to enrage the local population to such an extent that they now believed that the army was just another arm of the security forces of Stormont, and was not impartial in any way. Journalists were to be taken around the lower Falls, and the arms captured so far were to be shown to the public as 'justification for the action taken by the army'.[100] However, two Unionist MPs, Captain John Brooke and William Long, were also given a tour around the lower Falls area in a press vehicle to view the scene. This sight alone alienated many Catholics, who now believed that they were part of a subjugated people, with the Unionists as their masters and the army as their tool of repression.

Raids on houses continued into Saturday night, although not on the level of the previous evening. People were back in their houses after the two-hour shopping interlude. The GOC had decided to suspend the Curfew at 9 a.m. on Sunday morning so that people could go to mass. By now, however, word had got out of the lower Falls about the conditions that the people were living in and that basic foodstuffs like bread and milk were non-existent. It was at this point that the women of west Belfast decided to break the Curfew from the outside. One witness describes the scene.

Word came up the road that all the people were kept indoors; they couldn't get out for bread or milk. A lot of them had small babies ... people decided they would have to do something about it ... when one crowd gathered another crowd gathered and we said 'we are going down to try and break the curfew'.[101]

Many groups of women and children gathered at corners and in streets, and began a march down from Ballymurphy to the lower Falls. These women carried bread, milk and baby food. The group was in the hundreds as it marched towards the Falls around 9 a.m., passing soldiers at the barricades who were at a loss for what to do. That evening, at 5 p.m., a second march was organised. Estimates vary as to the exact number involved, but the CCDC estimate of 3,000 is not an exaggeration, considering that witnesses remember 'rivers of people' coming into the lower Falls. It was through these women, with their prams, that most of the still hidden weapons were allegedly taken out of the lower Falls; the army was in no position to begin to search every person and pram.[102]

According to Republican folklore[103] the Curfew was broken by the women marching down from Ballymurphy, but the army command had already decided, albeit confusingly as many soldiers were unaware of it, not to reimpose the Curfew after the 9 a.m. mass. However, the women brought sustenance to a population almost half starved by the Curfew, burst through the ranks of the army who were still manning the roads in and out of the lower Falls, and gave moral support and a sense of belonging and comradeship that would support the population of the lower Falls and of the Falls area in general in the difficult and violent months ahead.

'Geoff' remembers the scene as thousands of people marched on the lower Falls. As the Curfew began, his car was taken out of the area. He had two cans of petrol in the boot, as fuel was difficult to come across. The army took these out of the car. Later, as the lower Falls was being fed by the people outside the Curfew, his car was used to ferry food around the area.[104]

The people of the lower Falls suffered at the hands of the army; of that, there is no doubt. The army went in with a force and purpose not seen in Northern Ireland up to that point. The army command had a point to prove, the Unionists wanted action against the Catholic areas and the Westminster government wanted to placate Unionism. The army are not policemen, and sending so many troops into a residential area with CS gas and Saracens was a dangerous exercise. Catholic alienation, already nurtured through decades of misrule by Protestants, was now almost complete.

IV

Initially the army command stated that fourteen bullets were fired by the army in the lower Falls that weekend. Later on this figure was revised to 1,454 rounds, along with 1,385 CS canisters and 218 CS cartridges. The army command treated the situation as they saw it, a military operation to wrest control of the lower Falls from the IRA, whether Provisional or Official. At a meeting of the JSC on 6 July the GOC remarked that the 'weekend search exercise had been completed satisfactorily'. The issue of complaints, and there were many, was dealt with by setting up complaints centres in Springfield Road and Hastings Street police centre. More importantly for the army command and Stormont, the issue of the publicity surrounding the events was to be dealt with by showing the seizure of arms and weaponry from the area and balancing it against the searches the previous October in the Shankill area. In this way the army command could show that the 'exercise' in the lower Falls was not anti-Catholic.[105] There was one fundamental and extremely important difference, however. Unionists in Stormont did not put severe pressure on the army command to 'sort out the Shankill'.[106]

A request for information was given to the army command in Northern Ireland by the author under the Freedom of Information Act. This included looking for information on the number of troops, the use of firearms by the army, and the regiments that were present. The information received was limited: no information could be found with regard to the number of troops that were actually on the ground or of what battalions were in operation. The Ministry of Defence supplied the names of the brigades that were in Belfast at the time, and the number of bullets that were fired by the soldiers. This information is already in the public domain.

V

After the dust had settled from the events of the weekend, the CCDC conducted a survey using students to ascertain just how much damage, both mentally and physically, the Curfew had done to the people of the lower Falls. This was carried out anonymously in order to gain as truthful an account as possible. Anonymity was also the surest way to protect many of the citizens who were involved in the initial rioting from the army and police. In this survey, and subsequent TV and radio interviews, the people of the lower Falls told of the period when the area was under curfew. The survey was conducted in great detail, including issues such as loss of earnings, cruelty to animals and loss of liberty, as well as more serious accusations of sectarian abuse and religious bigotry. However, there are instances in the survey results where the army is commended for the way it conducted the searches and this has to be taken into account too.

There follows a small sample of the major complaints that the people of the lower Falls gave the researchers, including the streets that they lived in. The author is extremely grateful to Robert McClenaghan for permission to use this material:

> **Alma Street**: Pinned down. Hemmed in.
> **Cape Street**: Wife unable to get clothes from house on release from hospital. Kept in all night while their children were alone in Turf Lodge. Mother could not get out to hospital. Food damaged by gas. Gas destroyed drink and clothes. Gas caused diarrhoea.
> Food shortages were reported from nearly all the houses surveyed. There were no fridges in the houses and fresh food like milk and bread was bought daily.
> **Albert Street**: Baby without milk. No food and no shilling for meter.
> **Balkan Street**: No bread. No food.

The amount of CS gas used was a major issue. Clouds of it were still drifting around the lower Falls long after the situation had quietened down. According to the CCDC, one resident in five in the area that was under curfew regarded the gas as the main complaint against the army.[107]

> **Dunmore Street**: 'Being old I got chesty.'
> **Springview Street**: Effects of gas on baby.

Soldiers' reactions to the situation once the area was under curfew were also taken into account. These give an interesting insight into the behaviour of the troops once they got into the lower Falls.

> **Clonard Street**: 'If you don't take your head in I'll blow it off for you.' [Soldier's reported words. This closely resembles a story mentioned in Thomas Hennessey's *The Evolution of the Troubles*, in which future IRA volunteer, Mairead Farrell, overheard a soldier talking to a woman in this way in a shop where they were hiding from the trouble.][108]
> **Balaclava Street**: Abuse from soldiers.
> **Cape Street**: Made man lie down in street. Men kept kneeling for twenty minutes. Language in street very bad. Soldiers abusive.

The *Story of the Falls Curfew* pamphlet also talks about the financial hardship that the Curfew caused. People were trapped in the area and could not go to work, and those who had overtime or worked weekends also lost money. Pubs and shops were also looted; virtually no public house in the area was left alone. People talked of soldiers taking money from houses: 'One woman had left her wages in her apron pocket, and returned to find them gone.'[109]

Once again the conduct of individual soldiers was complained about. Their apparent disregard for the people of the lower Falls was a major issue.

> During the Curfew soldiers behaved with no regard for the population of the area. Soldiers fired CS gas 'straight into people's homes, were firing at people', and billeted in people's homes, including Patrick Elliman's.[110]

Billeting was a major issue to the family of Patrick Elliman. When family members went to his house to gather some items, they found soldiers had broken down the door and had been inside. One of them had left his shaving items there. It was clear to the family that troops had used the house as somewhere to bed down for the night. A bottle of whiskey had also been taken.[111]

While there was a lot of criticism regarding the behaviour of the troops, there was also praise. The CCDC said that 130 houses in the area reported good behaviour from the troops.

> **Alma Street:** Very courteous. Very nice. Quite civil. No complaint. Did not touch money that was lying around.
> **Mary Street:** Courteous – An English regiment. Courteous and friendly. Permission asked.
> **Omar Street:** Civil enough. Friendly. Courteous. Polite.
> **Cullingtree Road:** Officer very kind, let old woman and her son out. Asked permission to search. Very civil.
> **Lady Street:** Loaf and jam brought by soldier. Soldier got food (for us). Soldier apologised for search.
> **McDonnell Street:** Soldier brought milk, bread and cigarettes. Soldiers all right.
> **Grosvenor Road:** Special guard mounted throughout the night to see no harm came to man suffering from Multiple Sclerosis.

It is clear that many of the soldiers asked for permission to enter houses, were very courteous to people and were very fair. It is interesting to note that the English troops apologised for the behaviour of the Scottish troops, according to *The Story of the Belfast Curfew*.[112] There was a wide spectrum of discipline

exhibited by the troops across the various areas, be it good or bad, which ultimately drew comment from soldiers regarding the conduct of other troops.
The Scottish regiments seemed to be, according to witnesses and members
of the British army, the main instigators in the aggressive house-to-house
searches in the lower Falls that weekend.

The army command was not particularly interested in complaints, however. It was more interested in the public interpretation of the Curfew,
and how people would react to the army's handling of the situation. The
GOC, at the JSC meeting on 6 July, talked about the 'inevitable aftermath of
complaints' from the area.[113] Many in army command nevertheless secretly
blamed unreliable information held by the Special Branch of the RUC,
which was always going to be directed at the Catholic community.[114] On
8 July members of the CCDC handed in a list containing some 200 written
complaints about the troops' behaviour to the complaints centre situated
at the Springfield Road police barracks. The list contained allegations of
wanton destruction, the use of obscene language and evidence of religious
bigotry. Some soldiers serving in the army thought the Curfew and the subsequent destructive searches were a major error of judgement. Others just
thought that the army had got tough with the lower Falls, and dreaded the
consequences. Hamill quotes a priest who said at the time: 'Unfortunately
while some regiments behaved excellently, others didn't. There was a fair
amount of … not brutality, but extreme inconvenience.'[115] The priest went
on to say: 'the Provos were regrouping and getting ready and it all stemmed
from that lower Falls Curfew'.[116] Catholics were now firmly convinced that
the army was there to back Stormont. The days of tea and cakes were over.
The Provisionals were preparing for action.

Although Stormont was extremely concerned about the effects of the
house-to-house searches, the deaths and the ensuing adverse publicity, the
Protestant community was in effect elated. Another IRA 'nest' had been taken
out and as far as they were concerned the troops had done a good job. There
follows a Unionist version of the events of that weekend in July:

Friday, July 3 – Troops move in to seal off 13 streets in Belfast's Crumlin
Road area and build the city's second 'peace line'. A senior Scotland
Yard detective flies to Belfast to follow up gun-running investigations.
Hours later 3,000 troops dramatically swoop on the Lower Falls area in
an arms search, and IRA terrorists launch a full-scale gun battle on them.
A military curfew is clamped down as at least three people die, – two of
them snipers claimed to have 'been shot by Army marksmen' – scores are
injured and hundreds are detained while the troops relentlessly carry out

house-to-house searches. Among the terrifying arsenal ferried out by the truckload through the Army security net which closes the largely Roman Catholic area off are sub-machine guns, one believed to be of Russian origin, rifles, carbines and self-loading pistols. Some of the weapons are found hidden in a sewer while others are thrown out of house windows in panic as the soldiers comb the area. The trouble begins when troops searching a house in Balkan Street, one of a maze of streets between the Falls and Grosvenor Roads, find an arms cache consisting of 15 pistols, a rifle, a submachine gun and ammunition. A mob begins stoning the troops. Soon a full-scale riot is going on and within minutes stones, bottles and home-made plastic and gelignite bombs are being hurled at the soldiers. The rioters hijack buses and drive them across street entrances to form barricades. Pneumatic drills and an excavator are used to dig up the road. Nineteen soldiers and one policeman are injured as vicious volleys of bullets zip up side streets. Elsewhere in the city more injuries as diversionary explosions damage the newspaper offices of the 'News Letter,' two petrol stations, a savings bank and a parochial house.

By 5 a.m. the Army reports they are in complete control of the curfew-blanketed area – part of the constituency represented at Westminster by Republican Labour MP Gerry Fitt and at Stormont by Northern Ireland Labour member Paddy Devlin. The ban on movement is lifted for two hours in the evening to allow housewives to buy fresh food supplies. Later Army headquarters announce that the curfew will be lifted the next morning 'for an indefinite period' so that people can go to church. But the military emphasise that the relaxation does not mean a major withdrawal from the area. The systematic search for arms goes on as the heavy Army guard which had earlier clamped down on the streets, effectively transforming the area into a ghost town, remains.[117]

A ghost town it certainly was.

5

AFTERMATH

In Stormont, Dublin and Westminster the Curfew raised as many questions as it allegedly answered. The Republic, derided by nationalists in Belfast for not doing enough during August 1969, was now in a difficult position. There was a real possibility that the Irish government could be seriously destabilised or even fall due to hostile public opinion.[1] Lynch throughout the beginning of the Troubles repeatedly stated that reunification was the only solution to the issues facing Northern Ireland. However, even this decades-old stipulation was not enough for the hawks in his cabinet, or the nationalists in the south, who wanted direct action.

On 6 July, Lynch sent Patrick Hillery, minister for external affairs, to the Falls to ascertain exactly what the situation was, and also to attempt to placate the rising tensions at home. Hillery's visit was not done through the normal diplomatic channels; he visited as a 'citizen'. Chichester-Clark was furious. This visit by a serving member of the Republic's government at a time of high tension was, he believed, a rash and dangerous thing to do. Under pressure of his own, he responded by sending off a curt letter to the media:

> I am astounded that the Foreign Minister of any state should show such a lack of courtesy as to visit Northern Ireland without reference to me or the Northern Ireland government —the more so in the present very serious situation. I cannot regard such a visit as helpful and I deplore it.[2]

The above letter, with its omission of even the name of Hillery's 'state', duly appeared in the press. Chichester-Clark, however, wrote a slightly different original draft:

> Normally I would have expected Dr Hillery to inform me in advance of his intention to visit any part of the United Kingdom, including Northern

Ireland; not to have done so, particularly in present circumstances, is a serious diplomatic discourtesy. Had he observed the ordinary form no doubt a visit could have been arranged. However, that may be, he had an opportunity to see for himself the facts of the situation and will be in a position to inform his government that there has been a great deal of misrepresentation. He will know that a very serious situation arose; a relatively small group of people, who are I believe described of the Falls Road community as 'lunatics', have embroiled the district in a situation which has led innocent people to suffer hardship. This, I am sure, Dr Hillery will have observed for himself.[3]

Referring to sections of the Falls community as 'lunatics' and implying that some of the residents also saw them that way showed just how out of touch the Unionist establishment was in understanding the complexities of Northern Irish society and of the Catholic community of the lower Falls in particular. These 'lunatics' were, in the eyes of the people, the defenders of the area from the army and the security forces of Stormont.

Dr Hillery replied to Chichester-Clark in terse terms, reiterating the party line that it was by peaceful means that the unification of Ireland should be brought about. He also pledged support for northern Protestants in unification: 'There is no need for the northern majority to fear for its identity or its interests in a united Ireland as these will be respected and cherished by all Irishmen.'[4]

None of this eased the tensions building either side of the border. The Taoiseach was now in a difficult position. In the Dáil on 7 July he fielded questions about the situation in Northern Ireland. He also announced the visit of Dr Hillery to the Falls:

> Yesterday at my request the Minister for External Affairs visited the Falls Road area of Belfast, the intention being to reduce tension in the area by demonstrating the Government's interest in the welfare of the people of the area and also to obtain confirmation, at first hand, of the information we had already received, and to ascertain the feelings of the people. They had been forcibly dispossessed of weapons that they held for their defence. I do not condone the unauthorized possession of arms by anyone but the people of the Falls area know that weapons, probably more up-to-date, and greater in quantity, are held by militant Unionists. So far no effective action seems to have been taken to disarm them. There was fear, there was apprehension amongst the people of the Falls. They felt isolated. People of the will turn almost anywhere for help. It is vitally important that this fear be not exploited by subversive elements for their own ends. If a situation developed in which such people would turn to subversive elements there would be a

very grave threat to peace and security not only of the people in the Falls but in the Six Counties as a whole and possibly in the rest of the country.

Yesterday's visit was an initiative for peace and while it may have been devoid of diplomatic niceties it was undertaken in full accord with our policy of seeking a peaceful solution of the whole problem, and this policy has not changed.

The Government have also arranged to inform the Heads of Mission of all countries represented here of the Government's views on the present situation in the north. The Minister for External Affairs will visit London tomorrow for further conversations.[5]

He also stated that he was in constant contact with the British about the partiality of leaving one side of the community defenceless, in view of the approach of the climax of the marching season:

No undertaking has been given by the British Government about further disarming. We are continuing to press vigorously our views in this respect. We have had no indication as to whether parades will be cancelled or curbed in any way. As the Deputy is aware, the British Home Secretary is meeting this afternoon representatives of the Orange Order, who are responsible for holding these parades. It may be that no announcement will be made in advance of the meeting. As I have just indicated, the Minister for External Affairs will be visiting London tomorrow and he will no doubt raise this question again.[6]

Nationalists, however, were still clamouring for some sort of direct action. Lynch was being accused of 'abandoning defenceless Catholics to their fate' in the north of Ireland[7] by elements of the nationalist community. In Belfast the reaction of the PD to the events of the weekend was one of anger directed not at the south, but at what they saw as the core of the problem, British imperialism and its ally in the Unionist government of Northern Ireland:

The disarming of the lower Falls leaves the area completely at the mercy of the British army and the government which they serve. Successive Unionist Governments have always used the Falls as a 'hostage' against unrest. They did it very successfully in the unemployed riots of the 1930s, when there was a possibility (danger in the eyes of the government) that Catholic and Protestant unemployed might unite against their Tory [Unionist] oppressors. The last thing any oppressive government wants to see is people preparing to defend themselves. The British army remained true to imperial traditions of attacks on working class and national movements, traditions which were fully lived up to in Aden and Malaya and which were given their best expression in the Falls this weekend. For at the end of the day, the army stands for the continued exploitation of this country by imperialism.[8]

Moreover, Dr Hillery's 'secret' visit to the Falls had created a political ministorm between Dublin and Stormont, or more pointedly, between Hillery and Chichester-Clark, and it was rattling on. Lynch subsequently made a speech in the Dáil on 28 July in which he stated:

The primary objective of the visit of the Minister for External Affairs to the Falls Road area of Belfast was to reassure the minority by making it quite clear and beyond dispute that this Government intended to exert to the full their influence in support of the just claims of the minority in the north.[9]

In order to further placate the minority in the north, and to mollify nationalist opinion in the south, he also added:

So far as the future of our whole country is concerned, I should like to repeat what I have said already. It is my aim, it is the Government's aim, that Ireland should be united. I stated my motive recently in a television broadcast and it is that, in this island, there shall never again be fear, turning to hatred, turning to bloodshed. This implies quite clearly and deliberately that, in our view, Ireland will be united when the main Irish traditions are able to build together a new Irish society to their mutual good.[10]

The secretary of state for foreign and Commonwealth affairs in London, Sir Alec Douglas-Home, had his own opinions on the visit. In parliament on 7 July he made them clear:

When he called on me on 29th June Dr Hillery expressed the grave concern of the Government of the Republic of Ireland at the very difficult situation in Northern Ireland. It is natural that he should wish to keep himself informed, but I should have expected him to have consulted Her Majesty's Government in advance if he wished to make a visit. Not to have done so, particularly in present circumstances, is a serious diplomatic discourtesy. His visit has magnified the difficulties of those who are working so hard for peace and harmony in Northern Ireland. I am inviting Dr Hillery, who is visiting the Chancellor of the Duchy tomorrow on other matters, to call on me.[11]

Chichester-Clark, however, as with nearly all of Northern Ireland's prime ministers since partition, never really took seriously the vocal dissentions about partition from the Republic. Southern Irish politicians had been talking about the 'reunification' of Ireland for decades. This was, in part, why a siege mentality was still present amongst Protestants in Northern Ireland. Protestant opinion was what mattered most to Chichester-Clark, and the Unionists were very happy in the days after the Curfew. The army seemed to be on the side of Unionism, now that the Tories, traditional British allies of Unionism, were in power in London. The arrests made and the weapons seized were substantial. A total of 337 were arrested, 21,000 rounds of ammunition were seized along with 'twenty eight rifles, two carbines, fifty-two handguns, fourteen shotguns, 100 incendiaries, 250lb of gelignite [and] a grenade'.[12] Weapons were also found at the headquarters of the CCDC in Leeson Street, an event which ensured that the tentative relationship it had with the army before the Curfew was now destroyed. Along with the find, it was alleged that some of its members had fled to the safety of the Republic.[13] This was a sizeable haul. However, many arms were smuggled out of the area in the initial stages of the Curfew, and many more afterwards under babies in prams.

II

In London, the government looked on with disdain. Barely a week before, the army command was under severe pressure for not showing force in the Short Strand. Now, in the eyes of many, it had acted with too much force. Heath's attempts to reassure the Republic's government about its intentions towards the Catholics in the north were set back.[14] Heath believed that Lynch in Dublin was more than likely the best person to work with in placating nationalist and Catholic opinion in Northern Ireland.

The GOC was criticised privately by London for his handling of the Curfew, with the conclusion that from now on all planning for searches in Catholic areas of Northern Ireland had to go through the London government first,[15] a move that took on great significance as the weeks went by. Catholics in Northern Ireland, however, were angry; the process of complete alienation was now well under way. The government in London had allegedly shown Catholics that it sided with the Unionists. Catholics had been left without weapons for defence, the army had shown its true colours and only the IRA could defend them now. Fitt and Devlin, also outraged at the behaviour of the army during the Curfew, paid a visit to the home secretary in London to complain in person. Fitt argued with Maudling that the

Conservative administration had sided with the Unionists in demanding a hard line against Catholic areas.[16] Maudling just toed the party line that there had been no change to the policies already implemented by the previous Labour government. In the Westminster parliament there were few who argued that the actions of the army over the weekend were not productive in saving future lives. The Northern Irish government was of the same thinking.

In Dublin the debates around the Curfew continued. Many TDs were now calling again for United Nations (UN) intervention in the situation, a process that was begun in the traumatic days of August 1969. Many also believed that an observer from the UN should have been present in Northern Ireland, an idea to which Britain would certainly have said an emphatic 'no'. Lynch was extremely worried in the days and weeks after the Curfew that southern nationalist opinion would finally tip the balance between a stable government in the south or civil war, if there was any more trouble. He was especially concerned about the Orange parades due to occur on 13 July and wished to see them banned, something that Hillery pushed for during his discussions with the British ambassador to Ireland, John Peck. Debates in Dublin also raged along the familiar lines of the 'injustices' done by the British Empire and Britain's role in the Troubles, weeks after the ending of the Curfew. Mr Keating TD summed up the mood in the Dáil at this time when he said:

> For the ordinary people of England I have nothing but friendship but for the ruling classes who have partitioned Ireland, who have brought 'hangers-on' in both parts of Ireland, I have nothing but implacable animosity. They have spread an empire throughout the world which may not exist as the colour red on the map anymore but it still exists in economic and social terms.[17]

Partition was the issue and also the problem, in Dublin. Unification was the answer, as usual.

It would, however, with hindsight, be easy to criticise the role played by the Dublin government in the aftermath of the Curfew. Catholics in the north, cut off by partition and living under an alien regime, had many reasons to be angry at Lynch for his moderate attitude towards Stormont. But what, in reality, could Lynch have reasonably done? Taoiseach of a conservative state in perpetual recession since its creation, lacking in military resources and seen by the outside world as heavily influenced by the Catholic Church, there was little he could do other than placate the minority in the north. Offers of being the 'guarantor' and 'protector' of northern nationalists were just that – offers. Lynch was seriously at risk of losing his government after the events of the Curfew, the hawks in the Dáil were after blood and civil war in the north seemed on the horizon. Lynch had to mollify both the Catholics in the north and their other assumed 'protector', the government in London. The fact that his government survived and civil war did not materialise meant he had done exactly that.

The main objective of the parliament in London now was to attempt to bring some semblance of 'normality' to Northern Ireland. Heath, as mentioned, thanked Lynch publicly for the simple expedient of being able to communicate with the nationalists in the north. To this end, on 11 July, he sent a letter to Lynch to assure him that many of the proposed marches were to be routed away from sensitive Catholic areas and that the forces of law and order would act against any trouble, regardless of which side instigated it.[18] Lynch's moderate tone in his subsequent speech also calmed nationalist nerves in the north, and the marches of 13 July passed off without any major incidents.

This enabled Heath to take on the hawks in the Stormont government. Lynch wanted an outright cessation of marches across Northern Ireland, Heath wanted to build on the burgeoning relationship with the Republic's government, and Chichester-Clark wanted an end to the 'no go' areas of Belfast and Derry, which attracted severe criticism from the hawks. A compromise was reached:

> ... the balancing formula came from General Freeman and Sir Arthur Young in a rare show of unanimity, namely that the No-Go areas would remain for the time being, but that the RUC would assume a gradual, low-key presence in the Bogside and Falls Road. In return, all marches would be banned for twelve months (reduced to six at Chichester-Clark's request, but importantly covering the Apprentice Boys march scheduled for August).[19]

This compromise seemed to suit all. Lynch got his ban on provocative marches and Chichester-Clark got his 'no go' areas. More importantly, Heath thought that he had seen light at the end of the tunnel, but in effect he only created more difficulties. To introduce the RUC back into areas that they had been forced out of nearly a year before was showing the Catholics that there was going to be no immediate change in the nature of the state under Stormont. The RUC was seen as the 'chief agent and symbol of Unionist authority' in Northern Ireland.[20] As Michael Morgan stated:

> ... in re-asserting Unionist state authority, the British increasingly identified themselves with the Unionist cause. In so doing, they confirmed and validated Republican perceptions among the northern Catholic population. The former outside arbiter [the British government] became direct participant

and this, in turn, stimulated a 'nationalist' re-definition of the conflict amongst the Catholics. What had been seen as a specific Catholic/Unionist opposition now became seen in terms of a general Irish/British one.[21]

There are some who believe that Heath's motives were a bit more cynical. Since August 1969, troops had been in Northern Ireland in force. Heath wanted to bring them home, or at least withdraw them to their barracks. That way, episodes like the lower Falls Curfew would not come up again to embarrass the government. The British government's foot was firmly entrenched in the 'Irish bog', and Heath wanted to release it. He clearly hoped that this strategy would work. The RUC would take over many of the duties that now were undertaken by the army, the troop levels would drop off, Stormont could bring in radical reforms at its own pace, and Catholic opinion and anger towards Unionism would wane.

The problem was, although Heath wanted to take his foot out of the bog, the fact that the troops were there ensured that he could not. The British government was now firmly entrenched in Northern Ireland. Any deviation from this agenda was going to cause a serious degeneration of the situation. While the Provisional IRA asserted that only British withdrawal would see them halt their violence, the Protestants of the state ensured that any withdrawal would end in disaster. Writing in the 1990s, Cruise O'Brien gave his own analysis of the idea of the British pulling out of Northern Ireland, even at this point in the Troubles:

> The terrifying prognostication – at least for Irish people – is British disengagement, which is the primary object of the [Provisional] IRA. It can be predicted, with a probability amounting almost to certainty, that British disengagement would be followed by civil war in Ireland. The process had already begun in August 1969 and was halted only by the deployment of British troops. British withdrawal would 'unfreeze the film' of August 1969, but now with nothing to stop the blaze. The Protestant majority would attempt, as it did then, to impose its own idea of law and order, through its own security forces, in the Catholic areas, which would resist. The Republic would be drawn in and civil war would ensue. The casualties in a week would probably exceed the number of victims of political violence in Northern Ireland in the past fifteen years and large numbers of people, both Catholic and Protestant, would also be rendered homeless. The whole thing would end in a new border in a new place with homogenous populations – Catholic and Protestant – on both sides.[22]

The ban on processions in Northern Ireland ran from July 1970 to February 1971. Sporadic violence still occurred within this time but was markedly down on previous months. In Stormont, Chichester-Clark continued trying to push through with reforms. Catholic middle-class opposition to the violence was given a boost in August with the formation of the Social Democratic and Labour Party (SDLP). Formed by moderate politicians such as John Hume from Derry and Gerry Fitt from Belfast, it appealed to those Catholics who supported the aims of the civil rights movement but not the violence of the IRA. Nevertheless, the formation of the SDLP was perhaps six months too late. The ordinary, working-class Catholic in the lower Falls was now listening to the Provisional IRA, not the more moderate politicians. The Falls Curfew had inflicted so much damage on the psyche that, where in 1969 they might have listened, in August 1970 they did not. The Provisional IRA was now talking to the people behind the mental as well as physical barricades of the past twelve months. As Michael Morgan stated:

> Perceptions and identities changed: the Catholic community now saw themselves not so much as 'Catholics', but as 'nationalists'. The idea of 'the nationalist people', the future power base of the Provisional IRA, replaced that of the embattled Catholic community.[23]

More ominous for the future, though, was the threat of internment being introduced in Northern Ireland. In the previous IRA campaign, internment was introduced on both sides of the border. This had the effect of damp-ening down the full effects of the IRA offensive, and ultimately ended the campaign. This time around, the government of Northern Ireland could not expect the same cooperation from the Republic. Internment was one of the tools that Stormont had in its arsenal of repressive measures under the Special Powers Act. At a meeting of the Northern Ireland cabinet on 20 July the idea of internment was mooted:

> The Minister of Home Affairs said that this policy was kept under regular review, but hitherto the view had been taken that the adverse repercussions would outweigh any likely benefit. It also had to be acknowledged that, with the army so deeply involved in the security situation, action of this sort could not be taken without consultation with Whitehall.[24]

Seven months later this consultation did occur, and internment was intro-duced. It turned out to be one of the most damaging errors of judgement that the Stormont government made. Hundreds were arrested on outdated

1. Picture of Eamon DeValera. (National Photo Company Collection, Library of Congress (c. 1920))

You may fire after due warning

7. **Against a person carrying a firearm,** but only if you have reason to think that he is about to use it for offensive purposes

and

he refuses to halt when called upon to do so, and there is no other way of stopping him.

8. **Against a person throwing a petrol bomb** if petrol bomb attacks continue in your area against troops and civilians, or against property, if his action is **likely to endanger life.**

9. **Against a person attacking** or destroying property or stealing firearms or explosives. if his action is **likely to endanger life.**

10. Against a person who, though he is not at present attacking, has:

a. in your sight killed or seriously injured a member of the security forces or a person whom it is your duty to protect

and

b. not halted when called upon to do so and cannot be arrested by any other means.

11. If there is no other way to protect yourself or those whom it is your duty to protect from the danger of being killed or seriously injured.

You may fire without warning

12. **Either** when hostile firing is taking place in your area, and a warning is impracticable, **or** when any delay could lead to death or serious injury to people whom it is your duty to protect or to yourself; **and then only:**
a. against a person using a firearm against members of the security forces or people whom it is your duty to protect

or

b. against a person carrying a firearm if you have reason to think he is about to use it for offensive purposes.
Note: "Firearm" includes a grenade.

2 and 3. Yellow cards from 1970, given to the author for use by 'Dave' (unidentified soldier) in 2011.

Action by guards and at road blocks/checks

13. Where warnings are called for they should be in the form of specific challenges, as set out in paragraphs 14 and 15.
14. If you have to challenge a person who is acting suspiciously you must do so in a firm, distinct voice, saying "HALT—HANDS UP." Then:
a. if he halts, you are to say "STAND STILL AND KEEP YOUR HANDS UP."
b. ask him why he is there and, if not satisfied, call your Commander immediately and hand the person over to him.
15. If the person does not halt at once, you are to challenge again saying "HALT—HANDS UP" and, if the person does not halt on your second challenge, you are to cock your weapon, apply the safety catch and shout: "STAND STILL I AM READY TO FIRE."
16. The rules covering the circumstances for opening fire are described in paragraphs 7-12. If the circumstances do not justify opening fire, you will do all you can to stop and detain the person without opening fire.
17. At a road block/check, **you will NOT fire on a vehicle simply because it refused to stop.** If a vehicle does not halt at a road block/check, note its description, make, registration number and direction of travel.
18. In all circumstances where you have challenged and the response is not satisfactory, you will summon your Commander at the first opportunity.

Revised January 1971
RESTRICTED

RESTRICTED

Instructions by the Director of Operations for Opening Fire in Northern Ireland

1. These instructions are for the guidance of Commanders and troops operating collectively or individually. When troops are operating collectively soldiers will only open fire when ordered to do so by the Commander on the spot.

General Rules

2. Never use more force than the **minimum** necessary to enable you to carry out your duties.
3. Always first try to handle a situation by other means than opening fire. If you have to fire:
a. Fire only aimed single shots.
b. Do not fire more rounds than are absolutely necessary to achieve your aim.
4. Your magazine must always be loaded with live ammunition and be fitted to the weapon but unless you are about to open fire no live round is to be carried in the breech, and the working parts must be forward.

Warning before firing

5. **A warning must always be given before you open fire.** The only circumstances in which you may open fire without giving warning are described in para 12 below.
6. A warning should be as loud as possible, preferably by loud-hailer. It must:
a. Give clear orders to stop attacking or to halt, as appropriate.
b. State that fire will be opened if the orders are not obeyed.

4. Shankill Troubles. (© Fribber 1970, Wikimedia Commons)

'GOD REST YE MERRY GENTLEMEN'

5. Postcard from 1970, given to the author for use by 'Dave' (unidentified soldier) in 2011.

6. Sir Edward Carson. (J. Beagles & Co. Ltd, (*c.* 1900))

7. Fire at Woolworths. (©Albert Bridge (geograph.org.uk), 1972)

8. S. Hogan Flying Column No. 2. (Courtesy of CAIN (Conflict Archive on the Internet), University of Ulster)

9. Ardoyne 1970s. (© Ronnie Bell)

10. Women being searched while troops stand guard. (© *Belfast Telegraph*, 1970)

11. Smoke still coming from the rubble. (© *Belfast Telegraph*, 1969)

12. Military Policeman stands guard over youths. (© *Belfast Telegraph*, 1970)

13. Divis St Murals. (© Ardfern, 2011)

Ulster's
Solemn League and Covenant.

Being convinced in our consciences that Home Rule would be disastrous to the material well-being of Ulster as well as of the whole of Ireland, subversive of our civil and religious freedom, destructive of our citizenship and perilous to the unity of the Empire, we, whose names are underwritten, men of Ulster, loyal subjects of His Gracious Majesty King George V., humbly relying on the God whom our fathers in days of stress and trial confidently trusted, do hereby pledge ourselves in solemn Covenant throughout this our time of threatened calamity to stand by one another in defending for ourselves and our children our cherished position of equal citizenship in the United Kingdom and in using all means which may be found necessary to defeat the present conspiracy to set up a Home Rule Parliament in Ireland. ¶ And in the event of such a Parliament being forced upon us we further solemnly and mutually pledge ourselves to refuse to recognise its authority. ¶ In sure confidence that God will defend the right we hereto subscribe our names. ¶ And further, we individually declare that we have not already signed this Covenant.

The above was signed by me at...
"Ulster Day," Saturday, 28th September, 1912.

——— God Save the King. ———

14. The Ulster Covenant. (Wikimedia Commons)

15. July 1970. (© *Belfast Telegraph*, 1970)

16. July 1970. (© *Belfast Telegraph*, 1970)

EVICTION SCENE. 1767. W.L.

18. Family evicted by their landlord. (Lawrence Collection, National Library of Ireland)

19. Troops getting ready for another performance. (© Kasper Howard, 1970)

20. British soldiers on the interface. (© Kasper Howard, 1970)

21. Ulster Volunteers, 1914. (Wikimedia Commons)

22. A brooding, sullen lower Falls in 1970. (©Kasper Howard, 1970)

evidence, all of them Catholics. The death toll in the months following the introduction rose rapidly, and alienated even middle-class moderate Catholics from having any truck with the Northern Irish state.

The British establishment was now the enemy of a Catholic community with a revived, and collective, identity. The garrison in Northern Ireland had been reinforced to deal with the increase in unexpected violence and finding itself in a difficult position, was criticised from all quarters for their actions and inaction at times. The perception of being a unionist-led force was evident. The Irish government, for all the rhetoric about 'not standing by', did just that.

6

THE 'STICKIES' ECLIPSED

'The overwhelming desire of the great majority of all the people of the
north is for an end to military actions by all sides.'
Official IRA ceasefire statement, May 1972

I

The Official IRA, buoyed by its stand against the troops and the army statement that they had come up against 'determined and organised armed
resistance'[1] in the lower Falls, began progressively to gain recruits. People
joined, in part, for revenge. But it was also for the excitement. Many recruits
were unemployed, with few or no prospects, especially since the start of the
conflict. Joining the IRA was the next logical step in a process of revenge and
attack, and also of alleviating boredom. In Dublin, the role of the volunteers
of the Officials was recognised. The leadership released a statement in the
days after the Curfew, praising 'the courageous stand made by the volunteers/
auxiliaries of the IRA, and the people who fought shoulder to shoulder with
them against the overwhelming odds of 3000 elite troops in their effort to
disarm the people'.[2]

While there was no shortage of recruits in the initial days after the Curfew,
a full-scale operation against the British army by the Officials was not on the
cards. The leadership in Dublin baulked at the idea of open warfare with the
British; instead, to placate the volunteers a number of revenge attacks on the
army were authorised.[3] Nevertheless, new recruits were still coming in and
lessons in bomb making and the use of guns were common in the lower Falls
after the Curfew.[4] Auxiliary organisations were built up in all the Catholic
areas and surveillance was carried out on the British army in preparation.[5]

The problem was, as Hanley and Millar suggest, that events were now over-taking any plans for a well-planned and thought-out response to the situation by the Officials.[6] Their volunteers were getting impatient; they wanted to retaliate. The army was still conducting searches, although at this point not on the scale of the Curfew. But continuing they were, and it was beginning to agitate those involved.

On 31 July, Daniel O'Hagan, a 19-year-old youth, was shot dead by the army in serious rioting in the New Lodge area of Belfast, another case cur-rently under review by the HET. As is usual in these situations, there are conflicting stories as to the exact nature of his death. The army said he was lighting a petrol bomb; the eye witnesses said he was unarmed. At a meeting of the JSC (Joint Security Committee) at Stormont on 3 August, the GOC mentioned that 'very fair warning' was given before the shooting.[7] Cardinal Conway, however, in a meeting with the Minister of Community Relations in September, was apprehensive about the death, and the effects it had on the Catholic community. Mr W. Slinger took the notes of the meeting:

> He [the cardinal] was very perturbed by O'Hagan's death because earlier he had pleaded with the authorities not to make a Catholic martyr … He said the reaction to the shooting had been so sharp because it had occurred in an incident which had started from stone throwing.[8]

Nevertheless, he was shot dead by an army marksman. It was fast becoming clear to many that the army was not acting in a role of benevolent peace-keeper; it was actively waging war against any form of insurgency, in the Catholic community in particular. Cardinal Conway went on to say:

> He hoped that 12 months peace would be possible and that, as he put it, there would not be an over-reaction by the security forces to incidents although he realised how difficult a job the army had had. In this context the Cardinal instanced the Curfew in the lower Falls and the shooting of young O'Hagan. In these cases he said there was a very strong feeling among his people and that errors of judgement had been made in high places.[9]

These 'errors of judgement' made in high places would make sure that there would not be twelve months of peace; not for twenty-five years at least.

The months after the Curfew saw the Officials limit themselves to random attacks against the army, while at the same time continuing with their fund-raising activities. Relations with the Provisionals, however, were dete-riorating. Clashes over territory were the main reason, but there were others.

The Officials were also gathering information on security arrangements in Britain and there were plans to 'revamp' their operations there.[10]

The deteriorating relations with the Provisionals came to a head in March 1971 when the Officials launched an attack on the British army in Ballymurphy. There were few Officials in Ballymurphy; it was a strong Provisional IRA base. The Provisionals were not happy that there was fighting on their so-called turf without their knowledge or participation. Confrontation broke out between the two wings of the IRA, and shooting matches occurred while the army watched, according to Coogan, 'delighted'.[11] However, behind the scenes many were also critical of the Marxist path that the leadership of the Officials was taking. Some members thus drifted away to the Provisionals or even left the organisation and went back to their own lives. The leadership was on a path of change, though, and was not deviating. The more Marxist leaning they became, the more they believed that the time for a radical change in Ireland had not yet arrived. As Boyer Bell states:

> The Officials did not believe a revolutionary situation existed in Ireland and said so. The Officials, in order to deny the Provisionals, became, day by day, more radical, more orthodox Marxist, less Republican. Gardiner Place [OIRA headquarters] attacked those within Republican ranks that attacked them, gave up the old agendas, concentrated on all-Ireland analysis, on other priorities, on lesser realities than the day to day events in Northern Ireland.[12]

In the months after the Falls Curfew, the Official IRA began to lag well behind the Provisionals in gaining support from the Catholic community. In February 1972, after the horrific events in Derry known as 'Bloody Sunday', the Official IRA left a car bomb at the headquarters of the Parachute Regiment at Aldershot, in England. It exploded, killing seven civilians, one of whom was an army chaplain. The Officials completely missed their target of soldiers of the regiment. Widespread revulsion of the attack was levelled at the organisation. Shortly after, the Officials declared a ceasefire, save for 'defensive purposes'. Attacks would continue, however, for a number of years and a new, more militant, organisation was to rise from the ceasefire and take its place. The Irish National Liberation Army (INLA) went on their own murderous path throughout the 1970s and 1980s, in some cases outdoing the Provisionals in their barbarity. The Officials' star, rising briefly during the Curfew, had waned. Remnants of their political wing formed the Workers Party, fought elections in the Republic and followed a socialist and constitutional path that still exists today.

II

In direct contrast to the Officials was the Provisional IRA, which had no qualms about taking the 'war' to the British. Billy McKee, David O'Connell, Seán MacStíofáin and the rest of the Provisional leadership relished the idea. In this way they believed that Stormont would be more amenable to change, and might even be abolished in favour of a united Ireland, if the British felt that the disadvantages outweighed any advantages of staying. Their political wing, Provisional Sinn Féin, was also expanding, taking in young, articulate and intelligent individuals who would change the course of Republicanism in the following decades and bring the organisation to the negotiating table on a number of occasions.

Recruits flooded in to the Provisionals not only because of their militancy, but also, like the Officials, for revenge. The Provisionals, however, were not tied down with a Dublin leadership determined to go down a Marxist road of agitation and political theory, hence the flow of young recruits eager to get their hands on a gun and hit back. Devlin recalls the days after the Curfew and the reactions amongst the Catholic youths in the lower Falls:

> Overnight the population turned from neutral or even sympathetic support for the military to outright hatred of everything related to the security forces … Gerry Fitt and I witnessed voters and workers in the Docks and Falls constituencies turn against us to join the Provisionals.[13]

Tim Pat Coogan gives an interesting account of the rise in Provisional support at this time:

> I attended a big IRA funeral in Milltown cemetery the following September (of a Provisional who had blown himself up) and conducted such an intensive personal survey into allegiances that one polite young man came up to me to enquire if I was with the Special Branch! The overwhelming majority of men present were Provisionals and they all gave the Falls Road Curfew as their reason for joining.[14]

The Provisionals were fresh, they were arming and they were ready to take the war to the whole structure of the British presence in Ireland in order to win the Republic, declared from the steps of the GPO in Dublin in Easter 1916. They considered themselves part of the traditional Republican movement, using force to rid the country of the British presence. A 'call to arms' was issued in early 1970:

We declare our allegiance to the 32 County Irish Republic proclaimed at Easter 1916, established by the first Dáil Éireann in 1919, overthrown by force of arms in 1921 and suppressed to this day by the existing British-imposed Six-County and 26-County partition states ... We call on the Irish people at home and in exile for increased support towards defending our people in the North and the eventual achievement of the full political, social, economic and cultural freedom of Ireland.[15]

The only problem was that, although they were arming, it was not fast enough. David O'Connell (Daíthí O'Conaíl) had travelled to New York at the beginning of 1970 to attempt to set up a supply line for weapons, and this was to bear dividends in the months and years to come as literally 'thousands' of guns were subsequently transported to Ireland.[16] The money for these weapons was raised through robberies, fund raising and, as many would believe, from a 'section' of the Irish government of Jack Lynch and Fianna Fáil, despite the sacking of two ministers from his government for alleged gun running in early 1970.

However, while the Provisionals were rearming, home-made explosives were the order of the day. Unreliable and dangerous to transport, these bombs were made in the garages and kitchens of volunteers. Other forms of explosives were acquired from various sources in both Northern Ireland and the Republic. Quarries were a favourite source of gelignite, and many were raided and relieved of their stock. Volunteers, however, took great risks to their own personal safety in the building of bombs and improvised hand grenades. Many of the early weapons were also products of the previous IRA campaign in the early 1960s. As such, they were often old and unreliable. Brendan Hughes recalled: 'A lot of the ammunition and weapons ... were not reliable ... you would have misfires, or you would have damp ammunition or it was just burnt out, too rusty ... but this [was] early 1970, and there wasn't a great deal of operational activity.'[17]

Thus, a string of bomb attacks in County Armagh and in Lurgan were attributed to the Provisionals. It started to become clear to both the GOC and Stormont that they were gearing up for renewed attacks. By October 1970 the Provisionals were bombing business premises as a prelude to an all-out offensive against the British presence. In February 1971 the Clonard area of west Belfast was next on the agenda for house-to-house searches by the army. This sparked off four days of serious rioting which Protestants also joined in.[18] A *World in Action* team filmed the event.[19] The house-to-house searches were once again instigated by pressure from Unionists and by ministers in London, who wanted to see tough action being taken against the PIRA. The lessons of the Curfew had not been learned, either by the army or by the establishment. The Provisionals' star was rising amongst disaffected Catholics.

Many youths, seeing their fathers and brothers being arrested, turned to the Provisionals. As Michael Lawrence and Rowan Smith suggest:

> PIRA's stock within the Catholic community rose in proportion to the decline in the army's popularity as the movement increasingly made its name as an energetic defence force … PIRA was different, but not that different. It was far more rooted in the north. It was more community based. It did offer a form of defence to the beleaguered Catholic populations in the city areas.[20]

The number of soldiers now on the streets of Belfast also gave the Provisional IRA many opportunities to hit back at their adversaries. As they gained strength after the Curfew, the emphasis shifted from defence to attack. Potshots were taken at army patrols in the Falls district, and rioting offered the perfect screen for attacks on soldiers. It was not until February 1971, however, that the first soldier[21] was killed in action in Northern Ireland. His name was Robert Curtis.[22]

Provisional thinking at this time was also directed at targeting businesses in the centres of the major towns and cities in Northern Ireland. In a subsequent bombing campaign that was intended to make the state ungovernable, the PIRA targeted mainly Protestant businesses, centres of transport and hotels. Belfast city centre subsequently came under military control, and persons were searched at different locations before they were allowed in. The PIRA campaign ultimately created difficulties for the whole population, not just the Protestants or the army.

Did the Falls Curfew hasten the rise of the Provisional IRA? The answer to that question is yes. Although it was the Officials who took on the British army that weekend, it was the Provisionals who benefited from the backlash. The ghosts of August 1969 were still with the Officials, and their Dublin leadership was seen to be out of touch with the events now engulfing Northern Ireland. The Provisionals claimed to be the sole defenders of Catholics in the face of alleged state-sponsored British aggression against them. By the winter of 1970 they had grown larger than the Officials in the areas of west Belfast where previously the Officials had reigned supreme.

Thus the Provisionals, buoyed with young radicals and intelligent, dedicated volunteers, were seen to be acting in support of the Catholics. Behind the barricades, though, Provisional volunteers patrolled the streets and estates, meting out summary punishments for juvenile crimes and misdemeanours. More serious crimes were dealt with harshly, involving kneecapping and even execution. In this way, the Provisionals established a core base in the Catholic areas of Belfast, Derry and many other areas of Northern Ireland that remained right up to the *Peace Process* of the late 1990s.

7

LEGAL OR ILLEGAL?

'Even though the civil authority should give direction to the contrary the commander of the troops, if it is really necessary, is bound to take such action as the circumstances demand.'
Manual of Military Law[1]

I

Unionists had much to be pleased about in the weeks after the Curfew. A considerable amount of arms was discovered in the raids in the lower Falls and the Orange marches of 13 July had passed off peacefully, with no significant trouble from either side. Chichester-Clark was now agitating for the resumption of normal RUC patrols in the Bogside, Derry, which since August 1969 had in effect seceded from the state. Regular patrols were also to resume in the lower Falls as the army consolidated its grip on the area. Anglo-Irish relations were also improving, with conciliatory speeches being made on both sides in an effort to relieve tension. However, the Curfew was still creating ripples. The centre of this tension now began to focus on the legality of the operation, and was to lead to denials, counter-denials and accusations of dubious interpretations of the law.

In Dublin, as the pressure on the government continued, the issue of the legality of the Curfew was raised in the Dáil for the first time. Dr Hillery was answering questions on the deteriorating situation in the north. Mr O'Leary TD asked:

Can the Minister say whether, in fact, events in the Falls Road over the weekend give sufficient reason to refer to the attitude of the military involved in the **illegal** curfew and whether these actions are not fit material for reference to the United Nations?[2]

Hillery, aware of the pressure on Lynch, dismissed the question with the usual governmental response: 'The Government are constantly considering the steps that might be taken in every situation that develops.'

Clearly the Curfew looked illegal from all angles to many on both sides of the Irish Sea. The military in Belfast had conducted an apparently illegal operation that was now attracting the attention of many people, and they wanted answers. On 6 July Gerry Fitt MP took his seat in parliament in London. He had put forward a question regarding the measures taken by the army on the weekend of the Curfew. He was still angry, and looking for answers. The reply given to Fitt, a veteran of many bruising parliamentary encounters both in London and Stormont, very much surprised him. Lord Balniel spoke on behalf of the Ministry of Defence:

> After a successful search for arms in the Falls Road area, the Army came under heavy attack from grenades and firearms and a street battle developed. More forces were deployed to remove obstructions and clear the area so that action could be taken by troops against hostile fire. During this period orders were repeatedly given to clear the streets under pain of arrest. The restrictions on movement thus imposed were maintained until 5 p.m. on Saturday and reintroduced from 7 p.m. on Saturday until 9 a.m. on Sunday. No formal curfew was imposed.
>
> Any searches carried out on Friday were in direct pursuit of persons engaged against the security forces. On Saturday searches were carried out only after production of a search certificate. Members of Her Majesty's Forces are empowered under Regulation 4 made under the Civil Authorities (Special Powers) Acts (Northern Ireland), 1922–1943, to search any premises which are under suspicion of being used for purposes prejudicial to the preservation of the peace or maintenance of order. Restrictions on movement were imposed in the interests of the safety of the population as a whole and to restrict the operations of armed criminals.[3]

This was the British government's official word on the matter, no doubt supplied by the GOC and his army command in Belfast.

Fitt immediately picked up on the statement that 'no formal curfew was imposed'. His reply was one of amazement:

> Does the Minister recognise that he has just made a most amazing statement when he said that no formal curfew was imposed? ... can he tell the House under what law were 10,000 people hemmed in in 50 streets, many of them old and infirm and many of whom had to go without food for 36 hours?

Under what law was this situation imposed in Northern Ireland? Further, when the Army were not being subjected to attack, which was about 1 o'clock or 2 o'clock in the early hours of Saturday morning, why was it necessary to maintain for another 24 hours this unwarranted restriction on the movement of defenceless people, and why were the hon. Members who represent the constituency in this House and in Stormont prevented from gaining access to the area to see for themselves what was happening?[4]

Lord Balniel merely repeated the opinion that 'no formal Curfew' was called. Fitt was a lone voice that day in parliament, save for a couple of dissenting voices and other MPs' reactions regarding the exemplary conduct of the army.[5] Parliament was supporting its army and its command. Firearms had been found, the army had acted in an impeccable manner, impartially and justly, and had done a courageous thing. All of these comments came from members of the House, many of whom were ignorant of the real situation and of the issues facing the people of the lower Falls during the Curfew.

Did Balniel tell the truth, either knowingly or unknowingly, to parliament that day? There are many who believed that he did not. When pressed for clarification by Fitt, Balniel said: 'As I have explained, no formal curfew order was imposed under Regulation 19 of the Special Powers Acts. The restrictions on movement were imposed by the military commander as an operational measure for the safety of the community as a whole.'[6]

The people of the lower Falls knew that a Curfew had been called. They heard the word many times over that weekend. The question now was whether the Curfew was indeed legal, and if it was not, what about the four people who had died over those three days?

The following press release concerning the Curfew was given to the media on 3 July, the day the initial raid occurred:

The Director of Operations, Lt Gen Sir Ian Freeland has declared that there is to be an immediate **curfew** until further notice in the area of the lower Falls bounded by:

In the North – Falls Road from the junction of Falls Road and Grosvenor Road to the junction of Falls Road and Albert Street.

In the East – Albert Street from the junction of Falls Road and Albert Street to the junction of Albert Street and Cullingtree Road.

In the South-East – Cullingtree Road from the junction of Cullingtree Road and Albert Street to the junction of Cullingtree Road and Grosvenor Road.

In the South – Grosvenor Road from the junction of Grosvenor Road and Cullingtree Road to the junction of Grosvenor Road and Falls Road.

All civilians in the locality are to get into their houses immediately and stay there. After military occupation anyone found on the street will be arrested.[7]

Witnesses tell of a helicopter overhead with a loudspeaker attached to its underside announcing a curfew. Furthermore, an army report for 3 July states that a curfew was called at 2200hrs.[8] Thus a curfew was indeed called and it was authorised by the GOC himself.

The Curfew was called without any prior communication with either Stormont or London. In the JSC meeting at Stormont on 4 July the GOC referred to the events in the lower Falls as a 'battle', involving a considerable number of troops. There is a mention of 'curfew' later on in his report, where there seems to be a concern about how to 'legalise' it retrospectively.[9] By the 6th, however, the GOC was using language such as 'search exercise' and 'clampdown' to describe the Curfew. Furthermore, there still seemed to be confusion over the actual legalities surrounding it. It seemed that there was a certain amount of awareness finally creeping in that the Curfew might not have been legal. In a short statement, the minister of home affairs said: 'Against the possibility of another curfew … [he] suggested, and the GOC agreed, that the GOCs Civil Adviser should consult with the Minister's Legal Advisor about the legalities involved in making the curfew order.'[10]

At a meeting of the Stormont cabinet on 7 July, the minister of home affairs again attempted to clear up the matter of the legality of the curfew. However, his brief discussion only served to add confusion to the situation:

> Reviewing events connected with the search for arms in the lower Falls district during the last few days, The Minister of Home Affairs explained that to have announced a formal curfew would have required the making of an Order which would have applied only from late on the Saturday (4 July), thus highlighting the situation and possibly giving rise to questions on the validity of the measures already taken. It had therefore been decided to act under the Special Powers legislation and common law.[11]

The press in the Republic were by now taking a keen interest in the events during and after the Curfew, and they also picked up on the legality aspect. The *Irish Times* reported in detail over a period of days that there seemed to be a continuing case of passing the issue from one department to the other. Andrew Whittaker reported on Wednesday 8 July that he was unable to find an answer from any department to his question: 'Under what statute did the civil authority give the military the power to impose a curfew?'[12] That is because there was none. Stormont, as mentioned, did not authorise the army to take the action that it did. Neither did Westminster. The only person who took the decision to curfew the area was General Freeland, and he acted alone.

In order to throw a blanket over the legality issue, the GOC began to concentrate on the masses of complaints that were now coming in to the two complaints centres. In his opinion the significant issue of the capture of so many weapons was being overshadowed by these complaints and the focus on the legality of the Curfew. The Stormont cabinet believed that there was a 'smear campaign' against the army, and blamed elements within the media who were sensationalising the more lurid stories of troop depredations in the lower Falls.[13]

There was no escaping the issue for Heath at Westminster either. As Geraghty states, it was viewed in London as a major error, 'an error of epic proportions.'[14] Apart from the issue of whether it was illegal or not, Heath believed that serious damage had been done by the Curfew to bridge building in Northern Ireland. Smith suggests that, alongside the arrest of the PD activist Bernadette Devlin for riotous behaviour and inflammatory speeches by the GOC, it could have had the effect of convincing Catholics that the Conservatives, now in power, could have another agenda, namely a policy of solving the problem with coercion.[15] Many Catholics did indeed believe this. So did much of the youth in the lower Falls, in part encouraged by the Provisionals, who were now concentrating on ensuring that the lower Falls and the Catholic areas of west Belfast knew exactly who the enemy was.

However, the legality aspect of the events of the Curfew would not go away. According to Hennessey, the situation in London immediately after the Curfew was that the government was unsure about whether the GOC had acted legally or illegally:

> In an attempt to find out, the Director of Law Reform in London was reduced to consulting a few statute and text books and talking to the Attorney General and Ministry of Home Affairs on the telephone. The Director believed that the army did possess power to impose restrictions of the kind that it did.[16]

However, it was still a fine balancing act.

II

On 18 January 1971 Gerald Kaufman, Labour MP for Ardwick in Manchester, queried the legality of the Curfew with Ian Gilmour MP, the under secretary of state for defence. Kaufman had been trying for months to bring up the legality of the Curfew in parliament:

> I am grateful that I have at last the opportunity to raise on the Adjournment this subject of the events in Belfast during the weekend 3rd to 5th July, 1970. Hon. Members may ask, why am I raising events of July, 1970, in January, 1971? The answer is that I have been trying to do so ever since October, and I have only just succeeded in the ballot. Indeed, until I succeeded, I began to think that the ballot for the Adjournment took place rather on the lines of the allocation of prizes under Premium Bonds.
>
> Secondly, hon. Members may ask why this subject has been raised by me, a Member for an English constituency, when the events occurred in Northern Ireland in the constituency of my hon. Friend the Member for Belfast, West (Mr Fitt) who, I understand, will be trying to catch your eye, Mr Deputy Speaker. The answer is that my interest in this subject began originally when a constituent of mine whose sister lives in the area affected wrote and asked me to take up the matter of his sister being prevented during the period under discussion from visiting her niece in hospital. That is why I have taken an interest, and my interest has grown the more I have learned about this matter.

Kaufman then continued to tell parliament about the different versions of events of the Curfew and described the contents of the press release that Freeland had given to the local newspapers:

> There are differing versions of what took place in the Lower Falls area on 3rd July leading to the restrictions of movement. It is known that there was a search for arms, and this was followed by what the noble Lord the Minister of State described on 6th July in this House as a 'street battle'. For the sake of argument, let us accept that his description of what took place is accurate. But then what followed? General Freeland issued a press release, which is extremely important. It began: The Director of Operations, Lt-General Sir Ian Freeland, has declared that there is to be an immediate curfew until further notice in the area of the Lower Falls. It ended: All civilians in the locality are to get into their house immediately and to stay there. After military occupation anyone found on the street will be arrested. The key words are, 'an immediate curfew' and 'will be arrested'.
>
> After the issue of that Press release a helicopter flew over the area from which the following words were called out: This area is now under curfew. You are to go to your homes and remain there. Anyone found on the streets

will be arrested. That restriction on movement started from 10 o'clock on the Friday night and lasted until the Sunday morning. During that time thousands of people, perhaps as many as 10,000, were placed under what amounted to house arrest. Hundreds of men were prevented from going to work at a time when they particularly needed the overtime and were eligible for it. It is estimated that they were deprived of £3,500 in income. Many people were deprived of food for many hours. Houses were ransacked. People were stopped from going to mass and confession. Sick children were prevented from going to hospital. A wedding was prevented from taking place. A man was fatally shot.[17]

Kaufman was clearly aggrieved at what he saw as an aggressive act committed against the houses of residents of the lower Falls. He was also aggrieved at how the army had handled the people of the area, and how it seemed that the army had no regard for the unwell and disabled living there. Kaufman went on to discuss what he had discovered after searching for a legal precedent for the actions of the GOC.

Maitland in his *Constitutional History of England* says that the common law obliges the citizen to aid in suppression of unlawful force. This may just cover the situation but does not cover the action taken, namely, what amounted to a curfew. Wade and Phillips in their *Constitutional Law* say: In time of invasion or insurrection on a wide scale ... the military ... are then entitled to give directions to and impose restrictions upon civilians in order to fulfil their duty to repel invaders or suppress rebels. This covers the action taken, but does not cover the situation that obtained. There was certainly no invasion from anywhere. There was no insurrection on a wide scale. The Minister in his letter does no more than to say that it was a situation of riot.[18]

Kaufman then went on to say:

The hon. Member for Berwick-upon-Tweed [Antony Lambton, Conservative] spoke about preserving the peace and protecting life and property. If the troops were seeking to protect life and property, not only did they signally fail but it was they themselves who violated life and property. The only lives taken that night were the four lives taken by troops. There was one life taken in the curfew area, that of Patrick Elliman. They were the only lives taken during the curfew period.

Why cannot he come here tonight and admit that General Freeland lost his head on that day? There is much evidence, including his disgraceful telephone conversation with the Administrator of St Peter's Parish, Father Murphy, with whom he opened a telephone conversation with the words 'Father Murphy, you are now under my orders'. Why cannot the Minister admit that General Freeland took action he had no right to take?[19]

These were strong words, but they reflected the views held in certain quarters at the time, even by other members of parliament. These viewpoints showed that many believed that the Curfew was illegal, even under common law, and had been far too heavily administered.

Mr Gilmour replied:

The hon. Gentleman made a great deal about the legality of curfew. He has corresponded with me about that subject. However, I am afraid that the hon. Gentleman remains determinedly unconvinced about what I said. It is true that the restrictions were described by General Freeland as a curfew, for the simple and understandable reason that 'curfew' is a word which everybody understands. In a battle situation … it is a word which would be used in any circumstances. It is important, in a situation such as I have outlined, that everybody should know straight away what they are meant to do; in other words, to get indoors. Therefore, 'curfew' was an entirely sensible word to use … The fact that the restrictions were imposed under the common law, not under the Emergency Regulations, seems a very minor point, with respect to the legal learning of the hon. Gentleman. But the fact that they were imposed under the common law does not make them any less legal.[20]

Did shouting the word 'Curfew' give it legal credence? Gilmour seemed to be creating the illusion that a 'curfew' was not ordered; only the word was used in order to inform the population to get indoors. The session in parliament ended at twenty-four minutes past twelve, and with it any serious debate in the 'Mother of Parliaments' about the legality of the Falls Curfew.

Aside from arguments in parliament about the proper use of the English language, the issue of the legality of the Curfew has never been satisfactorily settled. There has been no official inquiry into the deaths of the four civilians, no apologies for the damage caused and no prosecutions of soldiers. Many questions therefore remain. If the Curfew was called in haste by the GOC, why did it continue until Sunday morning, by which time things had calmed down? Did the GOC use this time, once he had the area under military occupation, to strike a major blow at the IRA in the area? Campbell and Connolly go into incredible detail in their paper about the legal implications of the Curfew, sometimes getting bogged down in legal and academic jargon, but the answer is the same. There was probably no legality associated with the Curfew, Campbell and Connolly state, 'after the first few hours'.[21]

The four civilians who died were killed by the army. There are witnesses to at least three of these deaths. They all say that the army killed them. If the Curfew was illegal, where do the families of these people stand?

Many people in Belfast who were present at the time of the Curfew and of the shootings refer to them as the first example of a 'shoot to kill' policy by the British army. This is a strong and incriminating statement, but many believe it. Witness stories are told, people believe them, and the myth is then built up. However, was it the first episode? The army had been told to toughen up, it had been criticised for the previous weekend's operation and this was the first major shoot-out in the Falls, a hotbed of both wings of the IRA.

A few weeks later a young man was shot dead in a riot. By February 1971 two more had been shot dead. By August 1971 it was the turn of Ballymurphy, when within two days eleven people were shot dead by British troops.[22] Some believe that the Falls Curfew was the turning point; soldiers were now operating a policy of shoot to kill, with devastating consequences for Northern Ireland over the next two years.[23]

Thus the Falls Curfew began to fade in the mindset of a majority of the people of Northern Ireland, save for those who were directly affected by it. The country as a whole began to experience violence unparalleled in its history. Bombs followed bombs, random shootings occurred and the Provisional IRA began to assert itself on the streets of Belfast, turning the centre into a fearful and dangerous place. The British army command at Lisburn, rather than learning from the debacle of the Curfew, became more repressive, in Catholic eyes, in its role as a 'peacekeeping force'. Stormont remained, the RUC remained unreformed and the army was showing Catholics that it was not impartial. Their only lifeline was the emerging Provisionals, who began to hit back with a vengeance.

CONCLUSION

The Falls Curfew was illegal. The Stormont and London governments knew it. General Freeland knew it. The military takeover of a residential area without gaining the proper authorisation was undoubtedly an error. This error emanated from the upper echelons of the Stormont government, which wanted to see direct action taken against the lower Falls, and the London government, which after years of negligence was now struggling with the complexities of the problems facing Northern Ireland. Chichester-Clark had to be seen to be getting tough with the situation; hawks such as Brian Faulkner and William Craig were waiting in the wings. So was the preacher who believed that pure evil spouted from every Catholic, Ian Paisley. The GOC bowed to pressure to 'get tough'.

The army, stung by the heavy criticism of the Short Strand incident, was always going to respond in the way it did in the lower Falls. But soldiers are not policemen. They are trained in such a way that at the first sign of gunfire or any other weapons they will respond aggressively. That is the nature of their job. Policemen are not trained for a 'battle' situation, as General Freeland so euphemistically called the Curfew. In describing it as a 'battle', Freeland was attempting to give some legitimacy to the operation. The Falls area and the Clonard suffered heavily from Protestants, in the guise of the RUC and the 'B' Specials, in August 1969. They had seen them burn houses, beat people and attack businesses. Who was left to defend the people of the lower Falls from another attack? Faith in the army was draining before the Curfew, due to house searches and the continuance of the Stormont government. In Catholic eyes the police were not to be trusted. They decided to defend the area themselves, with whatever weapons they had.

In March 1971 the civil advisor to GOC Northern Ireland wrote to Chris Johnson of the Ministry of Defence in London to enquire about 'the responsibilities of the Westminster and Stormont Parliaments and Governments in respect of control of the army'.[1] Even at this late stage, nineteen months after the troops went into Northern Ireland, the army command were still looking for clarification from London about their role in the state. The reply was received on 12 May. In quoting from the Government of Ireland Act 1920, Hockaday said: '[This] empowered the Northern Ireland parliament to make laws for the peace, order and good government of Northern Ireland but specifically excluded the power to legislate about the armed forces and defence matters generally.'[2] In other words, the ultimate responsibility for the army lay in Westminster and the London government. He then went on to talk about the legal and executive responsibilities of the ordinary soldier on the streets of Belfast:

> [Legal responsibility] The soldier's responsibility for his actions under the civil law, whether common law or statute (e.g. the Special Powers Acts), is to the courts of Northern Ireland.
> [Executive responsibility] The soldier acts under higher military authority up to the chain of command as far as the Defence Council and ultimately Her Majesty. The Secretary of State is the Minister responsible to Her Majesty for everything connected with the performance of their military duties by the armed forces of the Crown.[3]

This shows that at the time of the Curfew the Stormont government had little or no control over the army.[4] Soldiers were responsible for their actions in the courts, but Westminster was ultimately in charge.

The GOC had warned about the 'Honeymoon Period' coming to an end late in 1969. He correctly envisioned that, while the Catholics were happy to have the troops as a buffer between them and the Protestants, sooner or later in the political vacuum there would be trouble. The British Labour government under Harold Wilson, traditionally a party that advocated Irish unity, knew that the troops would not be welcome if they stayed indefinitely. The attitudes of the troops who were in the built-up areas were also a main cause of Catholic alienation. Many felt that the number of soldiers on the streets of Belfast was too many, and that this added to the tensions in Catholic areas. Soldiers stopped people for searches, arrested the wrong people with insufficient motive, and generally behaved like an occupying force. This was Catholics' pervading view of the army. They continued to see brutality and harassment, and they continued to be told that it was instigated by the Provisional IRA.

The ordinary British soldier on the street in Belfast did not see himself in this way. They saw themselves involved in a conflict that they initially did not understand, a situation that the politicians should have sorted out years ago.

The streets of Belfast were as alien as anywhere else they had been, but at the same time very familiar. This was because they were familiar. They were the same as any street in England, in Manchester, Leeds, Bradford or Birmingham. That was the most confusing part. These streets were in the United Kingdom.

They were soldiers, not politicians or policemen. It is true that some soldiers used excessive force, were openly abusive to Catholics and seemed to enjoy the role that they were put in. Soldiers were put under extreme pressure on the streets of Belfast, where nobody knew where the next bomb or bullet was going to come from. In the case of the Falls Curfew, however, were the soldiers to blame? The GOC ordered them in, under pressure from Stormont, and the London government was still aloof from the complexities of the situation.

Many of the troops who went into the lower Falls were brutal, and carried out violent and excessive actions, no doubt fuelled by previous encounters such as the rioting in Ballymurphy, the Crumlin Road and the Shankill, to name a few instances. There is no doubt about that. Witness statements and photographic evidence all add credence to it. But that does not mean that they all took part in it. The majority behaved with respect, and even helped some of the residents. The consensus amongst many historians is that the army command, Westminster and Stormont were to blame for the aggression in the lower Falls. They are the ones who accelerated Catholic alienation in the area and hastened the rise of the Provisional IRA.

II

Many historians also argue that a majority of Catholics initially undertook a policy of self-alienation from the state, and in this respect 'missed out' on the benefits that being part of the United Kingdom could bring. Another angle to this self-exclusion is that Catholics did not want to gain employment in the civil service, or any form of governmental employment, as that would show their adherence to the state.[5] As Jonathan Tonge suggests: 'According to Unionists, Nationalist disloyalty led to self-exclusion, as Catholics refused to cooperate with what they regarded as an illegitimate state.'[6]

Catholics were over-represented in the poorer sections of society because as Catholics they were more than likely to be unemployed. Initial discrimination in employment, where it was Protestant businesses that would not employ Catholics, fed the discrimination in the voting franchise. It was a knock-on effect. Catholics had fewer educational prospects due to the standard of teaching in Church-run schools, and therefore were under-represented in higher education right up to the 1960s.

During the birth of the state, serious violence between Catholics and
Protestants occurred in Belfast and other districts. The sheer terror involved,
and the lack of any help from the new government, added credence to
Catholics opting out of the state altogether. The years of 1921 to 1923 were
perhaps the most traumatic for Catholics in Northern Ireland and undoubtedly fed the fires of 1969 through a collective memory:

> The Orange mobs, many of them drunk with looted whiskey, began
> early and worked late. When all the Catholic shops in the Newtownards
> Road area were cleaned out, they even looted a few belonging to their
> own co-religionists.[7]

Protestants were, and to a degree still are, bound by their history. For generations they were landowners, members of parliament and landlords. The
native Catholic Irish were subordinate to this. This arrogance within the
Protestant establishment carried on into the new Northern Irish state.
Catholics were to be looked down upon, given menial jobs, poor houses
and limited representation in government. The Unionist government,
however, was treating members of its own religion in much the same way.
Working-class Protestants in Northern Ireland were also penalised by the
very laws that the ruling elite created to keep down Catholic progression.
The Protestant working class suffered the same discrimination in local elections as Catholics. This disenfranchisement did not penalise on grounds of
religion, but on grounds of poverty:

> While it is generally agreed that there was discrimination against national-
> ists, its extent and whether they alone suffered discrimination is debated.
> The right to vote is the one that has attracted most criticism. Given the
> electoral rules, around a quarter of adults had no vote in Northern Ireland
> as the franchise was only granted to ratepayers and their spouses. It is not
> the case that as a result of these rules only nationalists were denied the vote,
> poor Protestants were also disenfranchised. But nationalists were dispropor-
> tionately disadvantaged as they were statistically over-represented among
> the poorest sections of society.[8]

As we have seen, Unionist government propaganda convinced working-class
Protestants that the real threat to their way of life came from the Catholic
minority. Thus the laws that also penalised them were forgotten in the fog of
hatred towards the Catholics. This hatred and suspicion was born out of centuries of mistrust of each other, but was also a product of the siege mentality

against the rise of Irish Catholic nationalism, which increased at the advent of the Northern Irish state.[9] Protestant belief that Catholics/nationalists were 'disloyal' went back centuries, and became more apparent as the Unionist-dominated state began its policy of discrimination.

By the advent of O'Neill to the premiership Northern Ireland was an extremely divided and sectarian state, with a segregated and discrimina-tive society. O'Neill was one of a long line of elite Protestants who became prime minister. Completely out of touch with the grass roots of Northern Irish society, his initial attempts at reconciliation with the Catholic minor-ity, while commendable, were inadequate. His own party as well as the more militant Protestants would have major difficulties with this too:

> Prime Minister Terence O'Neill was disconnected from the Protestant working class and many viewed his reforming agenda as undermining the Union and encouraging the disloyal nationalist community in its attempts to destroy Northern Ireland. Ian Paisley was more in touch with the Protestant working class and emerged as one of the most vocal and influen-tial of O'Neill's critics.[10]

The attitudes of the army, the RUC and the government in general to Catholics began to change as the Troubles continued. Catholics were now being treated as one unit, tarred with the brush of the IRA, in the house-to-house raids and stop-and-search practices. After the Curfew, recriminations for the damage caused were being firmly laid, as we have seen, at the door of the army. The media were blamed for this, as the following report from a meeting of the cabinet at Stormont shows:

> The similarity of the smear campaign now being mounted against the army to that launched against the police on previous occasions was noted and Ministers regretted the tendency of certain important sections of the press to play up the alleged depredations of the troops and to ignore the main issue of a very substantial arms cache which was desperately defended by the residents.[11]

The Reverend Dr Ian Paisley, demagogue and 'Demon Doctor', as Brian Faulkner rather passionately referred to him one day in 1974,[12] did more to alienate Protestants from rapport with Catholics than any discriminative legislation from Stormont. By the time of the Curfew, even the Stormont government recognised this. Working-class Catholic reaction to the state of Northern Ireland in the aftermath of the Curfew was now one of complete alienation. Although the 'no go' areas were being slowly infiltrated by the security forces, and a heavy military presence was still apparent in the lower Falls, the soldiers were not welcome any more. Gone were the cups of tea and cakes, the warm smiles and the photo opportunities. In their place were reels of barbed wire and sandbags.

Protestants, fed a diet of sectarianism and mistrust of Catholics, were in the wake of August 1969 and the subsequent violence ready for retaliation against the Catholic community, whom they saw as one with the IRA and those who wanted to destroy the 'Constitution of Ulster'. Many articles and essays were written at the time from a Loyalist point of view, each one of them pointing the finger of blame at Catholics. One such article, written by S. S. Herron and entitled 'Forget 1690 and 1916', shows the hatred that many Protestants now felt:

> Forget the Dutchman and the crucial battle for British freedom fought and won on Irish soil at the Boyne River. This was the advice of Mr Harold Wilson, leader of Her Majesty's Opposition at Westminster as he addressed the people of Northern Ireland. He might as well have told us to forget Adam and Eve. How can we forget history when history has made us what we are? Can England forget Nelson, Wellington or Churchill? Can freedom loving people ever forget the illustrious champions of the freedom they now enjoy? What of the immortal band of Christian statesmen and the noble army of martyrs who laid down their lives rather than submit England to the tyranny of popery? Mr Wilson's vitriolic anti-Ulster speech would have stuck in his throat if the great mass of his Liverpool constituency voters had been Protestant Loyalists instead of Catholic Irish Republicans.[13]

These were coarse words about how a significant number of Protestants felt, not only towards Wilson for his alleged pro-Catholic speeches, but towards Catholics as well. Protestant history was brought up to remind the reader that Protestants have an illustrious past that is inextricably linked with England. To be asked to forget it is to throw that link away. The civil rights movement and the alleged nationalist/Catholic-inspired violence of the previous two years was, Protestants believed, also an attempt to sever them from their shared past with England. In this respect their hatred of Catholics was justified in their eyes. Their subsequent paramilitary groupings would show even more hatred over the next twenty-five years.

III

Over the past few years historians have begun to look at the Troubles in a new light, encouraged to do so by the amount of archival material that has come into the public domain. This has ultimately opened up questions on various aspects of the history of the Troubles that until a few years ago would have been treated as 'fact'. The scale of discrimination against the Catholic community in Northern Ireland and its subsequent alienation is one of those areas that have received attention.

Christopher Hewitt, while not denying that it occurred, believes that the claims of Catholic discrimination are exaggerated. He cites a survey by Budge and O'Leary of Belfast, in which they found that 28 per cent of Catholics and 18 per cent of Protestants were not allowed to vote in the local elections, giving a similar set of figures for Belfast.[14] Hewitt also suggests that although discrimination did occur in Protestant-owned firms, Catholics in business did the same. This fits in with the alienation and segregation of both Catholics and Protestants in Northern Ireland. As mentioned, Catholics avoided the instruments of the new northern state, tending to rely on their own businesses and educational facilities provided by the Catholic Church. Protestants, while adhering to the structures of Stormont, were constantly led to believe that Catholics were the 'enemy', by derogatory speeches from Stormont ministers and from visiting politicians in their own areas. Thus Catholics and Protestants segregated themselves in the state, helped in part by the Unionist government and the Catholic Church, with its all-Ireland focus.[15]

The issue of gerrymandering is another area that has been given plenty of attention by historians, it being claimed that gerrymandering may not have been as widespread as previously thought. However, the situation in Derry in the 1960s, where a Catholic majority of two to one in the city was governed by a majority Unionist council, speaks for itself, and was the clearest example of gerrymandering in Northern Ireland. Local government boundaries were redrawn shortly after the birth of the state in order to thwart any rise of nationalist-dominated councils in the west and south. There are many reports of how social housing allocation became a religious issue, not one of need. Hennessey states: 'In Fermanagh, where Catholics formed a slight majority of the population, it was claimed that of 1,589 post war council houses, 568 were let to Catholics and 1,021 to Protestants.'[16]

By the time of the Falls Curfew in 1970 discrimination in housing was the norm, and was breeding contempt amongst the people of the area towards the state, along with unfair employment practices, high unemployment and fear of the state's security apparatus. Hewitt, however, argues that

Catholic/nationalist councils also discriminated against Protestants. He gives an example of this discrimination. Newry, in County Armagh, is a couple of miles from the Irish border and is overwhelmingly Catholic and nationalist. Hewitt cites that out of 765 council houses, 743 were occupied by Catholics and 22 by Protestants.[17] He also goes on to state that there were no Protestants working for the council. The fact that Newry is predominantly Catholic may have an impact on this, and a local council representing equal Protestant and Catholic populations might have been a better example.

The first IRA ceasefire of August 1994 began the process of bringing Republicans in from the cold politically. It was welcomed warmly by the Catholics of west Belfast, who believed that the political processes involved would eventually bring about a united Ireland. In this way, equality would be achieved with their co-religionists in the south, rather than with the Protestants of the north. Here again, history played a part. Catholics, so long second-class citizens in Northern Ireland, firmly believed that equality within the United Kingdom was impossible. As nationalists, their mental as well as physical allegiances would be with a united Ireland, and the political structures of Northern Ireland and the United Kingdom could not accommodate this reality.

The United Kingdom, seeing the imbalance, began to work towards reducing the stranglehold that Protestants had on the economic and social structures of Northern Ireland, especially after the imposition of Direct Rule in 1972. Before the outbreak of violence in 1969 Protestants had a firm grip on the economy of the country. Protestants were more likely to own businesses, and in turn were more likely to employ 'their own'. A shift from traditional Protestant-owned businesses dominating the economy after 1972, coupled with an increase in public spending and the implementation of equality in employment legislation, ensured that Catholics were becoming on a par with Protestants.[18]

The Falls Curfew and incidents like it ensured that the alienation of the Catholic community in Northern Ireland was complete. For decades they were made to feel inferior in Northern Irish society, right from the upper echelons of the state. The onset of the 1960s and worldwide popular protest, coupled with an increase in Catholics attending university, set the Catholic community on the road to attempting to gain some sort of parity with Protestants through their basic demands,[19] but it was interrupted by the onset of the Troubles and the inevitable Protestant backlash against making any concessions to Catholics. By the mid-1970s Catholics were more alienated than ever. Repressive security measures in their areas, a legacy of pre-Direct Rule days, kept the flame of the Provisional IRA burning brightly, and also ensured that Catholics not only were alienated from Northern Irish society, but believed that they were somehow different, somehow belonging somewhere else.

The conflict in Northern Ireland can ultimately be traced back to the plantation days, when native Irish Catholics were instilled with a sense of inferiority about their religion and their place. These feelings prevailed down through the centuries and created a situation where Protestant descendants believed that they were superior to the Catholics in their midst. The partition of Ireland in 1921 cemented this belief – now this superiority was legitimate in their eyes. This has been discussed here and in many other places, but the subsequent debacle of leaving them in control of the state while turning a blind eye to the erection of numerous sectarian barriers to equality, which showed that the British government, while not supporting these policies, did nothing to alleviate the conditions for Catholics, has not. It is clear that this needs to be debated further to understand how Catholic alienation in Northern Ireland was also enhanced by British neglect.

The advent of the campaign for Home Rule, coupled with a fear that a Dublin Catholic parliament would bleed the area that they inhabited dry for the benefit of the rest of the country, was another main reason behind Protestant reaction. But a belief in the idea of being 'British' was another major factor. Krishan Kumar suggests that it is this sense of belonging across the Irish Sea that drives Protestants to believe that they have a joint identity with the British:

> Of mixed English and Scottish descent, they have long ceased to think of themselves as 'English', as they did up to the middle of the eighteenth century. But since the early twentieth century, and especially after the secession of the rest of Ireland in 1921, they have come to insist ever more strongly on their 'Britishness'. That was why they resisted the idea of a separate parliament for Ulster, as envisioned in the 1920 Government of Ireland Act. As Sir Edward Carson, the Unionist leader told the House of Commons in 1919, 'Ulster has never asked for a separate parliament. Ulster's claim has always been of this simple character: 'We have thrived under the Union, we are in sympathy with you; we are part of yourselves.'[20]

Protestants thus came to believe that they were in some way superior to the native, Catholic Irish in order to distance themselves from them. In this way their 'separate identity' would ensure that the government in London could not abandon them to a Catholic state where they would lose their status. The London government did not abandon them, but gave them their own parliament.

Thus Protestants ensured that their culture and traditions, based on their superiority over Catholics, would continue to thrive. This was a fundamental error by the London government, which underestimated how much the Protestant tradition in Northern Ireland was based on subjugation. As this Protestant 'tradition' continued in their own state, Catholics were increasingly sidelined into a sense of inferiority and alienation.

The above goes some way to explain the complexities of Northern Irish society within the timeframe of the Stormont government and before. Protestants used the systems supplied by the London government to ensure that they were always in the ascendency at the expense of their Catholic neighbours. The Catholic feeling of alienation and difference has prevailed to today. Although equality is assured in Northern Ireland and peace has somehow continued, there is still that sense of comradeship that was a feature of the early days of the Troubles and before. However, community organisations, area committees, cross-border councils and Catholic–Protestant partnerships have replaced the old, traditional needs for security. Sinn Féin, now the largest nationalist/Republican party in Northern Ireland, shares the post of first minister of the devolved assembly at Stormont with Unionists, something that would have been an impossibility as recently as twenty years ago. Enshrined in the Good Friday Agreement is equality, even if at some point there is a Unionist minority within the state.[21]

Today, parts of the Falls Road area and especially the lower Falls are radically different from in July 1970. In the case of the lower Falls many of the street names that had been there since the beginning of the twentieth century have gone, lost in an architect's office when the plans for a new, cleaner and healthier area were being drawn up. In their place are bigger, neater homes with inside toilets and bathrooms, front and back gardens, something the people of 1970 could only dream of.

With these bigger homes the authorities decided to do something about the numerous roads that went in and out of the lower Falls, offering ideal escape routes, hideaways and attack routes for both wings of the IRA in the early 1970s. Today there are only four main ways to enter the lower Falls by car, and then the driver is in a warren of cul de sacs, one-way streets and blocked exits. All of this was part of the plan when the designs were drawn up, albeit with a little bit of help from the British army. It was a case of cutting off the terrorists at their heart, denying them the mobility that a guerrilla army depends on. There are no more 'guerrillas' now, though. The lower Falls is peaceful, orderly and neighbourly.

The Catholic community in Northern Ireland have gained immense benefits in the years since the start of the Troubles. But the sense of not belonging is still there in many. Many still avoid Protestant areas; a few still avoid all contact with them. These Catholics are people who shared experiences together, shared the despair and destruction of the early Troubles, and the repression of the early attempts by the British army to restore law and order under the Unionist regime. They shared some of the most harrowing days of the Troubles, and felt their sense of alienation grow as each event served only to drive them into the arms of their 'protectors'. This process, while apparent before the beginning of the conflict, was hastened by the Falls Curfew. On 5 July 1970 Catholics believed that the British army was there to prop up the discriminative Stormont government and the hostile RUC, to protect British interests in Ireland and to repress them.

It is what their children and grandchildren believe today, although on a lesser scale than their parents. But they still believe. The rise of the Provisional IRA was hastened by the Curfew, which radicalised great swathes of young, articulate and intelligent Catholics in one go. But it also alienated them from Northern Irish society and the interaction with other beliefs and customs. They had seen their parents, brothers, uncles and friends maltreated, had seen grown men attempt to defend their area. This is why so many joined. This is why the Provisionals themselves became radicalised, became active.

At the time of writing the HET has not delivered its reports into the four deaths attributable to the Falls Curfew. If their findings confirm that they were killed for no other reason than being in the wrong area at the wrong time, then the whole issue of the legality of the Curfew should be the next inquiry, regardless of the cost. Maybe then the families of the deceased will get some recompense, and not see the names of their loved ones sullied. The Falls Curfew, in my mind illegal and brutal, is enshrined in the psyche of the Catholics of the lower Falls. It will remain there for generations yet.

EXPLANATIONS OF GROUPS, ORGANISATIONS AND TERMS

Act of Union: After the failure of the 1798 rebellion, the parliament in London decided to disband the Irish parliament in Dublin. This was mainly because of the threat of Catholics, if given the right to partake in parliament, becoming a majority, breaking the link with England and allying themselves with France. The Act came into force on 1 January 1801 and united Britain with Ireland, thus creating the United Kingdom of Great Britain and Ireland.

An Phoblacht: 'The Republic', a Republican newspaper first printed in 1906. It went out of print but after the split in the Republican movement in 1970 the name was revived. Originally it was only sold in the south of Ireland. It merged with another Republican newspaper, the *Republican News* in 1979, thereafter being called *An Phoblacht/Republican News*. It was the sole voice of Republicanism in Ireland after members of Republican groups were banned from the airwaves. Today it is a monthly newspaper fully under Sinn Féin's wings.

Apprentice Boys: An organisation founded in 1814 to commemorate the lifting of the 'Siege of Derry' in 1689 by forces loyal to the Protestant King William. The siege was put in place by James II. Apprentice Boys march annually to commemorate this event. In 1969 the Apprentice Boys' march in Derry was the catalyst for nationalist rioting, culminating in the 'Battle of the Bogside', which lasted three days and instigated the intervention of British troops in Northern Ireland.

'Battle of the Bogside': An Apprentice Boys march in Derry on 12 August 1969 was the catalyst for three days of intensive rioting which culminated in British troops being deployed on the streets of Northern Ireland. Tension in the city had been on a razor's edge because of civil rights agitation for the past year. It finally exploded when Catholic youths began to stone the marchers. The RUC became involved, standing with their backs to the Protestants. Things degenerated with the RUC throwing stones back at the Catholics, then using CS gas. Barricades were erected at strategic points of entry into the Bogside. The area literally seceded from the state of Northern Ireland. This event was also the catalyst for serious sectarian rioting in other parts of Northern Ireland, Belfast being the place worst affected, with eight deaths over a period of two days.

Battle of the Boyne: King William's most famous battle and an inspiration for virtually all Protestants in Northern Ireland. On the river Boyne, about 3 miles west of the town of Drogheda in the Republic, was the site where the Protestant King William's armies defeated James, the Catholic King of England, who had been deposed by William and Mary, his Protestant daughter. This was not merely a Catholic versus Protestant battle, however. It was part of a wider European conflict, and there were many Protestants on the side of James and Catholics on the side of William and Mary. The 'Orange Order' was founded in William's memory, and every July Protestant areas of Northern Ireland celebrate his victory and the ascendency of the Protestant tradition in Ireland. A monument dedicated to the Protestant victory marked the site until it was blown up by the IRA in 1922.

CCDC: Central Citizens Defence Committee. Established in 1969, after the August riots in Belfast, this brought together the numerous defence and community groups that had formed in Belfast. Jim Sullivan and Billy McMillan were involved in its creation. The CCDC was involved in regular talks with the army about the dismantling of the barricades in Catholic areas after August 1969. Discussions were ended abruptly by the army after the Curfew, as arms were found at the CCDC's headquarters in the lower Falls. The CCDC was pivotal in cataloguing the excesses of the troops in the lower Falls Curfew.

Dáil: The Irish parliament (Dáil Éireann), which was formed in 1919 after a British general election in which Sinn Féin won 75 per cent of the available seats in Ireland. Sinn Féin members would not take their seats in Westminster, but instead set up their own parliament in Dublin. Declared illegal by the British, it was restored as the parliament of the Irish Free State after 1921.

Fenians: A group of secret revolutionaries in the United States and Ireland in the mid-nineteenth century who aimed to overthrow British rule in Ireland. In the States they were invariably formed from members of the Irish diaspora, who had emigrated during the Famine years. Protestants use the word in a derogatory sense, usually by tagging the word 'bastard' on the end.

Gaeltacht: areas of Ireland where the predominant language is Irish. These areas are mainly to the west of the country, although there are isolated areas in the south and east. In Catholic areas of Belfast, the Irish language and culture is now heavily promoted. The 'Gaeltacht Quarter' is one such area, centred on the Falls Road.

GOC: General Officer Commanding, in charge of the British army in Northern Ireland. Responsible to the Ministry of Defence in London, the GOC in 1970 was seen to be heavily influenced by the Unionist government.

HET: Historical Enquiries Team, formed in 2005 to investigate the many unsolved murders of the Troubles. From 2008 the team began to investigate the deaths attributable to army actions between 1970 and 1973.

Home Rule: The principle of a limited form of self-determination within a dependency of another country. In the case of Ireland, it was seen as a practical solution to Ireland's desire to run her own affairs. Home Rule became part of British political life in the late nineteenth century. It finally became law in 1914, but was shelved at the outbreak of the First World War and abandoned in the face of Unionist criticism and rebellion in Ireland after 1920.

IRA: Irish Republican Army. Formed from the Irish Republican Brotherhood and various other groups, the IRA came to prominence during the Irish War of Independence, 1919–21. It split over the provisions of the treaty with the British that brought about Partition. The IRA lost much, if not all, of its military prowess after the failure of 'Operation Harvest' in 1962. It embarked on a socialist path up to 1969, and was heavily criticised for its 'failure' to defend Catholic areas of Belfast in August 1969. In 1970 it split again into 'Provisional' and 'Official' wings. The Officials lost support to the Provisionals after the Falls Curfew, and the latter then became the dominant Republican paramilitary group. The IRA's Military wing called an indefinite ceasefire in 1972. In this book, PIRA denotes Provisionals and OIRA denotes Officials.

IRB: Irish Republican Brotherhood. This was a secret society formed in the latter half of the nineteenth century, dedicated to the establishment of an Irish Republic. It had American connections and took part in the failed Easter Rising of 1916.

Irish Volunteers: Formed in 1913 in direct response to the growing tensions among Protestants in the north and the creation of the Ulster Volunteer Force (UVF). It was among many groupings that fought in the Easter Rising in 1916, eventually morphing with various other groups to form the Irish Republican Army (IRA).

JSC: Joint Security Committee. This was a committee of Northern Ireland's Stormont government, containing army and RUC representatives. Set up after the British army became involved in August 1969, it met on a regular basis, sometimes three or four times a week, as the situation in Northern Ireland grew worse.

Loyalist: Term used for those who support the present union of Northern Ireland with the United Kingdom and who are prepared to use violence in order to achieve their aims. They are almost exclusively Protestant. Paramilitary groupings associated with Loyalism are the Ulster Volunteer Force (UVF), the Ulster Freedom Fighters (UFF), the Loyalist Volunteer Force (LVF), the Ulster Defence Association (UDA) and the Red Hand Commandos (RHC). Many more subsidiary groups were active during the Troubles and have not been mentioned here.

Nationalist: The majority of the Catholic population of the north of Ireland are classed as the 'nationalist community'. They hold a belief in 'Irishness' within their culture but do not resort to violence in their agitation for a united Ireland. Notable nationalist MPs have included John Hume and Austin Currie, later to found the Socialist and Democratic Labour Party (SDLP) with Paddy Devlin and Gerry Fitt, the party's first leader.

PD: People's Democracy. This organisation was formed by a group of students at Queens University, Belfast, in October 1968 in reaction to the political turmoil engulfing Northern Ireland and particularly the civil rights march on 5 October in Derry. Its principles were similar to the civil rights movement: fair allocation of housing, an end to gerrymandering and 'one man one vote'. The PD was most famous for the Belfast to Derry march in January 1969, which was repeatedly attacked by Loyalists. The organisation followed a socialist path for much of the 1970s.

Proportional Representation: An electoral system that allows a broad base for minority parties to have a voice. Under a completely proportional system, if a party won 20 per cent of the preferred votes, it would win 20 per cent of available seats. PR was abolished in the Stormont parliament by 1929.

Republican: Irish Republicans are considered by some as more prone than nationalists to use violence to reach their goals. They are associated with the aim of ending the partition of the island of Ireland and establishing a Socialist Republic of Ireland. Mostly Catholic, they are mainly drawn from the working-class areas of Northern Ireland, of which the Falls district and the Bogside are but a couple of examples. Groups associated with Republicanism's violent strain are the Provisional IRA (PIRA), the Official IRA (OIRA) (under permanent ceasefire since 1972), the Irish National Liberation Army (INLA), the Real IRA (RIRA) and the Continuity IRA (CIRA). Splinter groups are a feature of the violent strain of Republicanism; thus there are many more not mentioned here.

Ribbonmen: A secret organisation formed in opposition to the abject poverty that many farmers and workers lived in. Reports of their activities go as far back as 1815. Ribbonmen attacked landowners' properties and tithe collectors. They became increasingly sectarian, attacking Protestant Orange Lodge meetings, as the nineteenth century wore on.

RUC: Royal Ulster Constabulary, formed on 1 June 1922 out of the remnants of the Royal Irish Constabulary (RIC). Classed as acutely sectarian by the Catholic community in Northern Ireland, the RUC was replaced by the Police Service of Northern Ireland (PSNI) after the Good Friday Agreement of 1998.

Solemn League and Covenant: Ulster Covenant. This was a covenant signed by nearly half a million people in the north of Ireland in 1912 against the 'Home Rule' Bill for Irish independence. Ulster Protestants believed that it would be detrimental for Ireland if a parliament was set up in Dublin. The full text of the Covenant is:

> BEING CONVINCED in our consciences that Home Rule would be disastrous to the material well-being of Ulster as well as of the whole of Ireland, subversive of our civil and religious freedom, destructive of our citizenship, and perilous to the unity of the Empire, we, whose names are underwritten, men of Ulster, loyal subjects of His Gracious Majesty King George V., humbly relying on the God whom our fathers in days of stress and trial confidently trusted, do hereby pledge ourselves in solemn Covenant, throughout this our time of threatened calamity, to stand by one another in defending, for ourselves and our children, our cherished position of equal citizenship in the United Kingdom, and in using all means which may be found necessary to defeat the present conspiracy to set up a Home Rule

Parliament in Ireland. And in the event of such a Parliament being forced upon us, we further solemnly and mutually pledge ourselves to refuse to recognize its authority. In sure confidence that God will defend the right, we hereto subscribe our names. And further, we individually declare that we have not already signed this Covenant.

Taigs: Originally a nickname for an Irishman along the lines of 'Paddy' and 'Mick'. In modern times, it has been used as a derogatory term for Catholics in Northern Ireland.

Taoiseach: (Leader) Prime Minister of the Republic of Ireland (literally pronounced 'tee-shock'). The term came into use after the enactment of the 1937 Constitution.

The 'Treaty': The agreement between members of Sinn Féin and the British government bringing about the birth of the Irish Free State in December 1921. Its jurisdiction applied to twenty-six of its thirty-two counties, the other six forming the state of Northern Ireland. For all its apparent faults, the Treaty was a watershed in British political life. Ireland was treated with far greater respect than the other dominions within the British Empire. As Eleanor Hull stated:

> It would appear, therefore, that the Irish Free State stands in a privileged position among the Dominions of the British Empire both as to origin and constitution. It did not arise in a British Act of Parliament but by the Irish enactment of the Dáil, though the British Act was necessary to give it the force of law in Great Britain. Thus the Irish view that all power resides in the citizen and that the political sovereignty of the people is also the legal sovereignty, gains a sanction from the terms of the Constitution. The Constitutional assembly had a free hand in drawing up the machinery of Government within the terms of the Treaty, and the admission of representatives of the Free State to the League of Nations and of her independent representatives at Washington, Paris, Berlin, and the Vatican, countries which also have sent their Ministers to Dublin, are a recognition of the equal status that she enjoys.

The problem was, though, and to a degree still is, 'Partition'.

Unionist: Describes those who hold a desire to maintain the constitutional link with the United Kingdom. Most are Protestants, although there are

Catholics who are also Unionist. They wish to achieve their aims through mainly democratic means.

United Irishmen: Initially formed to campaign for parliamentary reform in the Irish parliament of the late eighteenth century, this group soon evolved into a more radical organisation. Involved in the 1798 rebellion, it was noted for its non-sectarian make-up: its aim was to unite 'Catholic, Protestant and Dissenter' in a united Irish Republic.

UVF: Ulster Volunteer Force. Formed in 1912 to oppose with arms the formation of a Home Rule parliament, it saw action at the Battle of the Somme in the First World War. The UVF was revived in 1966 as a paramilitary organisation led by 'Gusty' Spence. It was responsible for the death of a Catholic barman on the Shankill Road in 1966, and began to increase its paramilitary activities after 1970, in direct response to the increase in IRA activity.

Whiteboys: A rural society, in the eighteenth century, which demanded non-payment of rent by rural farmers. It generally defended rural farmers' rights over land and opposed price hiking.

APPENDIX A:
CHRONOLOGY OF MAJOR EVENTS

1542: The parliament of Ireland enacts a law that makes Henry VIII King of Ireland.

1594: War in Ulster as O'Neill attempts to remove the authority of Elizabeth I.

1601: Battle of Kinsale: Considered the last major battle which ensured English domination over the Irish. Spanish troops land in depleted numbers to aid the rebels but are defeated by the English, under Lord Mountjoy. O'Neill's lands in Ulster are carved up amongst English and Scottish Protestant settlers, the beginnings of the plantations.

1620: Plantations begin in the counties of central Ireland, most notably Kings County and Queens County (Offaly and Laois).

1641: Rebellion in Ireland. Sectarian conflict erupts between Irish Catholics and English Protestants.

1649: Cromwell lands in Ireland to clear up the remnants of the Royalist forces. Massacres at Drogheda and Wexford by soldiers of Cromwell's 'New Model Army'.

1655: By now at least 50,000 Irish Catholics have been sent to the Caribbean as slaves since Oliver Cromwell began his subjugation of Ireland. Many more are told to move to the more barren west, to Connaught, where the native Irish are now to live.

1690: Battle of the Boyne in County Meath between forces supporting the deposed King James, and soldiers belonging to the Protestant King William. King James's armies routed.

1791: Foundation of the United Irishmen by Rowan Hamilton, Napper Tandy, Wolfe Tone and others. Aims to bring Protestants and Catholics together in a new Ireland.

1795: The foundation of the 'Orange Order' after a localised battle involving Protestant and Catholic groups in County Armagh. They take their name from William of Orange and celebrate his Battle of the Boyne victory over the Catholic King James. Catholics were, and still are, barred from joining.

1798: The United Irishmen rebellion, led by Wolfe Tone, ends in failure.

1801: Act of Union between the parliaments of England and Ireland, as a direct response to the 1798 Rebellion. New country to be called the United Kingdom of Great Britain and Ireland.

1814: Foundation of the Apprentice Boys of Derry, celebrating the Siege of Derry in which the armies of King James attempted to storm the city. It was ended by the forces of King William.

1829: The Catholic Relief Act is passed, allowing Catholics to sit in parliament. Commonly referred to as Catholic Emancipation.

1841: The population of Ireland stands at just over 8 million.

1845: The beginning of the Irish Famine (an Gorta Mór) with the failure of the potato crop.

1846: A Poor Law is enacted by parliament, with the creation of a Poor Law Board. Famine enters its second year.

1848: Rebellion against British rule by the 'Young Ireland' movement ends in failure.

1851: Population of Ireland is now just over 6 million, 2 million down on the 1841 Census.

1858: The Irish Republican Brotherhood is formed.

1861: The Census of this year shows that the population of Ireland had decreased to just over 5.5 million.

1871: Population of Ireland is now under 5.5 million.

1879: Beginning of the 'Irish Land Wars'.

1880: Charles Stuart Parnell, MP for Meath, is made chairman of the Irish Home Rule Party.

1881: Population now stands at 5 million.

1891: In the 1891 Census the population of Ireland is shown as just over 4.5 million.

1893: The Gaelic League is formed.

1896: Formation of the Irish Socialist Republican Party by James Connelly, aspiring to create an Irish workers' republic.

1901: Census shows a decrease of 400,000 on previous one. Population is now 4,400,000.

1905: Advent of Sinn Féin ('we ourselves') by Arthur Griffiths. Dedicated to the creation of an independent Irish Republic, free from British interference.

1912: Formation of the Ulster Volunteer Force UVF by Edward Carson, a Dublin lawyer opposed to Home Rule. Formed to defend Ulster from Home Rule and a Catholic-dominated Irish Parliament.

1913: Formation of the Irish Volunteers in an attempt to thwart the rise of a Protestant-dominated militia force in the north of Ireland.

1914: Beginning of the First World War. Home Rule Act suspended for the duration.

1916: The Easter Rising. Working on the old adage that 'England's difficulty is Ireland's opportunity', the IRB stages an insurrection in Dublin, hoping for support from around the country. The insurrection fails and the leaders are executed, thus creating martyrs for the Irish cause. The Battle of the Somme. The Ulster 36th Division, with many UVF men, suffers heavy casualties.

1918: In the general election after the war Sinn Féin wins the majority of seats allocated to Ireland. The Unionists win seats in the north-east of the country and in Trinity College, Dublin. Sinn Féin refuse to sit in the Houses of Parliament, setting up their own parliament in Dublin. Start of the Anglo-Irish war (War of Independence). The 'Black and Tans' sent to Ireland to aid the police force. Embark on an orgy of destruction, burning the town of Balbriggan and razing the centre of the city of Cork in reprisal acts.

1920: Black and Tans kill twelve and injure scores more at a football match in Dublin in reprisal for the killing of fourteen undercover agents by the IRA earlier that day.

1921: Truce called between the British government and the IRA. Subsequent negotiations create the Irish Free State and Northern Ireland. IRA splits into pro- and anti-Treaty wings. Sectarian violence continues in Belfast with the expulsion of Catholics from their houses in mixed areas. Around 400 Catholics killed in this period. Opening of Northern Irish Parliament. Lord Craigavon appointed Northern Ireland's first prime minister.

1922: Civil war in the south. Anti-Treaty forces (IRA) against pro-Treaty forces under the command of Michael Collins. The vast store of historical records held at the Four Courts in Dublin destroyed by bombardment. Collins subsequently killed in County Cork. Expulsion of Catholics from homes in Belfast continues. Introduction of the Special Powers Act by the Northern Irish government, to be reviewed annually. Formation of the Garda Siochana (civic guard), the Free State police force, to replace the old Royal Irish Constabulary. New force is disarmed, and remains so.

1923: End of civil war in the south, anti-Treaty forces defeated. Stabilisation of the new state. Expulsion of Catholics from their homes in Belfast continues. Protestants evicted as well, though not on the scale of Catholics.

1925: Boundary Commission ends after an alleged leak to the press. The border between the Irish Free State and Northern Ireland to remain the same, leaving a substantial number of Catholics on the northern side.

1926: Census in Northern Ireland shows that Catholics make up fewer than 35 per cent of the state of Northern Ireland.

1932: Riots in Belfast involving Protestants and Catholics working together against lack of monetary relief for the unemployed.

1936: Census in the Irish Free State shows the population to be just under 3 million. A Census the following year in Northern Ireland shows the population as 1.2 million.

1937: The Irish Free State declares itself a republic in all but name by enacting a new constitution, replacing the king as head of state with the president and changing its name to the Gaelic 'Eire'. The constitution, however, comes under scrutiny for its territorial claim to Northern Ireland:

Article 2: The national territory consists of the whole island of Ireland, its islands and the territorial seas.

Article 3: Pending the re-integration of the national territory, and without prejudice to the right of the parliament and government established by this constitution to exercise jurisdiction over the whole territory, the laws enacted by the parliament shall have the like area and extent of application as the laws of Saorstat Éireann [Irish Free State, 26-county area] and the like extra-territorial effect.

1938: Agreement reached between Britain and the Free State over an economic dispute in operation since 1932. The 'Land Question' is finally solved with the Free State making a final payment of £10 million to settle British claims. The three 'Treaty Ports' of Cobh, Berehaven and Lough Swilly, held by the British as part of the Treaty settlement in 1921, are returned to the Free State, against the wishes of Winston Churchill who continued to criticise the decision throughout the ensuing war.

1939: Declaration of War on Germany by Great Britain and France. Northern Ireland immediately offers her support. The south declares herself neutral in a defiant show of her independence. This period became known as the 'Emergency' in the Free State. Severe criticism of her policy of neutrality from Britain and Northern Ireland.

1940: France, Belgium, the Netherlands, Norway and Denmark fall to the Germans. Britain stands alone against the Germans after the British Expeditionary Force is heavily depleted in France. IRA contacts opened with the Abwehr, the German intelligence service. IRA launches renewed campaign with a raid on a British army camp. Lord Craigavon dies.

1941: Belfast is heavily bombed in the 'Belfast Blitz' as the Germans attempt to impede British shipbuilding at Harland and Wolff. Many residential areas of the city are bombed, however. Catholics and Protestants share the basement cellar in Clonard monastery in west Belfast to escape the bombing. Fire engines from the south are sent north to help the Belfast fire service cope with the fires. Dublin is bombed as well and, although the German government apologises for the 'mistake', there are persistent rumours that the Germans sent a warning to Ireland to stay neutral. The United States of America enters the war on the side of the British, as the Japanese launch an attack on Pearl Harbor in Hawaii. Alleged offer of an end to partition by Winston Churchill to DeValera if he enters the war on the Allied side. DeValera does not take the offer seriously. Criticism of DeValera, however, from the British and the Americans for allowing the German and Japanese embassies in Dublin to remain open.

1942: American troops land in Northern Ireland as a prelude to the invasion of North Africa. DeValera protests at the Americans' actions, saying that the United States should have asked for permission before. A renewed IRA campaign begins.

1943: Americans land substantially more troops in Northern Ireland in preparation for D Day.

1945: Death of Adolf Hitler and ending of the Second World War. DeValera heavily criticised for offering his condolences on the death of Hitler to the German ambassador in Dublin. Labour government wins election in Britain. Advent of the 'Welfare State'. Formation of the Anti-Partition League.

1948: Declaration of the 'Republic of Ireland'. Britain responds with the Ireland Act, guaranteeing Northern Ireland's status within the United Kingdom as long as her parliament so wishes.

1954: The Flags and Emblems Act becomes law. Now the RUC could take down any flags they considered to be a breach of the peace (in other words, the Irish Tricolour).

1956: Beginning of 'Operation Harvest', the IRA's border campaign, with attacks on RUC stations along the border with Northern Ireland. Northern Irish government interns hundreds of known Republicans.

1957: Internment without trial introduced in the south by DeValera against the IRA, despite an order from their leadership banning any military action against the Republic's security forces.

1962: The IRA's campaign ends in failure. The leadership issue the following statement:

The leadership of the Resistance Movement has ordered the termination of the Campaign of Resistance to British occupation launched on

12 December 1956. Instructions issued to Volunteers of the Active Service
Units and of local Units in the occupied area have now been carried out. All
arms and other materiel have been dumped and all full-time active service
volunteers have been withdrawn ... Foremost among the factors motivat-
ing this course of action has been the attitude of the general public whose
minds have been deliberately distracted from the supreme issue facing the
Irish people – the unity and freedom of Ireland.

1963: Captain Terence O'Neill assumes the role of prime minister of
Northern Ireland. Begins a policy of attempting to bring Catholics and
Protestants closer together.

1965: O'Neill invites the Taoiseach of the Republic, Sean Lemass, to talks
in Belfast. This was the first time that two Prime Ministers of Northern
Ireland and the Republic met on a formal basis. Widely criticised in
Unionist circles. Ian Paisley denounces the summit.

1966: Easter Rising 50th anniversary marches in Belfast by Republicans and
nationalists. Creates tension in Catholic and Protestant working-class areas.
The Ulster Volunteer Force (UVF) reforms and issues a warning that all
known IRA men will be shot without mercy. First sectarian killing of the
present Troubles. Catholic man, Peter Ward, shot dead outside a pub on the
Shankill. Gusty Spence of the UVF accused of his murder.

1967: Formation of the Northern Ireland Civil Rights Association (NICRA).
Demands an end to inequalities in housing, local election voting and
employment on religious grounds.

1968: Formation of People's Democracy (PD) by students at Queens
University, Belfast. Aims similar to NICRA. Civil rights marches dominate
the political agenda of Northern Ireland. In October a march is attacked
by the RUC. Television cameras make sure that the aggression is widely
broadcast, attracting widespread criticism of the Northern Irish government. O'Neill now under extreme pressure for the speedy conclusion of
reforms. Makes 'Ulster at the Crossroads' speech. Resigns after election
shows deep cracks in party and Protestant support for his reform policies.
Chichester-Clark becomes prime minister of Northern Ireland. Continues
reform policy.

1969: Four-day PD march from Belfast to Derry in January attacked at
Burntollet by off-duty 'B' Specials and Loyalists. Tension mounts in Derry
and Belfast. Summer season round of marches creates sporadic rioting.
Rioting in Belfast at the beginning of August. Apprentice Boys march in
Derry on 12 August creates intense tension. Rioting starts, initially between
Catholics and Protestant marchers; the RUC begins to fight Catholics.

Battle of the Bogside begins. Jack Lynch, prime minister of the Republic, gives an inflammatory speech on television. Irish army 'hospitals' moved to border areas. Serious rioting in Belfast along interfaces. Catholics burned out of Bombay Street and various other parts of west Belfast. British soldiers called in 'temporarily' to relieve pressure on RUC. Begin to erect 'peace line'.

1970: Provisionals formed after split in IRA. Rump of IRA now called the Officials. Serious rioting in Ballymurphy housing estate after Orange march. First time army comes into conflict with Catholics. First signs of pressure on army command from Stormont government, which wants tougher action on Catholic 'no go' areas, set up after August 1969. Heavy violence in the Crumlin Road and Short Strand areas of Belfast, five Protestants killed in June. By now, heavy criticism of army from Unionist circles concerning lack of toughness. Falls Curfew begins, approximately 3,000 troops descend on the lower Falls in a search operation for IRA weapons. Subsequent ban on marches for six months by Chichester-Clark. Provisional IRA steps up its campaign.

1971: Robert Curtis is the first soldier to die in the current Troubles, shot in the New Lodge area in February. Three more soldiers are killed in March. Brian Faulkner becomes prime minister of Northern Ireland. In August, internment is introduced in Northern Ireland; over 300 people are arrested in the initial stages, all Catholic. Widespread rioting ensues. In December, Loyalists bomb McGurk's bar in the New Lodge area of Belfast, killing fifteen Catholics.

1972: 'Bloody Sunday' on 30 January. British soldiers shoot and kill thirteen civilians after a banned civil rights march in Derry. One of the injured dies a few months later. Widespread revulsion at the event. The British embassy in Dublin is burned down. Westminster subsequently demands control of all security in Northern Ireland. Brian Faulkner refuses and resigns. The government imposes Direct Rule. From this point all matters relating to Northern Ireland are within the domain of the London parliament.

APPENDIX B:
CONTEMPORARY SOURCES

There have been various government-initiated tribunals and reports over the years concerning the Troubles in Northern Ireland. Many of these attempted to get to the bottom of just why the violence began when it did. Others focused on the need for reforms of government and the police. Some, but certainly not all, are listed below with a short summary of their main points to give the reader an idea of how Northern Ireland convulsed from one political and social crisis to another in the late 1960s.

The Cameron Enquiry was commissioned by the then prime minister of Northern Ireland, Terence O'Neill, to investigate the causes of the disturbances leading up to the ill-fated march by the civil rights movement on 5 October 1968 and the subsequent upsurge in violence. It was to also investigate the various committees, groups, bodies and organisations that had sprung up over the period, and to ascertain the effects, if any, these had on the ensuing violence.

The Hunt Report was commissioned in late August 1969 by Chichester-Clarke, under pressure from Harold Wilson in London, in an attempt to examine the whole structure of the RUC and the notorious 'B' Specials. It was published in October 1969. Upon its publication there were three nights of rioting in the Shankill area of Belfast in protest at the disbandment of the Specials and of the disarming of the RUC. The first security forces death of the Troubles occurred at this point when an RUC officer by the name of Victor Arbuckle was shot dead by Protestants.

The Scarman Tribunal, which reported in April 1972, was commissioned on 27 August 1969 by the Northern Irish government and provides perhaps the best record for historians seeking to ascertain exactly what happened over the course of the year before August 1969. Moreover, the detailed breakdown of the events leaves the reader in no doubt that it is not a one-sided document.

All of the main events in the progression of the Troubles up to that point are listed, and discussed in an impartial and balanced way.

As well as listing the main conclusions of these reports, this appendix contains a number of other relevant documents. These include: the text of the Proclamation of the Irish Republic, read at the start of the Easter Rising; short summaries of the Civil Authorities (Special Powers) Act 1922 and the Flags and Emblems (Display) Act (Northern Ireland) 1954; the wording of the Downing Street Declaration of 1969; a series of letters written in the 1960s to Sir Alec Douglas Home, the then British prime minister, from the Campaign for Social Justice in Northern Ireland concerning discrimination in local authorities; and a selection of quotes from prominent members of Northern Irish society. These documents go a long way in explaining to the reader how Northern Ireland functioned in the mid to late 1960s.

Cameron Report

The Cameron Report was commissioned on 3 March 1969 to investigate the causes of the widespread disturbances in Northern Ireland in the preceding months, most notably the events on 5 October 1968 when RUC officers baton-charged a civil rights march in Derry. It was also commissioned to look into the various groups that had sprung up in the country and their relationship to the trouble. Some of the main points of its conclusions are set out below.

1) The route [of the march] proposed on behalf of the Civil Rights Association was one commonly followed by 'Protestant' and 'Loyalist' marches in Londonderry. The local Unionist headquarters objected to the [route of the] march as offensive to a great majority of the citizens residing on the route, and also to any meeting near the War Memorial or any place closely associated with the siege of Londonderry. There was also a threat of counter demonstration by the Middle Liberties Young Unionist Association. A third written protest came from the General Committee of the Apprentice Boys of Derry. It was dated 30th September and argued that the march was objectionable, since it was alleged that Civil Rights was only a cover for a parade of the Republican and Nationalist movements, and that it would show no respect for the War Memorial in the Diamond. It contained no reference to any conflicting plans or proposals by the Apprentice Boys for a march or demonstration to be held on the same day, at the same time and on the same route. Yet on 1st October the same organisation served notice of an 'Annual Initiation Ceremony', whose participants would march in procession on the afternoon of 5th October from the Waterside Railway Station via the Diamond to the Apprentice Boys Memorial Hall. Such a procession would have taken place at virtually the same time as the advertised march of the Civil Rights Association. It may be true that private initiation of members could have been planned for that date, but we are quite satisfied in the light of the facts that this proposed procession was not a genuine 'annual' event, and we regard the proposal to hold it at the precise time indicated as merely a threat to counter demonstrate by political opponents of the Civil Rights march

2) On the evidence we think that nothing resembling a baton charge took place but that the police broke ranks and used their batons indiscriminately on people in Duke Street. This unfortunate situation was made worse by the fact that the other end of Duke Street (nearer the Waterside Station) was blocked by the party of police which had originally been stationed at Simpson's Brae but had moved down in rear of the march. This party had not been informed that the march was to disperse and their choice of position had the effect that the marchers felt themselves to be trapped. No specific orders were given to their party to let the marchers through and when a number of marchers hurried towards them some violence was almost inevitable. There is a body of evidence, which we accept, that these police also used their batons indiscriminately, and that the district inspector in charge used his blackthorn with needless violence. Rapid dispersal of the crowd was also assisted by the use of water wagons which were moved along Duke Street and then along Craigavon Bridge. There is no real doubt that they sprayed the dispersing marchers indiscriminately, especially on the bridge, where there were a good many members of the general public who had taken no part in the march. There was no justification for use of the water wagons on the bridge, while the evidence which we heard and saw on film did not convince us of the necessity of their use in Duke Street. By about 5 p.m. Duke Street was cleared.

The Northern Ireland Civil Rights Association did not directly plan or control the march which was left to a local and purely ad hoc Committee.

No properly thought out alternative plans of action were available if the march was stopped by the police.

Stewarding was ineffective and no adequate communication system was available.

Some of the marchers were determined to defy the Minister's order. They accepted the risk that some degree of violence would occur, believing that this would achieve publicity for the Civil Rights cause, especially in Great Britain.

A section of extremists actively wished to provoke violence, or at least a confrontation with the police without regard to consequences.

The police were determined that the Minister's order should be made effective on this occasion and by a display, and, if necessary, use, of force to deter future demonstrators from defying ministerial bans.

Hooligan elements wholly unassociated with the Civil Rights demonstrators later took advantage of a minor clash in the Diamond to cause a serious riot with looting and damage to property – wholly unassociated with the Civil Rights demonstration itself or the clash in the Waterside.

The police handling of the situation in the Waterside was ill coordinated and ill conducted. The marchers' change of direction apparently took the police by surprise. The time available to take up a new blocking position in Duke Street was too short to permit the same disposition of police and tenders to be effected as that originally planned. The use of batons was probably unnecessary and in any event premature, as the major part of the demonstrators were obeying their leaders' advice to disperse quietly. The baton charge was lacking in proper control and degenerated into a series of individual scuffles, while the failure to inform the party of police moving down from Simpson's Brae, of the action being taken by the majority of the demonstrators in dispersing, led to the demonstrators being caught between two fires and to a flare up of further unnecessary violence.

A rising sense of continuing injustice and grievance among large sections of the Catholic population in Northern Ireland, in particular in Londonderry and Dungannon, in respect of, inadequacy of housing provision by certain local authorities, unfair methods of allocation of houses built and let by such authorities, in particular; refusals and omissions to adopt a 'points' system in determining priorities and making allocations, misuse in certain cases of discretionary powers of allocation of houses in order to perpetuate Unionist control of the local authority.

A growing and powerful sense of resentment and frustration among the Catholic population at failure to achieve either acceptance on the part of the Government of any need to investigate these complaints or to provide and enforce a remedy for them.

Widespread resentment among Catholics in particular at the continuance in force of regulations made under the Special Powers Act, and of the continued presence in the statute book of the Act itself.

Complaints, now well documented in fact, of discrimination in the making of local government appointments, at all levels but especially in senior posts, to the prejudice of non-Unionists and especially Catholic members of the community, in some Unionist controlled authorities.[1]

Hunt Report

In 1969, following the disturbances in August and the deployment of British troops on the streets of Derry and Belfast, the minister of home affairs in the Northern Irish government commissioned a report into the structure of the RUC. The Hunt Report was published on 10 October 1969 and ignited serious rioting on the Shankill Road because of its recommended changes of disarmament and the disbandment of the Ulster Special Constabulary (the 'B' Specials). The main conclusions are set out below.

(1) The RUC should be relieved of all duties of a military nature as soon as possible and its contribution to the security of Northern Ireland from subversion should be limited to the gathering of intelligence, the protection of important persons and the enforcement of the relevant laws.

(2) There should be a Police Authority for Northern Ireland, whose membership should reflect the proportions of different groups in the community.

(3) The Police Authority should be responsible, subject to the authority of the Minister of Home Affairs, for the establishment and maintenance of an adequate and efficient police force, for the appointment of the chief officer of police and certain senior officers, for buildings, vehicles and clothing.

(4) The Police Authority should have a particular duty to keep itself informed as to the manner in which complaints against the police are dealt with.

(5) The chief officer of police should submit an annual report to the Minister of Home Affairs and to the Police Authority.

(6) The chief officer of police should submit a report on any matter when required to do so by the Minister.

(7) The Minister of Home Affairs may call upon the Police Authority to require a chief officer to retire in the interests of efficiency, subject to certain safeguards.

(8) The RUC should be subject to inspection by Her Majesty's Inspectorate of Constabulary.

(9) A Police Advisory Board should be established for consultation between the Minister, the Police Authority, and all ranks of the force.

(10) The need to retain some police stations in border areas should be reviewed.

(11) The rank structure should be reviewed.

(12) The maximum term of duty in the Reserve Force should be three years.

(13) When the Reserve Force has to be deployed for crowd control, overtime should be payable where appropriate to all ranks.

(14) The Reserve Force should be renamed.

(15) A civilian welfare officer should be appointed to the RUC.

(16) The present policy for the general issue and carrying of firearms should be phased out as soon as possible.

(17) Certain weapons should be no longer part of the equipment of the RUC.

(18) The effective strength of the force should be increased as a first priority.

(19) The establishment of women police should be reviewed.

(20) A volunteer reserve police force should be set up.

(21) The establishment of a Cadet Corps should be considered.

(22) There should be O & M studies of the administrative process so as to reduce the time spent by members of the force on duties which could be done by civilians, or where modern equipment would help.

(23) The extent to which the police are engaged on extraneous duties or by private employers should be examined ...

(24) Armoured cars should cease to be part of the equipment of the RUC.

(25) The building programme should be reviewed.

(26) The practice of reserving a specific proportion of vacancies in the force for Roman Catholics should be discontinued.

(27) Vigorous efforts should be made to increase the number of Roman Catholic entrants into the force.

(28) The establishment of a central recruiting office at Police Headquarters, with a branch at Londonderry, and supported by nominated officers at County Headquarters and mobile touring teams, should be considered.

(29) Simplified application forms should be available at all police stations; in particular, applicants should not be required to disclose their religion on their initial applications.

(30) The programme of talks to sixth-formers should be extended and use should be made of other publicity media.

(31) The possibility of acquiring accommodation for training in Great Britain should be examined.

(32) The Home Office and the Scottish Home and Health Department should be asked to consider sympathetically any applications for places on courses of higher training.

(33) The procedure for dealing with complaints against the police should be changed.

(34) The chief officer of police should be made vicariously liable for wrongful acts committed by members of the force.

(35) Activities in the field of community and youth relations should be stepped up.

(36) Professional advice should be sought as to the organisation needed to improve public relations.

(37) A police liaison committee should be set up in Londonderry.

(38) The closure of certain small stations in difficult urban areas and in some rural areas should be reconsidered.

(39) The colour of the uniform should be changed to blue.

(40) Sergeants and constables throughout the force should wear numbers on their uniforms, as is already the practice in Belfast and Londonderry.

(41) The name of the force should not be changed.

(42) The Scottish system of independent public prosecutors should be adopted.

(43) There should be closer co-operation between the RUC. and the Home Office Police Research and Development Branch.

(44) Arrangements should be made for interchanges of personnel between the RUC and forces on the mainland.

(45) Members of the RUC should be encouraged to apply for posts with mainland forces, and vice versa.

(46) The Central Representative Body should be reorganised and associated with the representative organisations in Great Britain, so that members of the force can have the same right to be consulted about their pay, etc., as members of police forces in Great Britain.

(47) A locally recruited part-time force, under the control of the GOC, Northern Ireland, should be raised as soon as possible for such duties as may be laid upon it. The force, together with the police volunteer reserve, should replace the Ulster Special Constabulary.[2]

Grand Orange Lodge on the 'B' Specials

The Hunt Report's release in October 1969 unleashed a wave of protest from the Protestant communities in Northern Ireland because of its recommendation to disband the 'B' Specials. By 1969 the Specials were discredited in Catholic eyes because of their almost exclusively Protestant make-up and of their sectarian actions. The Grand Orange Lodge of Ireland has this to say about the 'B' Specials and their demise:

An organisation calling itself the Northern Ireland Civil Rights Association came into being on February 1, 1967. Views differ according to one's political viewpoint and prejudices as to whether or not it was simply a republican or IRA front organisation. However, significantly one of its five demands was the disbandment of the B Specials. At the outbreak of the Troubles the USC had a strength of approximately 8,500 members. Of these, 3,000 were fully mobilised to assist the RUC. The remainder were part-time volunteers. Objectively, the USC played only a limited role in policing the Troubles, their primary responsibility being the guarding of key installations. The Cameron Report, appointed to examine the causes of the Troubles, published its report on 12 September and alleged that one of the causes of the Troubles was Roman Catholic resentment at the existence of the USC.

The following month saw publication of the Hunt Report which recommended inter alia that the RUC should become an unarmed police service and that the B Specials should be replaced by a new RUC reserve and a locally recruited part-time regiment of the British Army. Many Unionists would have readily concurred with Ian Paisley's observation that 'if you want to destroy a country pull out the teeth of her defence forces and she will be easy prey'. During its 50 years of service the B Specials came to occupy a unique place of mythic proportions within the Unionist community. They were regarded as the embodiment of the Northern Ireland state's ability to protect itself from internal and external threat. However, the recommendations of the Hunt Report were implemented. The USC was stood down on April 30, 1970.[3]

Not many Catholics saw them in this way. Allegations of mistreatment of Catholics, whether in stop-and-search procedures or the more serious charges concerning August 1969, spelt the death knell for the force.

The disarming of the RUC was in part because of its actions in April 1969 when it went on a rampage through the Bogside area of Derry after the arrival of the Belfast to Derry marchers. It was short-lived however: the RUC was rearmed in February 1971, albeit initially only in Belfast.

The Plain Truth

In June 1969 the Campaign for Social Justice in Northern Ireland issued a pamphlet entitled The Plain Truth, highlighting discrimination in Northern Ireland against the Catholic community. Examples of discrimination were given for Dungannon, Armagh, (London) Derry, Omagh, Lurgan, Fivemiletown and the County of Fermanagh. Examples were also given of discrimination in employment, council housing and local franchises. Below is a commentary from the pamphlet, along with quotes from eminent Unionists who held power in Northern Ireland.

Since 1920, when Ireland was divided, the Republic of Ireland has been a separate independent state, while Northern Ireland has remained an integral part of the United Kingdom. It is now loosely termed 'Ulster' although there were nine counties in old-time Ulster, three of which are now in the Republic of Ireland. The British Parliament in London first legalised this arrangement by the Government of Ireland Act, 1920 Office. London has since ruled Northern Ireland through its subordinate Parliament at Stormont, Belfast. Both London and Stormont have always been at pains to present the province as a happy, contented place, whereas in fact it contains a minority which has always been very hard pressed, and indeed denied rights which most of the free world has come to accept as a matter of course. The outside world was largely unaware of what was going on in Ulster mainly because the British press had always been discouraged from printing stories about it.

Some years ago when a British television group had a series of documentaries suppressed, the leader of the reporting team, Alan Whicker, declared 'No country deserves the Government you have here. This is the only place in the world where you can't report honestly without silly people kicking up about what is only the truth.' Since the 5th October, 1968, when a peaceful Civil Rights march was broken up by the police, the world has been looking at Northern Ireland on television, and reading about her in the press, first with incredulity, and then shock. Civil Rights activities have been opposed by various groups of militant Protestants. These people already have their civil rights, and do not wish to share them with others. They have caused the recent unrest by opposing democratic demands for change. This opposition has been effected mainly by violent counter-demonstrations, and by arbitrary police bans on Civil Rights marches in certain places, e.g., in the city of Londonderry.

Scarman Tribunal

The Scarman Tribunal was commissioned by the Stormont government to investigate the disturbances that had occurred in Northern Ireland in 1969. It was published in April 1972. It concluded that there was no attempt at an overthrow of the state by Republican subversives; however, it criticised the RUC in its handling of the riots, and maintained that they it have handled the situation better. It also concluded that the various defence committees were set up as a response to the riots, and were not the cause. Some highlights of its report are reproduced below.

In June 1968 the local Member of Parliament (NI), exposed a case of house allocation in Caledon in which there was discrimination in favour of an unmarried Protestant girl. The agitation which started over this case caught the imagination of the non-Unionist minority in the Province and greatly increased the standing and influence of the Northern Ireland Civil Rights Association. Events elsewhere in the world, particularly perhaps the student riots in France in the early summer of that year, encouraged the belief that a policy of street demonstrations at critical places and times could achieve results, if only because they would attract the attention of the mass media. The Government of Northern Ireland felt the pressures that NICRA and others were able to create, and responded first by outright resistance, and then by concessions. Thus Mr Craig, the then Minister of Home Affairs (NI), banned a demonstration scheduled to take place in Londonderry on 5 October. The ban was defied and a violent clash between police and demonstrators occurred. Further unrest followed in Londonderry. Then a reform programme was announced by the Government in November; but it was regarded as inadequate by the minority, and did not efface or diminish their feeling that the police would be used as a partisan force to suppress the political demonstrations of those opposed to the Northern Ireland Government.

With regard to the disturbances in Derry, the report criticised the following:

The lack of firm direction in handling the disturbances in Londonderry during the early evening of 12 August. The 'Rossville Street incursion' was undertaken as a tactical move by the Reserve Force commander without an understanding of the effect it would have on Bogside attitudes. The County Inspector did understand, but did not prevent it. The incursion was seen by the Bogsiders as a repetition of events in January and April and led many, including moderate men such as Father Mulvey, to think that the police must be resisted.

The decision by the County Inspector to put USC on riot control duty in the streets of Dungannon on 13 August without disarming them and without ensuring that there was an experienced police officer present and in command.

The similar decision of the County Inspector in Armagh on 14 August.

The use of Browning machine-guns in Belfast on 14th and 15th August. The weapon was a menace to the innocent as well as the guilty, being heavy and indiscriminate in its fire: and on one occasion (the firing into St Brendan's block of flats where the boy Rooney was killed) its use was wholly unjustifiable.

The failure to prevent Protestant mobs from burning down Catholic houses:-
In the Conway Street area on the night of 14/15 August: members of the RUC were present in Conway Street at the time, but failed to take effective action; In Brookfield Street on the night of 15/16 August: a police armoured vehicle was in the Crumlin Road when Brookfield Street was set on fire, but made no move.

The failure to take any effective action to restrain or disperse the mobs or to protect lives and property in the riot areas on 15 August during the hours of daylight and before the arrival of the Army.

The conduct which we have criticised was due very largely to the belief held at the time by many of the police, including senior officers that they were dealing with an armed uprising engineered by the IRA. This was what all their experience would have led them to expect: and when, on 13 August, some firing occurred and a grenade was thrown in Leeson Street, Belfast, their expectation seemed to them to have materialised. In dealing with an armed uprising, the usual restraints on police conduct would not be so strong, while more attention would naturally be given to the suppression of the insurgents than to the protection of people's lives and property. In fact, the police appreciation that they had on their hands an armed uprising led by the IRA was incorrect. Direct IRA participation was slight; and there is no credible evidence that the IRA planned or organised the disturbances.

We are satisfied that the spread of the disturbances [in August 1969] owed much to a deliberate decision by some minority groups to relieve police pressure on the rioters in Londonderry. Amongst these groups must be included NICRA, whose executive decided to organise demonstrations in the Province so as to prevent reinforcement of the police in Londonderry. We were told that they intended to exclude Belfast from their plans; but we have no doubt that some activists, so far from accepting the decision, did co-operate with some in Londonderry to call for demonstrations in Belfast. There is clear evidence of such a call being made in Divis Street on the 13th.

Protestant participation in the disorders under review was largely that of violent reaction to disturbances started by Catholics, though there were exceptions. Their reaction was particularly fierce in Belfast in mid-August, when it took the form of violent eruptions into Catholic areas – the Falls, Divis Street, and Hooker Street. These eruptions, the course of which we trace in detail later in the Report, may with some justice be described as 'invasions' – given the 'ghetto' pattern of so much of Belfast.

Yet when one looks at the Protestant side of the sectarian divide, it is not very different from the Catholic side. There was no province-wide organisation sponsoring a policy of disturbance. The Orange Order and its lodges were determined to hold their parades and ceremonies, although well aware of the risks of violent reaction. Many Orangemen enjoyed provoking their opponents – just as those opponents enjoyed jeering at and disrupting Orange processions. The opportunities for communal disturbance were plentiful: but, while many Orangemen did little or nothing to reduce them, there was no riot or battle plan.

The only centre where there was evidence of a Protestant organisation actively participating in the riots was Belfast. Members of the Shankill Defence Association participated in the disturbances on the Crumlin Road and in the Falls, including the Protestant eruptions into Divis Street, Clonard and Brookfield Street, which led to the burning of Catholic homes; but this is not to say that the organisation planned the burnings, and we have no acceptable evidence that it or any other organisation was party to any such plan. The truth, we believe, was simply that, at a time when communal feeling was high, violent events released violent passions which men such as Mr McKeague did nothing to assuage and which proved to be beyond the ability of the people's leaders or the police to control.

In our judgment there was no plot to overthrow the Government or to mount an armed insurrection. But, although there was no conspiracy in the sense in which that term is normally used (for it is not possible to identify any group or groups of persons deliberately planning the riots of 1969), yet it would be the height of naivety to deny that the teenage hooligans, who almost invariably threw the first stones, were manipulated and encouraged by persons seeking to discredit the Government. While accepting that the major riots that occurred in Londonderry, Belfast, Armagh and Dungannon were not deliberately planned, we are satisfied that, once the disturbances started, they were continued by an element that also found expression in bodies more or less loosely organised, such as the People's Democracy, and various local Defence Associations, and in associating themselves with bodies such as NICRA and the several Action Committees. The public impact of the activities of this element was tremendously enhanced by the coverage given by the mass media of communication. We are satisfied that the great majority of the members of the RUC was concerned to do its duty, which, so far as concerned the disturbances, was to maintain order on the streets, using no more force than was reasonably necessary to suppress rioting and protect life and limb. Inevitably, however, this meant confrontation and on occasions conflict with disorderly mobs. Moreover, since most of the rioting developed from action on the streets started by Catholic crowds, the RUC were more often than not facing Catholics who, as a result, came to feel that the police were always going for them, baton-charging them –never 'the others'.

In fact the RUC faced and, if necessary, charged those who appeared to them to be challenging, defying, or attacking them. We are satisfied that, though they did not expect to be attacked by Protestants, they were ready to deal with them in the same way, if it became necessary. The Shankill riots of the 2/4 August establish beyond doubt the readiness of the police to do their duty against Protestant mobs, when they were the disturbers of the public peace.

But it is painfully clear from the evidence adduced before us that by July the Catholic minority no longer believed that the RUC was impartial and that Catholic and civil rights activists were publicly asserting this loss of confidence.

Understandably these resentments affected the thinking and feeling of the young and the irresponsible, and induced the jeering and throwing of stones which were the small beginnings of most of the disturbances. The effect of this hostility on the RUC themselves was unfortunate. They came to treat as their enemies, and accordingly also as the enemies of the public peace, those who persisted in displaying hostility and distrust towards them.

Thus there developed the fateful split between the Catholic community and the police. Faced with the distrust of a substantial proportion of the whole population and short of numbers, the RUC had (as some senior officers appreciated) lost the capacity to control a major riot. Their difficulties naturally led them, when the emergency arose, to have recourse to methods such as baton-charges, CS gas and gunfire, which were sure ultimately to stoke even higher the fires of resentment and hatred.[4]

Proclamation of a Republic

The 'Proclamation of a Republic' was read out on the steps of the General Post Office on Sackville Street (later O'Connell Street) by Padraig Pearse on 24 April 1916, beginning the 'Easter Rising'.

POBLACHT NA h-EIREANN
THE PROVISIONAL GOVERNMENT OF THE
IRISH REPUBLIC
TO THE PEOPLE OF IRELAND

Irishmen and Irishwomen:
In the name of God and of the dead generations from which she receives her old tradition of nationhood, Ireland, through us, summons her children to her flag and strikes for her freedom.
Having organized and trained her manhood through her secret revolutionary organization, the Irish Republican Brotherhood, and through her open military organizations, the Irish Volunteers and the Irish Citizen Army, having patiently perfected her discipline, having resolutely waited for the right moment to reveal itself, she now seizes that moment, and, supported by her exiled children in America and by gallant allies in Europe, but relying in the first on her own strength, she strikes in full confidence of victory.

We declare the right of the people of Ireland to the ownership of Ireland, and to the unfettered control of Irish destinies, to be sovereign and indefeasible. The long usurpation of that right by a foreign people and government has not extinguished the right, nor can it ever be extinguished except by the destruction of the Irish people. In every generation the Irish people have asserted their right to national freedom and sovereignty; six times during the past three hundred years they have asserted it in arms. Standing on that fundamental right and again asserting it in arms in the face of the world, we hereby proclaim the Irish Republic as a Sovereign Independent State. And we pledge our lives and the lives of our comrades-in-arms to the cause of its freedom, of its welfare, and of its exaltation among the nations.

The Irish Republic is entitled to, and hereby claims, the allegiance of every Irishman and Irish woman. The Republic guarantees religious and civil liberty, equal rights and equal opportunities of all its citizens, and declares its resolve to pursue the happiness and prosperity of the whole nation and of all its parts, cherishing all the children of the nation equally, and oblivious of the differences carefully fostered by an alien government, which have divided a minority in the past.

Until our arms have brought the opportune moment for the establishment of a permanent National Government, representative of the whole people of Ireland and elected by the suffrages of all her men and women, the Provision Government, hereby constituted, will administer the civil and military affairs of the Republic in trust for the people.

We place the cause of the Irish Republic under the protection of the Most High God, Whose blessing we invoke upon our arms, and we pray that no one who serves that cause will dishonour it by cowardice, inhumanity, or rapine. In this supreme hour the Irish nation must,
by its valour and discipline and by the readiness of its children to sacrifice themselves for the common good, prove itself worthy of the august destiny to which it is called.

Signed on behalf of the Provisional Government,
Thomas J. Clarke, Sean Mac Diermada, Thomas MacDonagh, P. H. Pearse, Eamonn Ceannt, James Connolly, Joseph Plunkett.[5]

Civil Authorities (Special Powers) Act (Northern Ireland) 1922

Perhaps the most notorious document to come out of Northern Ireland in the brief fifty-year rule by Unionists was the Special Powers Act. This piece of legislation alone was the bedrock of Unionist domination over Catholics in the state. Its abolition was also a major bedrock of the civil rights movement, and was a key demand even by moderates in the state. One of its most odious aspects was that it enabled indefinite internment without trial for 'any person whose behaviour is of such a nature as to give reasonable grounds for suspecting that he has acted or is acting or is about to act in a manner prejudicial to the preservation of the peace or maintenance of order'. For this reason it was invariably used against Republicans and other 'subversives', the majority of whom were Catholic. Nevertheless, it was not until 1973 that the Act was repealed. The Act was born in violence, and died in violence.

The Civil Authority may by Order:
Require every person within any area specified in the order to remain within doors between such hours as may be specified in the order, and in such case, if any person within that area is or remains out between such hours without a permit in writing from the civil authority or some person duly authorised by him, he shall be guilty of an offence against these regulations.
(1) Require all or any licensed premises within any area specified in the order to be closed, either altogether, or subject to such exceptions as to hours and purposes, and to compliance with such directions, as may be specified in the order
(2) Make such provisions as he thinks necessary for the prevention of the practice of treating in any licensed premises within any area specified in the order.
Any order of the civil authority under this regulation may be made to apply either generally or as respects all or any members of the police or other forces mentioned in the order, and may require copies of the order to be exhibited in a prominent place in any licensed premises affected thereby.
If any person contravenes or fails to comply with any of the provisions of an order made under this regulation or any conditions or restrictions imposed thereby, he shall be guilty of an offence against these regulations, and the civil authority may cause such steps to be taken as may be necessary to enforce compliance with the order.
In this regulation the expression 'licensed premises' includes any premises or place where the sale of intoxicating liquor is carried on under a licence.
The civil authority may make orders prohibiting or restricting in any area
(a) The holding of or taking part in meetings, assemblies (including fairs and markets), or processions in public places;
(b) The use or wearing or possession of uniforms or badges of a naval, military or police character, or of uniforms or badges indicating membership of any association or body specified in the order;
(c) The carrying in public places of weapons of offence or articles capable of being used as such
(d) The carrying, having or keeping of firearms, military arms, ammunition or explosive substances; and

(e) The having, keeping, or using of a motor or other cycle, or motor car by any person, other than a member of a police force, without a permit from the civil authority, or from the chief officer of the police in the district in which the person resides.

The civil authority may by notice prohibit the circulation of any newspaper for any specified period, and any person circulating or distributing such newspaper within such specified period shall be guilty of an offence against these regulations.[6]

Flags and Emblems (Display) Act (Northern Ireland), 1954

An Act to make provision with respect to the display of certain flags and emblems.

Be it enacted by the Queen's most Excellent Majesty, and the Senate and the House of Commons of Northern Ireland in this present Parliament assembled, and by the authority of the same, as follows:-

Display of Union Flag.

1. Any person who prevents or threatens to interfere by force with the display of a Union flag (usually known as the Union Jack) by another person on or in any lands or premises lawfully occupied by that other person shall be guilty of an offence against this Act.

Removal of Provocative Emblems.

2. (1) Where any police officer, having regard to the time or place at which and the circumstances in which any emblem is being displayed, apprehends that the display of such emblem may occasion a breach of the peace, he may require the person displaying or responsible for the display of such emblem to discontinue such display or cause it to be discontinued; and any person who refuses or fails to comply with such a requirement shall be guilty of an offence against this Act.

(2) Where –

(a) A requirement under the preceding subsection is not complied with; or

(b) The person responsible for such display is not readily available; or

(c) No person, or no person responsible for such display and capable of complying with such a requirement, is present on or in any lands or premises whereon or wherein such an emblem is being displayed;

A police officer may without warrant enter any such lands or premises, using such force as may be necessary, and may remove and seize and detain such emblem.

(3) It shall be a good defence to any proceedings (whether civil or criminal) against a police officer or constable in respect of anything done or omitted to be done for the purpose or in the course of carrying into effect the provisions of this section, to prove that anything in respect of which the proceedings have been instituted was done, or as the case may be omitted, in good faith for the purpose or in the course of carrying into effect any of those, provisions.

(4) In this section the expression 'emblem' includes a flag of any kind other than the Union flag, and the expression 'police officer' means an officer, head-constable or sergeant of the Royal Ulster Constabulary.

(1) Any person guilty of an offence against this Act shall be liable –

(a) On summary conviction, to a fine not exceeding fifty pounds or to imprisonment for a term not exceeding six months;

(b) On conviction on indictment, to a fine not exceeding five hundred pounds or to imprisonment for a term not exceeding five years; or in any case to both the fine and the imprisonment hereinbefore respectively provided.

(2) A court before which a person is convicted of an offence under section two of this Act may order any emblem in respect of which he is so convicted, and which has been seized and detained under that section, to be destroyed or otherwise disposed of.

Restrictions on Prosecutions.

4. Where any person is charged with any offence against this Act the court may, if it thinks fit, order him to be remanded in custody or on bail, but save as afore said further proceedings on such a charge shall not be taken against him without the consent of the Attorney General for Northern Ireland.

5. This Act may be cited as the Flags and Emblems (Display) Act (Northern Ireland), 1954.[7]

Downing Street Declaration 1969

There follows the text of a statement issued by the British and Northern Irish governments after a meeting in Downing Street on 19 August 1969 in which the British government reiterated its continuing support and commitment to the parliament of Northern Ireland after the August 1969 disturbances.

DECLARATION

(1) The United Kingdom Government re-affirm that nothing which has happened in recent weeks in Northern Ireland derogates from the clear

pledges made by successive United Kingdom Governments that Northern Ireland should not cease to be a part of the United Kingdom without the consent of the people of Northern Ireland or from the provision in Section I of the Ireland Act 1949 that in no event will Northern Ireland or any part thereof cease to be part of the United Kingdom without the consent of the Parliament of Northern Ireland. The Border is not an issue.

(2) The United Kingdom Government again affirm that responsibility for affairs in Northern Ireland is entirely a matter of domestic jurisdiction. The United Kingdom Government will take full responsibility for asserting this principle in all international relationships.

(3) The United Kingdom Government have ultimate responsibility for the protection of those who live in Northern Ireland when, as in the past week, a breakdown of law and order has occurred. In this spirit, the United Kingdom Government responded to the requests of the Northern Ireland Government for military assistance in Londonderry and Belfast in order to restore law and order. They emphasise again that troops will be withdrawn when law and order has been restored.

(4) The Northern Ireland Government have been informed that troops have been provided on a temporary basis in accordance with the United Kingdom's ultimate responsibility. In the context of the commitment of these troops, the Northern Ireland Government have re-affirmed their intention to take into the fullest account at all times the views of Her Majesty's Government in the United Kingdom, especially in relation to matters affecting the status of citizens of that part of the United Kingdom and their equal rights and protection under the law.

(5) The United Kingdom Government have welcomed the decisions of the Northern Ireland Government in relation to Local Government franchise, the revision of Local Government areas, the allocation of houses, the creation of a Parliamentary Commissioner for Administration in Northern Ireland and machinery to consider citizens' grievances against other public authorities which the, Prime Minister reported to the House of Commons at Westminster following his meeting with Northern Ireland Ministers on May 21 [1969] as demonstrating the determination of the Northern Ireland Government that there shall be full equality of treatment for all citizens. Both Governments have agreed that it is vital that the momentum of internal reform should be maintained.

(6) The two Governments at their meeting at 10 Downing Street today [19 August 1969] have re-affirmed that in all legislation and executive decisions of Government every citizen of Northern Ireland is entitled to the same equality of treatment and freedom from discrimination as obtains in the rest of the

United Kingdom irrespective of political views or religion. In their further meetings the two Governments will be guided by these mutually accepted principles.

(7) Finally, both Governments are determined to take all possible steps to restore normality to the Northern Ireland community so that economic development can proceed at the faster rate which is vital for social stability.[8]

Letters between the Campaign for Democracy in Ulster and the British government

Catholic alienation in Northern Ireland was, and to a degree still is, a product of the society in which they have lived since partition. The Protestants accepted the idea of a semi-independent state because they were then able to create a system that allowed them to hang on to the centuries-old illusion of supremacy over their Catholic neighbours. In that way, the cherished traditions of the past could be kept for the future. The London government remained aloof and ignorant, content to allow the state to manage its own affairs. An example of this aloofness is found in a series of letters exchanged between the Campaign for Democracy in Ulster and the British government and its prime minister, Sir Alec Douglas-Home, starting on 21 April 1964.

Dear Prime Minister,

During your recent visit to Northern Ireland, you indicated that discrimination could be dealt with by law; and that the rights of the minority could be protected by recourse to the courts, under the terms of the Government of Ireland Act, 1920. This organisation has irrefutable evidence of discrimination by Local Authorities, in the allocation of houses and jobs in certain areas in Northern Ireland. In the light of your remarks, we engaged the services of Solicitors and Counsel to investigate the possibility of having these acts of discrimination examined in a Court of Law. We have now been advised by Senior and Junior Counsel that the discrimination practiced by Local Authorities is not capable of review by the courts under the terms of the Government of Ireland Act, 1920, or any other Statutory Provisions.

We assume that your statement was made with some consideration of the legal position, and in the circumstances, we would be obliged if you would refer us to the specific provisions which you had in mind.

Yours respectfully,
BRIAN GREGORY, Secretary [Campaign for Democracy in Ulster]

Letter formally acknowledged 21st April, 1964

This is clearly an eloquently written letter, asking for clarification of points made. This is a common ploy by politicians – things are said in the heat of the moment in the hope that they are not followed up. The reply came two weeks later.

May 8, 1964

Dear Sir,

The Prime Minister has asked me to reply to your letter of April 13 asking for a reference to the provisions he had in mind in the course of some remarks made during his visit to Northern Ireland. The provisions are section 5 of the Government of Ireland Act 1920, which prohibits the Parliament of Northern Ireland from making laws interfering with religious equality, and section 8 (6), which prohibits religious discrimination in the exercise of the executive powers granted to the Governor of Northern Ireland. I should add, having regard to your letter that these provisions were relevant in the context of the remarks made by the Prime Minister in the course of replies to questions put at a press conference.

Yours truly,
M. H. M. Reid
The Secretary,
Campaign for Social Justice

Thus the reply is vague and unhelpful. The 'context' of his remarks is open to inter-pretation. Another letter is sent to the prime minister to gain more clarification of the Government of Ireland Act and its relationship to the Northern Irish parliament.

2nd June, 1964

Dear Prime Minister

Thank you for your letter of May 8 in which you state that Section 5 of the Government of Ireland Act provides against religious discrimination in enactments of the Northern Ireland Parliament and Section 8 (6) prohibits religious discrimination in the exercise of executive powers granted to the Government of Northern Ireland. This legislation does not, however, appear to prevent discrimination in the exercise of powers conferred or duties imposed by Acts of the Northern Ireland Parliament; and in particular it does not appear to give any redress against discriminatory acts by local authorities in the exercise of their powers.

It is this latter matter which is of most immediate concern in Northern Ireland. As we have stated in previous correspondence, we believe there is clear evidence that certain local authorities in exercising their functions have discriminated against people on the grounds of religion. We would be pleased to have your advice as to whether there is any existing legal process whereby persons in Northern Ireland can bring such cases of alleged religious discrimination before the Courts, and secure redress in the event of the allegations being established. If such provision is not at present available, we would like to know whether your Government would be prepared to initiate legislation, whether by way of amendment to the Government of Ireland Act or otherwise, which would enable cases of alleged religious discrimination by public authorities to be examined by the Courts and to be rectified where proved.

Yours respectfully,
BRIAN GREGORY, Secretary [Campaign for Democracy in Ulster]
Letter formally acknowledged 4th June, 1964

Once again evidence of discrimination against Catholics by local authorities is mentioned in a letter to the prime minister of the United Kingdom. The lack of legislation preventing the possibility of discrimination is discovered, and relayed to the prime minister in the hope that he can provide a solution. There was no reply. Another letter was sent to Downing Street.

24th June, 1964

Dear Prime Minister

While appreciating the demands which are made upon a Prime Minister's time, may we state with all courtesy that we are most anxious to have a considered reply to our letter of the 2nd instant, which you acknowledged on the 4th instant. We feel sure that you recognise the importance of the issues raised in our letter, and we trust that the delay in replying thereto is in some measure occasioned by the necessity of giving full consideration to these issues.

Yours respectfully,
BRIAN GREGORY, Secretary [Campaign for Democracy in Ulster]

This letter was once again eloquently written, asking for a quick reply. The reply was sent the next day.

June 25, 1964

Dear Sir,

I write on behalf of the Prime Minister to acknowledge the receipt of your letter of June 24.
The Prime Minister has asked the Home Secretary to look into the points that you raised and a further reply will be sent to you in due course.

Yours truly,
M. H. M. REID
The Secretary

30th June, 1964

Sir,

I am directed by the Secretary of State to reply to your letters of 2nd and 24th June which, as you know, have been forwarded to him. The matters raised in these letters appear to the Secretary of State to be within the field of responsibility which the Government of Ireland Act, 1920, has entrusted to the Parliament and Government of Northern Ireland, and it would not be proper for him to comment upon them. Her Majesty's Government have no legislation in view to amend the 1920 Act.

I am, Sir,
Your obedient Servant,
A. J. LANGDON
The Secretary

The government of the United Kingdom had, according to the letter, no responsibility for the laws 'entrusted' to the Northern Irish government. The British government hid behind the Government of Ireland Act 1920 to avoid the responsibility of investigating the alleged cases of discrimination against Catholics by the local authorities in Northern Ireland. Another letter was sent to Whitehall. The rest of the conversation is left to the reader.

13th August, 1964

Dear Prime Minister

As promised by you in your letter of June 25th, 1964, we have received a letter
from Mr Henry Brooke, copy of which is enclosed. It seems to us to leave
our original questions to you, in our letters of 13th April 1964 and 2nd June
1964, unanswered. Since there are upwards of half a million Roman Catholic
people in Northern Ireland who feel that they are suffering injustice by living
their lives at a disadvantage as compared with their Protestant fellow country-
men, and since, in the final analysis, you and your Government are responsible
for their welfare, may I take the liberty of pressing you for precise answers to
the questions posed.

Yours faithfully,
Mrs PATRICIA McCLUSKEY, Chairman [Campaign for Democracy in
Ulster]
Letter formally acknowledged 14th August, 1964

20th August, 1964

Dear Madam

The Prime Minister has asked me to reply to your letter of August 13.
    Referring to your previous letters, of April 13 and June 2, about allegations
of religious discrimination in Northern Ireland. As explained in the Home
Office letter of June 30, the matters you raise appear to be within the field of
responsibility of the Parliament and Government of Northern Ireland, and
are not, therefore, matters upon which the Prime Minister can properly comment. Nor is it possible for the Prime Minister to advise on the possibility of
initiating legal proceedings in Northern Ireland.

Yours truly,
The Chairman,
M. H. M. REID

25th August, 1964

Dear Prime Minister,

Thank you for your letter of 20th August, 1964, with reference to religious discrimination in Northern Ireland. We note your statement that the matters we raised 'appear to be within the field of responsibility of the Parliament and Government of Northern Ireland' and that therefore you cannot properly comment upon them. If by this statement you seek to disclaim responsibility in the matter, we must refer you to Section 75 of the Government of Ireland Act, 1920, by which the British Government retained overall responsibility for Northern Ireland affairs 'notwithstanding the establishment of the Parliament of … Northern Ireland'.

You further state in your letter that it is not possible for you to advise on the possibility of initiating legal proceedings in Northern Ireland. May we refer you to your reply of 8 May, 1964 to our letter of 13 April, 1964 and the remarks made by you on your visit to Northern Ireland and referred to by you in the same reply. You actually quoted the sections of the Government of Ireland Act to which your remarks referred. If your remarks and your letter of May 8 do not advise legal proceedings in cases of discrimination what other meaning do they bear? As this is a matter of the highest constitutional importance, we should be grateful for a clear statement on it. Would you please tell us therefore:

1. Do you still hold to the opinion that charges of discrimination against local and central government in Northern Ireland are capable of being tested in court under the Government of Ireland Act?

2. Are you now stating that the Government of Northern Ireland is the final judge in charges of discrimination brought against that government?

3. Do you hold that the Government of Northern Ireland is the responsible authority to which charges of discrimination against local government authorities should be referred?

We trust you will appreciate that our object in seeking clarification of these points is to eliminate causes of tension and frustration, and not to score points in an argument. We would urge upon you, therefore, the need for serious and immediate attention to the constitutional issues we have raised.

BRIAN GREGORY, Secretary,
Campaign for Social Justice

September 3rd, 1964

Dear Sir,

The Prime Minister has asked me to reply to your further letter of 25th August about allegations of religious discrimination in Northern Ireland. Section 75 of the Government of Ireland Act, 1920, preserves the supreme authority of the Parliament of the United Kingdom – not of Her Majesty's Government in the United Kingdom – over all persons, matters and things in Northern Ireland. Section 5 of the Act already prohibits the enactment by the Parliament of Northern Ireland of laws interfering with religious equality, and the Prime Minister sees no reason for asking the United Kingdom Parliament to legislate further on this matter.

Yours truly,
The Secretary

Quotes about the Catholic minority

There follows a list of quotes from prominent people in Northern Irish society, showing their views on the Catholic minority.

Sir Basil Brooke (later Viscount Brookeborough). Minister of Agriculture 1933–41, Minister of Commerce 1941–43, Prime Minister 1943–63

There were a great number of Protestants and Orangemen who employed Roman Catholics. He felt he could speak freely on this subject as he had not a Roman Catholic about his own place … He would appeal to Loyalists, therefore, wherever possible, to employ good Protestant lads and lassies. (*Fermanagh Times*, 13 July 1933)

He made certain remarks regarding the employment of Roman Catholics which created a certain amount of controversy. He now wished to say he did not intend to withdraw a single word of what he then said. (*Fermanagh Times*, 17 August 1933)

Thinking out the whole question carefully … I recommended those people who are Loyalists not to employ Roman Catholics, ninety-nine per cent of whom are disloyal. I want you to remember one point in regard to the employment of people who are disloyal. There are often difficulties in the way, but usually there are plenty of good men and women available, and the employers don't bother to employ them. You are disfranchising yourselves in that way. You people who are employers have the ball at your feet. If you don't act properly now before we know where we are we shall find ourselves in the minority instead of the majority. (*Londonderry Sentinel*, 20 March 1934)

Brian Faulkner MP. Minister of Home Affairs 1959–63, Minister of Commerce 1963–69, Minister of Development 1969 (subsequently Prime Minister 1971):

The Church of Rome, he warned, ran a world-wide organisation — the most efficient political undertaking in the world. It controlled newspapers, radio and television stations and a hundred and one other avenues of propaganda. It was able to give vigorous publicity to any cause it espouses … that it favours Irish Republicanism today as whole-heartedly as it has done for generations past is universally recognised. (*Northern Whig*, 13 July 1954)

There is no reason why Orangemen individually and collectively should not interest themselves in the economic welfare of the community; I mean by that statement we should be anxious to find employment for our brethren. (County Down, *Spectator*, 17 July 1954)

Of one thing, I for my part, have no doubt – if it should ever happen that Orangemen disassociate themselves from the political life of Ulster, both Ulster and the Orange institution are doomed … I have said before and I repeat today – the Orange Order is the backbone of Ulster. (*Irish News*, 13 July 1960)

Captain Terence O'Neill. Prime Minister 1963–1969:

Protestant girl required for housework. Apply to The Hon. Mrs Terence O'Neill, Glebe House, Ahoghill, Co. Antrim. (Advertisement in *Belfast Telegraph*, November 1959. Quoted by *Sunday Times*, London, 2 March 1969)

E. C. Ferguson MP (Resigned from Parliament in October 1949 to become Crown Solicitor for Co. Fermanagh):

The Nationalist majority in the county, i.e., Fermanagh, notwithstanding a reduction of 336 in the year stands at 3,684. We must ultimately reduce and liquidate that majority. This county, I think it can be safely said, is a Unionist county. The atmosphere is Unionist. The Boards and properties are nearly all controlled by Unionists. But there is still this millstone around our necks. (*Irish News*, 13 April 1948)[9]

Alderman George Elliott, Enniskillen:

We are not going to build houses in the South Ward and cut a rod to beat ourselves later on. We are going to see that the right people are put into these houses and we are not making any apology for it. (7 November 1963)

Senator J. E. N. Barnhill, Londonderry:

Charity begins at home. If we are going to employ people we should give preference to Unionists. I am not saying that we should sack Nationalist employees, but if we are going to employ new men we should give preference to Unionists.' (9 January 1964)

Sir James Craig. Prime Minister, 1921–40:

The Prime Minister [Sir James Craig]: The hon. Member says that all our appointments are carried out on a religious basis. I would like to go into this somewhat fully. The appointments made by the Government are made as far as we can possibly manage it of loyal men and women. Why not? And what objection can there possibly be to those who are upholding Ulster as part of the great British Empire and the United Kingdom, seeing that we have not got saturated through the place those who acquiesce in the policy of the hon. Members opposite, of endeavouring to break down the machinery of government given to us by the British people? Surely nothing could be clearer than that. If a man is a Roman Catholic, if he is fitted for the job, provided he is loyal to the core, he has as good a chance of appointment as anybody else; and if a Protestant is not loyal to the core he has no more chance than a similar Roman Catholic.
Mr O'Neill: How do you test their loyalty?
The Prime Minister: There are ways of finding that out. The hon. Member knows just as well as I do there are ways of discovering whether a man is heart and soul in carrying out the intention of the Act of 1920, which was given to the Ulster people in order to save them from being swallowed up in a Dublin Parliament. Therefore, it is undoubtedly our duty and our privilege, and always will be, to see that those appointed by us possess the most unimpeachable loyalty to the King and Constitution. That is my whole object in carrying on a Protestant Government for a Protestant people. I repeat it in this House.[10]

NOTES

Preface

1 Max Arthur, *Northern Ireland Soldiers Talking* (London: Sidgwick and Jackson, 1988), p. 2.
2 Arthur, p. 3.
3 This belief comes from a review of the booklet by 'Garibaldi' in *The Cedar Lounge Revolution*, an online blog that, in its own words is, 'an Irish blog with a[n] unashamedly, but undogmatically, left-wing view of the world'. It was also the belief of the army: www.cedarlounge.wordpress.com.
4 Author's correspondence with a resident of the Falls Road.
5 Caroline Kennedy-Pipe, *The Origins of the Present Troubles in Northern Ireland* (London: Longman, 1997), p. 53.
6 Colm Campbell, Ita Connolly, 'A Model for the 'War Against Terrorism'? Military Intervention in Northern Ireland and the 1970 Falls Curfew' *Journal of Law and Society* Vol. 30, No. 3, September, 2003 pp. 341-75.
7 Max Arthur, *Northern Ireland Soldiers Talking* (London: Sidgwick and Jackson, 1987), p. 26.
8 Daniel M. Wilson, 'Peace-Making: The Effectiveness of British Strategy in Northern Ireland, 1969–1972', thesis, 1979; www.dtic.mil.
9 Desmond Hamill, *Pig in the Middle* (London: Methuen, 1985), p. 143.
10 Gordon Gillespie, *Years of Darkness: The Troubles Remembered* (Dublin: Gill and Macmillan, 2008).
11 Hansard Parliamentary Debates HC Deb 18 January 1971 Vol. 809 pp. 680–92 www.hansard.millbanksystems.com/commons.
12 Gerry Adams, *Before the Dawn* (London: William Heinemann, 1996), p. 87.
13 Author's correspondence.
14 Joseph W. Bishop, 'Law in the Control of Terrorism and Insurrection: The British Laboratory Experience'; www.scholarship.law.duke.edu.
15 Michael Dewar, *The British Army in Northern Ireland* (London: Arms and Armour, 1985), p. 47.
16 Taken from http://news.bbc.co.uk/1/hi/6923699.stm.
17 Taken from HC Deb 18 January 1971 vol 809 cc680-92 http://hansard.millbanksystems.com/commons/1971/jan/18/northern-ireland.
18 Martin Dillon, *Trigger Man: Assassins and Terror Bosses in the Ireland Conflict* (Edinburgh: Mainstream, 2004).
19 Taken from HC Deb 18 January 1971 vol 809 cc680-92 http://hansard.millbanksystems.com/commons/1971/jan/18/northern-ireland.
20 Ibid.

21 This is Van De Bijl's own view, as mentioned in his book. It should not be treated as an official viewpoint. The official version of 'Operation Banner' was withdrawn from circulation when several inaccuracies were found in it.

22 Paddy Devlin, *Straight Left* (Belfast: Blackstaff Press, 1993), p. 131.

23 Peter Taylor, *Brits: The War against the IRA* (London: Bloomsbury, 2002).

24 Courtesy of *The Story of the Belfast Curfew* pamphlet.

25 Richard English, *Armed Struggle: The History of the IRA* (London: Macmillan, 2003), p. 136.

26 Author's correspondence with Robert McClenaghan.

27 Tony Geraghty, *The Irish War: The Hidden Conflict Between the IRA and British Intelligence* (London: HarperCollins, 2000), p. 38.

Chapter 1

1 Mary Kenny, 'Winston Churchill and Ireland'; www.mary-kenny.com/published_articles/winston-churchill-ireland. Kenny also includes an interesting anecdote about Churchill's views on reunification. 'In November 1948, Churchill met the Irish High Commissioner, subsequently Ambassador, John Dulanty in London: Winston said to him – "I still hope for a United Ireland. You must get those fellows from the North in, though you can't do it by force. There is not, and never was, any bitterness in my heart towards your country."'

2 Taken from *A History of Ireland* by Eleanor Hull at www.libraryireland.com.

3 The 'Pale' was an area of territory that encompassed the area around Dublin on the east coast, up to the town of Dundalk, near the present-day border with Northern Ireland and inland for roughly 40 miles. It was the only area that the English could hold on to in Ireland in this period. Heavily fortified, it was often raided by the native Irish stealing cattle.

4 John Darby, 'Conflict in Northern Ireland: A Background Essay'; www.rhsroughriders.org

5 Richard Aldous and Niamh Puirsell, *We Declare: Landmark Documents in Ireland's History* (London: Quercus, 2008), p. 43.

6 Most notably Barbados.

7 See 'Explanations of Groups, Organisations and Terms' for a brief explanation of the battle.

8 These laws started off in a variety of forms: for example, in 1607 Catholics were fined for non-attendance at Anglican services. Thereafter there were laws banning Catholics from intermarriage with Protestants, foreign education, entering Trinity College in Dublin, entering the legal profession, voting, teaching and inheriting Protestant-owned land.

9 Rafferty, Oliver P., *Catholicism in Ulster 1603–1983: An Interpretive History* (London: Hurst & Co., 1994).

10 Kee, *Ireland: A History*.

11 Known as 'An Gorta Mor' in Ireland: 'The Great Hunger'.

12 There can be no comparison between the two. The British establishment did not consciously set out to destroy the Irish race, although there are still some who believe that it was an attempt to control the rising population. The Nazi regime consciously, and brutally, set out to destroy the Jews.

13 The Potato 'Blight' is a disease caused by a fungal infection in the crop; it invariably spreads rapidly and is known to stay in the ground from season to season, as happened in the case of the Irish Famine.

14 Aldous and Puirsell, p. 80.

15 Ibid., p. 81.

16 Maire and Conor Cruise O'Brien, *Ireland, A Concise History* (London: Thames and Hudson, 1999), p. 105. O'Brien, an Irish intellectual, author and a subsequent supporter of Unionism, was classed as a revisionist writer of Irish history. He was also a vehement opponent of the Provisional IRA's campaign, although he ironically worked for the Irish government's anti-partition campaign in his early career.

17 Emyrs Jones, 'The Distribution and Segregation of Roman Catholics in Belfast', *The Sociological Review*, Vol. 4, Issue 2, pp. 167–189 (1956), p. 168.

18 Ibid., p. 181.

19 See 'Explanations of Groups, Organisations and Terms' for an explanation of Home Rule.

20 Mary Harris, 'Religious Divisions, Discrimination and the Struggle for Dominance in Northern Ireland', p. 210; www.stm.unipi.it.

21 An explanation, with the original transcript, is in 'Explanations of Groups, Organisations and Terms'.

22 Even with this four-county solution, guaranteeing Protestants an inbuilt majority, there would have been a significant Catholic population remaining, especially in the counties of Down and Armagh. Parts of Derry city were and are wholly Catholic, and thus would have had a justifiable claim to join the south at the time of the partition of the country. West Belfast had, and still does, contain a large Catholic population.

23 This saying is more closely associated with the First World War but it was also in use in previous decades.

24 Out of 102 Sinn Féin candidates put forward, seventy-three were returned, polling nearly 500,000 votes.

25 Even today the very name 'Black and Tans' evokes strong memories in Ireland. Recruited from First World War veterans, they were a brutal auxiliary force that wreaked havoc in Ireland during the War of Independence. Sent to Ireland to support the Royal Irish Constabulary, they soon became a law unto themselves. Their name comes from the improvised British army uniforms that they wore.

26 The Black and Tans were capable of some heinous crimes, as this quote details. 'The most infamous attack on the public came in November 1920. Many people had packed into Croke Park, Dublin, to watch a football match. In retaliation for the murder of fourteen undercover detectives by the IRA, the Black and Tans opened fire on the crowd, killing twelve people'; www.historylearningsite.co.uk.

27 The Irish Civil War began in June 1922 and ended in May 1923 when the anti-Treaty forces were ordered to 'dump arms' by DeValera. The war had a major effect on the psyche of the Irish people, dividing families and ensuring that politics in the new Irish state developed along the lines of Republicanism and a break from British influence in Ireland.

28 The commission failed as mentioned because of a leak to the press. Suspicion immediately fell on one of the representatives, who resigned shortly after. Much work was done by the Boundary Commission, including a comprehensive study of the border region, and it was almost certain that significant parts of the territory of Northern Ireland would have been ceded to the Irish Free State had the commission been allowed to carry on; www.dur.ac.uk/resources.

29 Taken from www.thepsychologist.org.uk/archive.

30 Hepburn, A. C. Northern Ireland" Taken from www.mrmichaelstuart.com/uploads/3/2/6/.../noirelandencartainfo.doc.

31 Oliver P. Rafferty, *Catholicism in Ulster, an Interpretive History* (London: Hurst and Company, 1994), p. 222.

32 Harris, 'Religious Divisions', p. 8.

33 Michael Farrell, *Northern Ireland: The Orange State* (London: Pluto Press, 1976).

34 The Special Powers Act became a permanent feature of Northern Ireland legislation in 1933. Subsequent editions only served to bolster the tools that the Unionist government could use. It was repealed in 1973 after the advent of Direct Rule.

35 Anders Boserup, 'Contradictions and Struggles in Northern Ireland', *The Socialist Register*, 1972, p. 8.

36 Not all Catholics and Protestants segregated themselves. There was an element of intermingling socially and personally, with many Catholics marrying Protestants.

But on the whole, marriage between them was frowned upon, especially by the Catholic Church, who insisted that the children of such marriages were to be brought up in the Catholic faith.

37 Thomas Hennessey, *A History of Northern Ireland* (London: St Martin's Press, 1997), p. 42.

38 A brief explanation of PR is available in 'Explanations of Groups, Organisations and Terms'.

39 For first-hand interpretations of this discrimination see *Northern Ireland, The Orange State* by Michael Farrell, *Straight Left* by Paddy Devlin and *Before the Dawn* by Gerry Adams. Many contemporary history books on the period also offer brief but detailed descriptions. Farrell especially gives a graphic account of the discriminatory aspects of successive Unionist governments.

40 Adams, *Before the Dawn*, p. 60.

41 Farrell, p. 94.

42 Christopher Hewitt, 'Catholic Grievances, Catholic Nationalism and Violence in Northern Ireland during the Civil Rights Period', *British Journal of Sociology*, Vol. 32, No. 3, September 1981, pp. 362–77.

43 Henry Patterson, *Ireland since 1939* (Dublin: Penguin, 2006), p. 181.

44 Ibid.

45 See Appendix B for more quotes.

46 It is surprising that Britain did not act more aggressively to Eire in this period, as she was still part of the Commonwealth and, in theory at least, recognised the king as head of state. The 'Treaty Ports', retained by the British after the Anglo-Irish war, were returned to Ireland in 1938 as part of a general Irish–British agreement. There was a great demand in England for the ports to be returned for the duration of the war but DeValera flatly refused, saying that it would breach Irish neutrality. Churchill was keen to get the Irish state involved, whether forcibly or not. A limited excursion by the British army into the south to recapture the ports would almost certainly have created insurgency in the country, however; the last thing Churchill would have wanted.

47 See the chronology in Appendix A for more information.

48 Ireland Act, 1949, Ch. 41; www.legislation.gov.uk, accessed 12 June 2012.

49 Hennessey, *A History of Northern Ireland*, p. 98.

50 English, *Armed Struggle*, p. 98.

51 Emigration from the Republic of Ireland in the 1950s was an acute problem, running at around 40,000 a year. Since the Famine of the late 1840s emigration had carried on, with varying numbers leaving yearly. These invariably followed the thousands who had left before them, and went to England, the United States, Australia and New Zealand. This created a 'brain drain' in the economy of the Republic, leaving it a mainly rural and poor country. Year on year the population of the country decreased.

52 John Conroy, *Belfast Diary: War as a Way of Life* (Boston: Beacon Press, 1987), p. 25.

53 Paul Rose, 'Backbencher's Dilemma', Chapter 12 in *The Northern Ireland Fiasco*; and 'Appendix' (a report by the Campaign for Democracy in Ulster on a visit to Northern Ireland in 1967) (London: Muller, 1981).

54 Rose, 'Backbencher's Dilemma'.

55 Ibid.

56 Ibid.

57 Ibid.

58 Taken from: 'Lord I Stonewall' (14 June 1968), from the *Tribune Magazine* Archive; www.archive.tribunemagazine.co.uk/article.

59 Boyd carries on in the same vein, showing that even in 1968 they were well aware that Westminster had neglected Northern Ireland for too long: 'Westminster, according to Lord Stoneham, is not going to say a word out of place to Stormont about the gerrymandering of Derry, restrictions on the local government franchise which favour the profit-taking

businessman above the taxpayer, or the disgraceful and widespread practice of religious discrimination in employment, housing and public appointments. Westminster is apparently content to live with these undemocratic practices and with measures such as Stormont's Special Powers Act and the Safeguarding of Employment Act even though they mean, as Harold Wilson admitted on April 30, that Her Majesty's Government is prevented from being a full signatory to "international human rights and other conventions." (ibid.).

60 Dillon, *Trigger Man*.

61 Ibid.

62 '*A Commentary by the Government of Northern Ireland to Accompany the Cameron Report incorporating an account of progress and a programme of action*'; taken from www.cain.ulst. ac.uk/hmso.

63 Devlin served a jail term for incitement to riot, was the youngest ever MP to sit in the Houses of Parliament and was a socialist activist. She also slapped the Northern Ireland Secretary, Reginald Maudling, across the face on the floor of the House of Commons when he stated that the army had shot in self-defence on 'Bloody Sunday'.

64 Captain Terence O'Neill, Unionist Party, Northern Ireland Prime Minister, May 1969. Reported in *Belfast Telegraph*, 10 May 1969. Accessed from www.cain.ulst.ac.uk/issues/ discrimination/quotes.

65 '*We Shall Overcome': The History of the Struggle for Civil Rights in Northern Ireland 1968–1978* (Northern Ireland Civil Rights Association (NICRA), 2 Marquis Street, Belfast BT1 1JJ). This book was published in 1978 to mark the tenth anniversary of the civil rights movement in Northern Ireland. Taken from www.cain.co.uk

66 Ian Kyle Paisley, son of a Baptist preacher, was the founder of the *Protestant Telegraph* which ceased publication in 1982. Known for his rabidly anti-Catholic preaching, he was heavily active in the 1960s counter-demonstrations against the civil rights marches.

67 Billy McMillan, the leader of the Belfast IRA, was the candidate in the election that prompted the display of the Irish Tricolour and was responsible for displaying it. He was also responsible for putting it back up after the RUC took it down.

68 NA PRONI FIN/30/P20 Minority Recognition and Representation.

69 Farrell, p. 250.

70 The Cameron Commission concluded: 'We are driven to think that the leaders must have intended that their venture would weaken the moderate reforming forces in Northern Ireland. We think that their object was to increase tension, so that in the process a more radical programme could be realized. They saw the march as a calculated martyrdom. In addition the riot of 3rd January in Guildhall Square, Londonderry which was wrongly attributed to the Civil Rights movement, still further damaged that movement in the public mind.' *Disturbances in Northern Ireland. Report of the Commission appointed by the Governor of Northern Ireland*. Taken from http://cain.ulst.ac.uk/hmso/ cameron.htm#chap9 (Accessed 31/1/2013).

71 NA PRONI CAB/9/B/205/8 '*Press Release*'.

72 Harris, p. 215.

73 In fact Wilson was known to be a supporter of Irish unity.

74 Peter Rose, *How the Troubles Came To Northern Ireland* (Basingstoke: Palgrave, 2001), p. 51

75 By 1970 he had become Lord O'Neill.

76 *Irish Times*, 9 November 1970. Quoted in Gordon Gillespie, *Years of Darkness: The Troubles Remembered* (Dublin: Gill and Macmillan, 2008), p. 15.

Chapter 2

1 Gerry Adams, *Falls Memories* (Dingle: Brandon Books, 1993), p. 2.

2 NA PRONI HA/32/2/55 Letter about sending in the troops.

3 Farrell, p. 92.

4 Adams, *Before the Dawn*, p. 7.

5 Adams, p. 22.

6 Devlin, *Straight Left*, p. 20.

7 Falls Think Tank, *Ourselves Alone? Voices from the Nationalist Working Class*, compiled by Michael Hall (Newtownabbey: Island Publications, 1996), p. 8.

8 Currently this amounts to about £2.5 billion.

9 The British Exchequer paid for it all, and the UK government also invested millions in industry in order to alleviate unemployment in the state. The advent of a welfare system in Northern Ireland greatly increased the differences between Northern Ireland and the Republic, which made partition all the more permanent.

10 This money went to industries in the east of the state; the south and west had little industry, so little investment. The south and west of the state had the most Catholics, hence there was higher unemployment amongst them as a whole.

11 This has been debated along the lines that the majority of the Catholic population were also east of the Bann, thus gaining more employment than their western counterparts.

12 Devlin, *Straight Left*.

13 Many working-class Protestants attest that Unionist politicians regularly visited the Shankill at times of tension, warning them about the dangers of Catholicism, and suggested avoidance at all times. Glen Barr, a former politician and UDA member from Derry, spoke about the time of the 1932 riots in Belfast. Protestant and Catholic working-class people had got together to demonstrate in defiance of the ban on gatherings. In an interview on the Thames Television programme *The Troubles*, he spoke about how 'the Unionist politicians very quickly moved into the Protestant ghetto areas and manipulated the situation again into a constitutional problem, whereby they were saying to the ordinary working class Protestant people, "Look, you can't connect with these Catholics, because what they are doing is only a front. The real reasons behind the labour unrest are that, quite simply, they want to destroy the state of Northern Ireland and take us into a united Ireland." And unfortunately, through fear, the Protestant working class believed what they were told, and very quickly the whole movement was divided again'; *The Troubles* (London: MacDonald Futura, 1980).

14 Gerry Adams, *Falls Memories* (Dingle: Brandon, 1993), p. 142.

15 Subsequently the Divis complex became notorious in the history of the Troubles as being a 'nursery' for hardened and committed terrorists.

16 There was also severe rioting in Newry, Armagh and Dungannon.

17 Brian Hanley and Scott Millar, *The Lost Revolution* (London: Penguin, 2010), p. 126.

18 The actual script read 'not standing *idly* by', but the word 'idly' was omitted from the TV monitor he was reading off in the RTE studios. Many subsequent histories of the Troubles have erroneously included the word in the text.

19 It created a hostile situation in the Dáil as well in a heated debate on 23 October 1969. Barry Desmond, TD, member of the Labour Party, was very critical of Lynch's movement of Irish troops to the border. 'I would point out to the Taoiseach that the movement of Irish troops at the Border, admittedly on humanitarian grounds, had, I think, an overt tendency to raise false hopes in the Bogside, to raise particularly false hopes in Belfast and to escalate a situation which admittedly we may now criticise by hindsight. However, the decision made was the Taoiseach's: he did not consult with leaders of the Opposition; he held his Cabinet meeting and made his decision. I felt at the time and I still feel – and I would have stated this had there been a meeting of Dáil Éireann in August – that this strategy of the Irish Government was an error of judgment, and I am glad to see that in many respects it has not been defended'. *Dáil Éireann*, Vol. 241, 23 October 1969, Situation in Six Counties; www.historical-debates.oireachtas.ie.

20 Ronnie Munck, 'The Making of the Troubles in Northern Ireland', *Journal of Contemporary History*, Vol. 27, No. 2 (April 1992), pp. 211–29.

21 Devlin, *Straight Left*, p. 105.

22 Interview in *The Troubles* (MacDonald Futura Publishers, 1980).

23 Devlin, *Straight Left*, p. 106.

24 Sean Murray, article in *An Phoblacht*, 23 July 2009.

25 Falls Think Tank, *'Seeds of Hope': An Exploration by the 'Seeds of Hope' Ex-prisoners* (Newtownabbey: Island Publications, 2000), p. 6.

26 Devlin, *Straight Left*, p. 107.

27 Hanley and Millar, p. 124.

28 Ibid., p. 127.

29 Patterson, p. 213.

30 A plaque has been put on the wall of Divis Tower at the bottom of the Falls Road to commemorate Patrick and the off-duty soldier who was killed there on the same night. History remembers Patrick Rooney because of his age; Hugh McCabe, the Catholic soldier, barely gets a mention.

31 It is important to note that the deaths of Patrick Rooney and Hugh McCabe occurred *before* the events in the Clonard district.

32 Many of these families subsequently moved south into the Republic, and were housed in military camps such as Gormanstown, in County Meath, until permanent accommodation was found. Many of them also stayed and built new lives in the Republic.

33 Devlin, *Straight Left*, p. 107.

34 Peter Taylor, *Provos, The IRA and Sinn Fein* (London: Bloomsbury, 1997), p. 59.

35 Adams, *Before the Dawn*, p. 110.

36 This was certainly one reason, but there were many more, including the Falls Curfew.

37 O'Brien, p. 176.

38 Desmond Hamill, *Pig in the Middle* (London: Methuen, 1985), p. 10.

39 He had originally called for a United Nations peacekeeping force.

40 Jack Lynch, *A Review of the Situation in the Six Counties* (Lynch, Jack. (1969) 'The Situation in the Six Counties of the North-East Ireland'. (Dublin: Irish Government).

41 Ibid.

42 Ibid.

43 Malachi O'Doherty, *The Pogrom Myth*; www.malachiodoherty.com/2009/08/12/the-pogrom-myth. Taken from *The Trouble with Guns, Republican Strategy and the Provisional IRA* (Belfast: Blackstaff Press, 1998).

44 Ibid.

45 O'Doherty, *The Pogrom Myth*.

46 Prince and Warner, p. 210.

47 English, *Armed Struggle*, p. 100.

48 *Violence and Civil Disturbances in Northern Ireland in 1969. Report of Tribunal of Inquiry*, April 1972. Taken from: www.cain.ulst.ac.uk/hmso/scarman.

49 From the author's personal notes (interview with 'Dave').

50 Ibid.

51 Nick Van Der Bijl, *Operation Banner, The British Army in Northern Ireland 1969–2007* (Barnsley: Pen and Sword Military, 2009), p. 27.

52 From the author's personal notes (interview with 'Dave').

53 In talking to the author, this was a major issue for him. He often thought about how his own family could cope with the situation and subsequently came to the conclusion that the ruling government in Stormont should have been brought to account in a court of law for allowing such a situation to develop. He also blamed the British

establishment for completely ignoring Northern Ireland and the government that ruled in its name.

54 J. Boyer Bell, *The Irish Troubles: A Generation of Violence* (New York: St Martin's Press, 1993), p. 127.

55 HC Deb 13 October 1969 Vol. 788 pp. 47–164; www.hansard.millbanksystems.com/commons.

56 Tim Pat Coogan, *The Troubles: Ireland's Ordeal and the Search for Peace* (New York: Palgrave, 2002), p. 111.

57 English, p. 106.

58 MacStíofáin believed in three phases that would guide the emerging Provisionals. The first one was the defence of local areas, coupled with rearmament; the second was combined defensive actions; and the third was be an all-out attack on the British presence in Northern Ireland.

59 Hamill, p. 21.

60 Ibid., p. 26.

61 The 'perception' amongst many Catholics at the time was that the military command was undertaking actions consistent with Unionist thinking. Therefore there is no proof that this was actually happening.

62 NA CAB/129/144.

63 Ibid.

64 Hamill, p. 25.

Chapter 3

1 'The Patriot Game', in Charles Carlton, *Bigotry and Blood* (Chicago: Nelson-Hall, 1977), p. 107.

2 Farrell, p. 270.

3 *Disturbances in Northern Ireland*, Report of the Commission appointed by the Governor of Northern Ireland, Conclusion.

4 *Disturbances in Northern Ireland*, Report of the Commission appointed by the Governor of Northern Ireland, Conclusion, Ch. 14.

5 Farrell, p. 266.

6 HMSO, *Report of the Advisory Committee on Police in Northern Ireland*.

7 Rose, p. 154.

8 John McGarry, *Northern Ireland and the Divided World* (Oxford: Oxford University Press, 2001), p. 9.

9 Henry Patterson, 'The British State and the Rise of the IRA', *Irish Political Studies*, Vol. 23, No. 4 (2008), pp. 491–51, p. 2.

10 McGarry, p. 7.

11 Ibid.

12 Michael Cunningham, *British Government Policy in Northern Ireland* (Manchester: Manchester University Press, 2001), p. 2.

13 Peter R. Neumann, *Britain's Long War: British Strategy in the Northern Ireland Conflict, 1969–98* (London: Palgrave Macmillan, 2004), p. 20.

14 Ibid.

15 Ibid.

16 Ibid.

17 From the author's personal notes ('Army John').

18 John Magee and Jack Magee, *Northern Ireland: Crisis and Conflict* (London: Routledge, 1974), p. 130.

19 Farrell, p. 269.

20 Some money earmarked for the relief of displaced people in Northern Ireland was

indeed directed towards the Provisionals for the purchase of weapons. Also, the Dublin government authorised the training of some of its troops for 'incursions' into Northern Ireland, ostensibly to protect Catholics.

21 Tim Ripley and Mike Chappell, *Security Forces in Northern Ireland 1969–92* (London: Osprey Publishing, 1993), p. 31.

22 Peter H. Merkl (ed.), *Political Violence and Terror: Motifs and Motivations* (London: University of California Press, 1986), p. 98.

23 *Seeds of Hope*, p. 10.

24 Farrell, p. 20.

25 Prince and Warner, p. 229.

26 Farrell, p. 272.

27 NA PRONI CAB/9/G/89/2. Stormont Castle Meeting. Notes on points to be discussed with the GOC 22nd April 1970.

28 Ibid.

29 Ibid.

30 The names on the list that were withheld were blanked out in the archives.

31 Ibid.

32 NA PRONI CAB/9/G/89/2. Stormont Castle Meeting. Notes on points to be discussed with the GOC 22nd April 1970.

33 Unionists have long believed this, along with the erroneous belief that NICRA wanted to lead them into a united Ireland by destabilising the state. Republicans and members of the IRA were in NICRA, but they mainly acted as stewards on marches.

34 Taylor, *Provos*, p. 74.

35 Michael A. Murphy, *Gerry Fitt: A Political Chameleon* (Cork: Mercier Press, 2007), p. 154.

36 Cunningham, p. 9.

37 *The Troubles* (MacDonald Futura Publishers, 1980).

38 Wichert, p. 145.

39 NA CAB/128/47 Conclusions of a meeting of the Cabinet held at 10 Downing Street, SW1 on Tuesday 23rd June 1970 at 11 a.m.

40 Ronald Weitzer, p. 126.

41 Peter Taylor, *Brits*, p. 46.

42 NA CAB/128/47 'Conclusions of a Meeting of the Cabinet' 26 June 1970.

43 Prince and Warner, p. 234.

44 Ibid., p. 237.

45 Taylor, *Provos*, p. 75.

46 Prince and Warner, p. 237.

47 Ibid.

48 Ibid., p. 241.

49 *An Phoblacht*, 9 March 2011.

50 Thomas Hennessey, *The Evolution of the Troubles* (Dublin: Irish Academic Press, 2007), p. 34.

51 Taylor, *Provos*, p. 77.

52 Prince, Warner, p. 251.

53 Stormont Papers, Vol. 76 (1970), pp. 1619–20.

54 Adams, *Before the Dawn*, p. 139.

55 Hennessey, *The Evolution of the Troubles*, p. 34.

56 Taylor, *Brits*, p. 48.

57 Hennessey, *The Evolution of the Troubles*, p. 34.

58 Neumann, p. 14.

59 Taylor, *Brits*, p. 48.

60 Hennessey, *The Evolution of the Troubles*, p. 36.

61 Prince and Warner, p. 241.

62 Hennessey, *The Evolution of the Troubles*, p. 37.

63 Patterson, *The British State and the Rise of the IRA*, p. 503.

64 McKee, as we have seen, was in fact at Mass that evening in Clonard.

65 Many witnesses spoke to the author and confirmed this viewpoint.

66 Stormont Papers, Vol. 76, pp. 1619–20.

67 Ibid.

68 Ibid.

69 Taylor, *Brits*, p. 48.

70 Hansard Parliamentary Debates, HC Deb 03 July 1970 Vol. 803 cc201-92.

71 Ibid.

72 Smith, p. 221.

73 Taylor, *Provos*, p. 78.

74 NA CAB/128/47 p. 3.

75 Criminal Justice (Temporary Provisions) Act (Northern Ireland) 1970, Chapter 22.

76 Citizen Press, *The Story of The Falls Curfew*, p. 7.

77 Brian Hanley and Scott Millar, *The Lost Revolution*, p. 156.

78 The possibility of another incursion into the Falls from the Shankill was part of the thinking of the Officials at the time. Mr Maguire, in whose house the weapons were found, was one such auxiliary who had done arms drills for a possible future Falls Militia. See *Sunday Times Insight Team Report*, p. 213.

79 Ibid., p. 156.

Chapter 4

1 From the author's personal notes (interview with 'Dave').

2 *The Story of the Falls Curfew*, p. 13.

3 From the author's personal notes (interview with unnamed witness).

4 Taken from *Three Days in July* (used with the kind permission of Robert McClenaghan), TAL Productions. The programme was produced by the Republican movement in Belfast to commemorate the 25th anniversary of the Falls Curfew.

5 *The Story of the Falls Curfew*, p. 14.

6 *Three Days in July*. Interview with Mr Maguire (courtesy of Robert McClenaghan).

7 Ulster: By the *Sunday Times Insight Team* (Harmondsworth: Penguin Books, 1972), p. 212.

8 Ibid.

9 *The Story of the Belfast Curfew* (CCDC, 1970), p. 10. The original booklet was given to the author by Robert McClenaghan in the Sinn Féin offices on the Falls Road in October 2011. As the Central Citizens Defence Committee has been defunct for over 40 years the author has used information from here with the express permission of Robert McClenaghan. Although the information about the events of the Curfew is from a singular viewpoint, wherever possible the author has checked the information out with other accounts and sources. The student survey at the end of the book, however, remains a valuable source of primary information as it was taken four weeks after the Curfew.

10 Warner, *The Falls Curfew Revisited*, p. 326.

11 *The Story of the Falls Curfew*, p. 14.

12 *The Story of the Belfast Curfew* (CCDC, 1970), p. 10.

13 Dewar, p. 47.

14 Warner, *The Falls Curfew Revisited*, p. 326.

15 Hanley and Millar, p. 157.

16 Taylor, *Provos*, p. 79.

17 Moloney, *Voices from the Grave*, p. 56.

18 From the author's personal notes (almost all the witnesses the author spoke to confirmed this).

19 Taylor, *Provos*, p. 78.

20 Warner, *The Falls Curfew Revisited*, p. 327.

21 From the author's personal notes (again, almost all the witnesses the author spoke to confirmed this).

22 *The Story of the Belfast Curfew*.

23 Ibid., p. 21.

24 O'Neill was subsequently found to be at least three times over the drink drive limit. Clearly if he was in any way inebriated this could have affected his thinking. The case is still subject to an HET review.

25 Ibid., p. 17.

26 *The Story of the Falls Curfew*, p. 17.

27 Ibid.

28 From the author's personal notes (interview with 'Dave').

29 From the author's personal notes (interview with Rita).

30 *Three Days in July*.

31 Hanley and Millar, p. 157.

32 'Pat' subsequently showed the author two large scars on her hands, inflicted by rubber bullets allegedly fired at 'point-blank range' by the army in another incident a couple of years later.

33 From the author's personal notes (interview with Pat).

34 *The Story of the Belfast Curfew* , p. 12.

35 Ibid.

36 Ibid.

37 *Three Days in July*.

38 From the author's personal notes (interview with 'Lorna').

39 From the author's personal notes (interview with unnamed soldier).

40 *The Story of the Belfast Curfew*, p. 13.

41 Devlin, *Straight Left*, p. 128.

42 In fact Sullivan had warned the GOC that he was not to 'come onto his patch' without his prior approval, a sure-fire way to rankle a general of the British army.

43 Devlin mentions this in his autobiography, calling it 'most remarkable' that the army went in at this time. Army searches were usually carried out in the dead of night, ostensibly to 'catch' the perpetrators at home.

44 Devlin, *Straight Left*, p. 128.

45 From the author's personal notes (interview with Robert McClenaghan).

46 Ministry of Defence, *Operation Banner*, p. 2.

47 It is reported in the Workers Party booklet, p. 20.

48 Ibid.

49 From the author's personal notes.

50 *The Story of the Belfast Curfew*, p. 13.

51 From the author's personal notes (interview with Pat McCotter).

52 Hanley and Millar, p. 157.

53 From the author's personal notes (interview with 'Dave').

54 Used with the kind permission of Danny Morrison, in an email to author.

55 From the author's personal notes (interview with Eamonn).

56 From the author's personal notes. Initially Eamonn did not want to be interviewed, and seemed as keen to find out information about the author as the author was about him. Eventually he began to reminisce about the Curfew. It was helpful that there were other people in the room, and that Eamonn did not feel under pressure.

57 From the author's personal notes. Rita is the niece of Patrick Elliman and was especially keen to talk to the author about her memories of her uncle, the Curfew and her own father, himself a victim of the army.

58 Eamonn remains very bitter about the whole episode, and reminded the author that this attitude of the authorities towards them and others is the reason why so many young people joined the IRA in those days. They felt that the whole system was against them by this point.

In a separate issue, many of the witnesses whom the author interviewed on this day showed their distaste for the current 'Peace Process', stating that Gerry Adams is now a TD in the Republic and Martin McGuinness is sitting in Stormont, the British are still in charge and there is no sign of a united Ireland after nearly forty years of fighting.

59 Hansard, http://hansard.millbanksystems.com/commons/1971/jan/18/northern-ireland.

60 The author interviewed 'two women in a pub' in the lower Falls in early January 2012. 'Gill' was the most vocal and angry about a period that she said changed her life forever and left her with a profound hatred of the British presence in Northern Ireland. 'Gill' is a classic example of how the Curfew radicalised many of the residents of the lower Falls through the army's mismanagement of the search operation.

61 The conclusions of the HET investigation into the death of Patrick Elliman should hopefully prove one way or the other who fired the lethal bullet. Debate still rages about the circumstances amongst some historians.

62 *Irish Times*, July 1970.

63 Ibid.

64 *Three Days in July*.

65 *The Story of the Belfast Curfew*, p. 15.

66 Geraghty, *The Irish War*, p. 36.

67 From the author's personal notes.

68 Hennessey, *The Evolution of the Troubles*, p. 39.

69 Ibid., cites DEFE 24/980.

70 *The Story of the Falls Curfew*, p. 21.

71 Ibid.

72 *The Irish Times*, 6 July 1970.

73 Devlin, *Straight Left*, p. 129.

74 *The Story of the Belfast Curfew*, pp. 29–31.

75 Hugh Jordan, *Milestones in Murder: Defining Moments in Ulster's Terror War* (Edinburgh: Mainstream, 2002).

76 From the author's personal notes (interview with Eamonn). However, there is no record of the KOSB being involved in the Curfew.

77 Devlin, *Straight Left*, p. 129.

78 From the author's personal notes (interview with 'Two women in a pub').

79 From the author's personal notes (interview with Robert McClenaghan).

80 From the author's personal notes (interview with 'Lisa').

81 Hennessey, *The Evolution of the Troubles*, p. 43.

82 Ibid., p. 44. Hennessey gives a good account of instances of damage that were caused by the army in its searches, but which are not mentioned in the CCDC report. Thus it is another good source of information, and more importantly, of opinion. He also discusses the legal aspect.

83 *Three Days in July*.

84 From the author's personal notes (interview with Helena Lanigan).

85 *The Story of the Belfast Curfew*, p. 13.

86 Max Arthur, *Northern Ireland Soldiers Talking* (London: Sidgwick and Jackson, 1988), p. 25. Max Arthur has a goldmine of information here about how the ordinary soldier felt

during his time in Northern Ireland. There are many examples in the book – but not necessarily from the Curfew, as information from soldiers about this event is somewhat limited.

87 Ibid., p. 26.
88 Ibid., p. 25.
89 From the author's personal notes.
90 Hamill, *Pig in the Middle*, p. 39.
91 From the author's personal notes (interview with Dave).
92 Ibid.
93 Arthur, *Northern Ireland Soldiers Talking*, p. 24.
94 Moloney, *Voices from the Grave*, p. 58.
95 NA HA/32/3/3 Security meeting at Stormont 4 July 1970.
96 Ibid.
97 Ibid.
98 *The Story of the Belfast Curfew*.
99 Ibid.
100 NA HA/32/3/3 Security meeting at Stormont 4 July 1970.
101 *Three Days in July*.
102 In contrast to this is an account in Hugh Jordan's book, *Milestones in Murder: Defining Moments in Ulster's Terror War*. In it he states that Billy McMillan, aware that the army were entering the lower Falls in force, organised a sizeable amount of women with prams to smuggle weaponry out. Babies were used to hide the weapons. This could be the explanation for the idea that weapons were smuggled out after the Curfew was finished in prams. (Jordan, *Milestones in Murder*, p.11).
103 According to *Saoirse*, the Curfew was '… only broken on Sunday, July 5 when courageous local women organised a march and broke through the shocked line of British soldiers after two days of gun battles.' This is a typical account throughout Republican literature. However, it is also an errornous one. www.saoirse32.dreamwidth. org/4767038.html.
104 From the author's personal notes (name withheld).
105 PRONI HA/32/3/3 Monday 6th July.
106 Although weapons searches were carried out in the Shankill and an equal amount of weapons were recovered, many in the lower Falls believed that the army was pro-Loyalist in their behaviour towards them. Army raids in the Shankill were probably less violent (author's personal notes).
107 *The Story of the Belfast Curfew*, p. 29.
108 Hennessey, *The Evolution of the Troubles*, p. 44.
109 *The Story of the Falls Curfew*.
110 From the author's personal notes (interview with Eamonn).
111 Ibid.
112 *The Story of the Belfast Curfew*, p. 38.
113 PRONI HA/32/3/3 6th July 1970.
114 Nick Van De Bijl, *Operation Banner*, p. 35.
115 Hamill, *Pig in the Middle*, p. 40.
116 Ibid.
117 *Ulster – The Facts: The Bullet and the Bomb versus the Better Life* … (Ulster Unionist Party, 1970).

Chapter 5

1 Smith, p. 227.
2 NA PRONI CAB/9/U/6/1.
3 Ibid.

4 NA PRONI CAB/9/U/6/1 Statement from Dr Patrick Hillery.

5 Taken from: *Dáil Éireann*, Vol. 248, 7 July 1970. Private Notice Questions: – Northern Situation; www.oireachtas-debates.gov.ie.

6 Ibid.

7 Hennessey, *The Evolution of the Troubles*, p. 45.

8 People's Democracy, *Free Citizen*, 7 July 1970.

9 www.oireachtas-debates.gov.ie; Vol. 28, 28 July 1970.

10 Ibid.

11 HC Deb 07 July 1970 Vol. 803 cc494-6; www.hansard.millbanksystems.com/commons/1970/jul/07/northern-ireland.

12 Nick Van De Bijl, *Operation Banner*, p. 35.

13 NA CAB/4/1532.

14 Smith, p. 226.

15 Warner, *The Falls Curfew Revisited*, p. 335.

16 Murphy, p. 152.

17 Dáil debates, 30 July 1970; http://www.oireachtas-debates.gov.ie/debates.

18 Smith, p. 230.

19 Ibid., p. 231.

20 Michael Morgan, 'How the British created the Provos', *Fortnight*, No. 275 (July– August, 1989), pp. 12–13.

21 Ibid., p. 13.

22 O'Brien, p. 176.

23 Morgan, *How the British Created the Provos*, p. 13.

24 NA PRONI CAB/4/1535 Conclusions of a Meeting of the Cabinet held at Stormont Castle on Monday 20th July 1970 at 3.00 p.m.

Chapter 6

1 Hanley and Millar, p. 158.

2 cedarlounge.files.wordpress.com; IRA Statement, July 1970.

3 Hanley and Millar, p. 158.

4 Ibid., p. 160.

5 Ibid.

6 Ibid., p. 159

7 NA PRONI HA/32/3/3. Meeting of the Joint Security Committee on 3rd August 1970 at Stormont Castle.

8 NA PRONI DCR/1/128 Meeting with Cardinal Conway 18th September 1970.

9 Ibid.

10 Hanley and Millar, p. 165.

11 Tim Pat Coogan, *The Troubles: Ireland's Ordeal and the Search for Peace* (New York: Palgrave, 1996), p. 137.

12 J. Bowyer Bell, *The Irish Troubles: A Generation of Violence 1967–1992* (New York: St Martin's Press, 1993), p. 185.

13 Devlin, *Straight Left*, p. 134.

14 Coogan, p. 129.

15 Taken from, Daniel M. Wilson 'Peace-making: The Effectiveness of British Strategy in Northern Ireland 1969–1972'; http://www.dtic.mil/dtic/tr/fulltext/u2/a255118.pdf. Other relevant points Wilson made are: 'Britain acknowledged the civil rights problem, and promised reform. Britain allowed the Stormont government, however, to dictate the pace and extent of reform. All civil rights reform was enacted gradually and by Stormont. Britain seemed to believe the reforms already promised by Stormont were sufficient to satisfy the majority of Catholics. At best, Catholics might have been suspicious of

Stormont's motives. In fact, Catholics viewed the reforms as too little too late and as desperate attempts by Stormont to maintain order. Significant reform was enacted by Stormont, however any real power sharing was not considered. Even after Stormont enacted election reform, they did not correct gerrymandered boundaries and did not promptly hold elections until the new system elections were scheduled for 1971. And, Britain seemed to believe the IRA was the problem, rather than recognising them as a symptom.' This analysis fits in well with Morgan's *How the British Created the Provos*, which speaks along the same lines.

16 *Armed Struggle*, p. 116.

17 Moloney, *Voices from the Grave*, p. 49.

18 Ed Moloney, *A Secret History of the IRA* (London: Penguin, 2002), p. 95.

19 The *World in Action* team filmed a street in the Clonard area of Belfast just after an army search of a property. The women of the community did not take this too well and started abusing the soldiers, culminating in stones being thrown by youths and a water cannon being used on the women. Soldiers abused the women back. Catholic alienation was certainly on the way in the Clonard district.

20 Michael Lawrence and Rowan Smith, *Fighting for Ireland? The Military Strategy of the Irish Republican Movement* (London: Routledge, 1997), p. 93.

21 In fact many soldiers were surprised that it took the IRA so long to kill a soldier, considering it was over a year since its formation.

22 Gunner Robert Curtis was involved in riot control at the junction of Lepper Street and the New Lodge Road when he was hit by a bullet from a burst of automatic fire, fired from a submachine gun. Contemporary reports tell that the rioting crowd threw a nail bomb then opened up to let the gunman shoot clearly. The crowd then gathered around him so he could get away. The gunman was almost certainly Billy Reid, a Provisional IRA member, who was killed three months later by the British army.

Chapter 7

1 Taken from Colm Campbell and Ita Connolly, 'A Model for the "War against Terrorism"? Military Intervention in Northern Ireland and the 1970 Falls Curfew', *Journal of Law and Society*, Vol. 30 (September 2003), pp. 341–75, p. 349.

2 www.oireachtasdebates.oireachtas.ie/Debates.

3 www.hansard.millbanksystems.com/commons; Lord Balniel speech to parliament 6th July 1970.

4 www.hansard.millbanksystems.com/commons; 6th July 1970. Gerry Fitt reply to Lord Balniel speech.

5 Denis Healey was one of these, and his statement goes a long way in supporting the theory that the army could do no wrong in the eyes of parliament. 'Will the hon. Gentleman accept that the overwhelming majority of hon. Members in both parties have nothing but admiration for the humanity and discipline with which the British Army has conducted itself under extreme provocation, and that we welcome the fact that he has indicated his readiness to investigate any specific complaints of misconduct which may be made? Indeed, is it not the case, as has been reported on the wireless, that the GOC has set up two centres in Belfast to which specific complaints may be made for investigation by the authorities?' (HC Deb 6 July 1970 Vol. 803 cc328–34).

6 www.hansard.millbanksystems.com/commons; 6th July 1970, Balniel reply.

7 *The Story of the Belfast Curfew*, p. 44.

8 Connolly and Campbell, p. 353.

9 PRONI HA/32/3/3 JSC Meeting 4th July 1970.

10 www.cain.ulst.ac.uk/proni/1970/proni_CAB-4-1532_1970-07.

11 CAB/4/1532 Cabinet meeting Stormont 7th July 1970.

12 *Irish Times*, Wednesday, 8 July 1970.

13 CAB/4/1532 7th July 1970.

14 Geraghty, p. 30.

15 Smith, p. 226.

16 Hennessey, *The Evolution of the Troubles*, p. 42.

17 HC Deb 18 January 1971 Vol. 809 cc680-92; www.hansard.millbanksystems.com/commons/1970/jul/06/northern-ireland.

18 Ibid.

19 HC Deb 18 January 1971 Vol. 809 pp. 680-92; www.hansard.millbanksystems.com/commons/1970/jul/06/northern-ireland.

20 Ibid.

21 Campbell and Connolly, 'A Model for the War against Terrorism?', p. 371.

22 The troops were part of the Parachute Regiment. This was also the time that Internment was brought in by the Stormont government, a very bloody time indeed.

23 Alongside the 'Ballymurphy Eleven' there were the 'New Lodge Six' and 'Bloody Sunday'. Bloody Sunday is the only one that has been investigated by a tribunal.

Conclusion

1 PRONI HA/32/2/35 Letter from Mr A. P. Hockaday to D. J. West, Civil Advisor to GOC Northern Ireland.

2 Ibid.

3 Ibid.

4 Soldiers in Northern Ireland were presumably working under the 'common law', since Stormont had no control over their actions. Stormont, however, had to pay for any damages that the army caused in house searches or in quelling disturbances, as the army was there 'in aid of the civil power', which was Stormont.

5 Michael Hout, *Following in Father's Footsteps: Social Mobility in Ireland* (Cambridge, Mass.: President and Fellows of Harvard College, 1989), p. 156.

6 Jonathan Tonge, *Northern Ireland: Conflict and Change* (London: Pearson, 2002), p. 27.

7 Taken from http://archive.org/stream/factsfiguresofbe00kenn/factsfiguresofbe00kenn_djvu.txt.

8 Taken from *The Outbreak of the Troubles*; www.pearsonhighered.com/assets/hip/us/hip_us.../1405801352.pdf.

9 Christopher McAll, *Class, Ethnicity, and Social Inequality* (Quebec: McGill–Queens University Press, 1992), p. 160.

10 Taken from www.pearsonhighered.com/assets/hip/us/hip_us_pearsonhighered/samplechapter/1405801352.pdf.

11 NA PRONI CAB/4/1532 Conclusions of a meeting of the cabinet held at Stormont Castle on Tuesday, 7th July 1970, at 11a.m.

12 This was during protests about the Sunningdale Agreement, which allowed Catholics to share power for the first time in Northern Irish history, the main one being about the Council of Ireland, which many Protestants saw as a sell-out to the Catholics. Faulkner made the comment in a burst of anger to a film crew after disturbances on the floor of the house at Stormont, when the Redcaps, the military police, were called to remove Paisley and his supporters.

13 S. S. Herron, *The Great Conspiracy to Destroy Ulster* (out of print paperback, c.1971).

14 Hewitt, 'Catholic Grievances, Catholic Nationalism and Violence in Northern Ireland during the Civil Rights Period'.

15 Sabine Wichert, *Northern Ireland Since 1945* (Harlow: Longman, 1991), p. 34.

16 Thomas Hennessey, *A History of Northern Ireland 1920–1996* (London: Macmillan, 1997), p. 129.

17 Hewitt, 'Catholic Grievances, Catholic Nationalism and Violence in Northern Ireland during the Civil Rights Period'.

18 John McGarry (ed.), *Northern Ireland and the Divided World: The Northern Ireland Conflict* (Oxford: Oxford University Press, 2001).

19 There were no demands from the marchers for a united Ireland in the days of the civil rights marches. They were demanding 'one man, one vote' and equality within the society in which they lived.

20 Krishan Kumar, *The Making of English National Identity* (Cambridge: Cambridge University Press, 2003), p. 245.

21 John McGarry (ed.), *Northern Ireland and the Divided World: The Northern Ireland Conflict* (Oxford: Oxford University Press, 2001).

Appendices

1 *Disturbances in Northern Ireland*, Report of the Commission appointed by the Governor of Northern Ireland. Published in Belfast by Her Majesty's Stationery Office, 1969. Taken from: www.cain.ulst.ac.uk/hmso/cameron.

2 Report of the Advisory Committee on Police in Northern Ireland, published in Belfast by Her Majesty's Stationery Office, 1969. Taken from: www.cain.ulst.ac.uk/hmso/hunt. htm.

3 *Orange Standard*: 'The Story of the Ulster Special Constabulary' (Article 6, May 2000). Taken from www.grandorangelodge.co.uk/press/Orange-Standard.

4 Government of Northern Ireland, *Violence and Civil Disturbances in Northern Ireland in 1969* (Report of Tribunal of Inquiry). Taken from www.cain.ulst.ac.uk/hmso/scarman.

5 Taken from www.organizedrage.com/2010/04/1916-irish-proclamation. This is the document that set Ireland on the road to a Republic. As Mícheál Mac Donncha suggests: 'The 1916 Proclamation stands as probably the single most important document in Irish history and one of the most significant documents in the history of progressive movements all over the world. In choosing to set out not only their motivation for an armed revolt against British rule but also the rights on which the Irish Republic would be based, the authors of the Proclamation left a lasting legacy.' Perhaps that 'lasting legacy' is Northern Ireland, and the impossibility of attaining a 32-county Republic by force.

6 Civil Authorities (Special Powers) Act (Northern Ireland), 1922; www.cain.ulst.ac.uk/ hmso/spa1922.

7 Flags and Emblems (Display) Act (Northern Ireland), 1954; www.cain.ulst.ac.uk/hmso/ fea1954.

8 Northern Ireland Text of a Communiqué and Declaration issued after a meeting held at 10 Downing Street on 19 August 1969. Taken from: www.cain.ulst.ac.uk/hmso.

9 'A commentary by the Government of Northern Ireland to accompany the Cameron Report - incorporating an account of progress and a programme of action', (12 September 1969), [PRONI Public Records CAB/9/B/308/2; 19 pages], [PDF; 3562KB]. Belfast: Public Record Office of Northern Ireland (PRONI); http://cain.ulst.ac.uk/ proni/1969/proni_CAB-9-B-308-2_1969-09-12_b.pdf.

10 Sir James Craig, Unionist Party, then Prime Minister of Northern Ireland, 21 November 1934. Reported in: *Parliamentary Debates*, Northern Ireland House of Commons, Vol. XVII, Cols. 72–73.

BIBLIOGRAPHY

Articles and documents

'A Commentary by the Government of Northern Ireland to Accompany the Cameron Report incorporating an account of progress and a programme of action'; www.cain.ulst. ac.uk/hmso. Courtesy of Merlin Press.

Bishop, Joseph W., 'Law in the Control of Terrorism and Insurrection: The British Laboratory Experience'; www.scholarship.law.duke.edu.

Boserup, Anders, 'Contradictions and Struggles in Northern Ireland', *The Socialist Register,* Vol. 9, 1972, pp.157-92.

Bourke, Richard, '"Imperialism" and "Democracy" in Modern Ireland, 1898–2002', *Boundary*, Duke University Press, Vol. 2, No. 31 (2004), pp. 101–2.

Colm Campbell, Ita Connolly, 'A Model for the "War Against Terrorism?" Military Intervention in Northern Ireland and the 1970 Falls Curfew', *Journal of Law and Society*, Vol. 30, No. 3, September, 2003 pp. 341-75. For a fuller account, see *The Trouble with Guns* (Blackstaff Press, 1998).

The Plain Truth, Campaign for Social Justice in Northern Ireland, Castlefields, Dungannon, 15 June 1969; www.cain.ulst.ac.uk/events.

Darby, John, 'Conflict in Northern Ireland: A Background Essay'; www.rhsroughriders. org; www.plutobooks.com

Disturbances in Northern Ireland. Report of the Commission appointed by the Governor of Northern Ireland (Belfast: HMSO, 1969); www.cain.ulst.ac.uk/hmso/cameron.

Farrell, Michael, *Northern Ireland: The Orange State* (London: Pluto Press, 1976).

Government of Northern Ireland, *Violence and Civil Disturbances in Northern Ireland in 1969* (Report of Tribunal of Inquiry); www.cain.ulst.ac.uk/hmso/scarman.

Harris, Mary, 'Religious Divisions, Discrimination and the Struggle for Dominance in Northern Ireland'; www.stm.unipi.it

Hepburn, A. C., 'Northern Ireland', www.mrmichaelstuart.com/uploads/3/2/6/.../noirelandencartainfo.doc

Hewitt, Christopher, 'Catholic Grievances, Catholic Nationalism and Violence in Northern Ireland during the Civil Rights Period: A Reconsideration', *British Journal of Sociology*, Vol. 32, No. 3 (September 1981), pp. 362–77.

Hull, Eleanor, 'A History of Ireland'; www.libraryireland.com.

Lynch, Jack, 'A Review of the Situation in the Six Counties' (Dublin: Irish Government).

Jones, Emrys, 'The Distribution and Segregation of Roman Catholics in Belfast', *The Sociological Review*, Vol. 4, No. 2 (1956), pp. 167–89.

Kenny, Mary, 'Winston Churchill and Ireland'; www.mary-kenny.com/published_articles/winston-churchill-ireland.

'Lord I Stonewall', *Tribune*, 14 June 1968; www.archive.tribunemagazine.co.uk/article.

Manual of Military Law, in Campbell, Colm and Connolly, Ita, 'A Model for the "War Against Terrorism"? Military Intervention in Northern Ireland and the 1970 Falls Curfew", *Journal of Law and Society*, Vol. 30, pp. 341–75.

Morgan, Michael, 'How the British Created the Provos', *Fortnight*, No. 275 (July–August 1989), pp. 12–13.

Munck, Ronnie, 'The Making of the Troubles in Northern Ireland', *Journal of Contemporary History*, Vol. 27, No. 2 (April 1992), pp. 211–29.

Murray, Sean, article in *An Phoblacht*, 23 July 2009.

O'Doherty, Malachi, 'The Pogrom Myth'; www.malachiodoherty.com.

O'Neill, Captain Terence, reported in *Belfast Telegraph*, 10 May 1969; www.cain.ulst.ac.uk/issues/discrimination/quotes.

Patterson, Henry, 'The British State and the Rise of the IRA', *Irish Political Studies*, Vol. 23, No. 4 (December 2008), pp. 491–511.

Smith, Jeremy, 'Walking a Real Tight-Rope of Difficulties, Edward Heath and the Search for Stability in Northern Ireland', *Twentieth Century British History*, Vol. 18, No. 2 (2007), pp. 219–53.

'Ulster – The Facts: The Bullet and the Bomb versus the Better Life …' (Ulster Unionist Party, 1970). Courtesy of *The Orange Standard*, official publication of the Grand Orange Lodge of Ireland.

Wilson, Daniel, 'Peace-Making: The Effectiveness of British Strategy in Northern Ireland, 1969–1972', thesis, 1979; www.dtic.mil.

Books

Adams, Gerry, *Falls Memories* (Dingle: Brandon, 1993).

Adams, Gerry, *Before the Dawn* (London: William Heinemann, 1996).

Aldous, Richard and Niamh Puirsell, *We Declare: Landmark Documents in Ireland's History* (London: Quercus, 2008).

Arthur, Max, *Northern Ireland Soldiers Talking* (London: Sidgwick and Jackson, 1988).

Bell, J. Bower, *The Irish Troubles: A Generation of Violence 1967–1992* (New York: St Martin's Press, 1993).

Bew, Paul, Peter Gibbon and Henry Patterson, *Northern Ireland 1921–2001: Political Forces and Social Classes* (London: Serif, 2002).

Central Citizens Defence Committee, *The Story of the Belfast Curfew*, 1970.

Conroy, John, *Belfast Diary: War as a Way of Life* (Boston, Mass.: Beacon Press, 1987).

Coogan, Tim Pat, *The Troubles: Ireland's Ordeal and the Search for Peace* (New York: Palgrave, 1996).

Cunningham, Michael, *British Government Policy in Northern Ireland* (Manchester: Manchester University Press, 2001).

Devlin, Paddy, *Straight Left* (Belfast: Blackstaff Press, 1993).

Dewar, Michael, *The British Army in Northern Ireland* (London: Arms and Armour, 1985).

Dillon, Martin, *Trigger Man: Assassins and Terror Bosses in the Ireland Conflict* (Edinburgh: Mainstream, 2004).

English, Richard, *Armed Struggle: The History of the IRA* (London: Macmillan, 2003).

Falls Think Tank, *Ourselves Alone? Voices from the Nationalist Working Class*. Compiled by Michael Hall (Newtownabbey: Island Publications, 1996).

Falls Think Tank, *'Seeds of Hope': An Exploration by the 'Seeds of Hope' Ex-prisoners* (Newtownabbey: Island Publications, 2000).

Foster, R. F., *Modern Ireland 1600–1972* (London: Penguin, 1989).

Geraghty, Tony, *The Irish War: The Hidden Conflict Between the IRA and British Intelligence* (London: HarperCollins, 2000).

Gillespie, Gordon, *Years of Darkness: The Troubles Remembered* (Dublin: Gill and Macmillan, 2008)

Hamill, Desmond, *Pig in the Middle* (London: Methuen, 1985).

Hanley, Brian and Scott Millar, *The Lost Revolution: The Story of the Official IRA and the Workers Party* (London: Penguin, 2010).

Hennessey, Thomas, *The Evolution of the Troubles* (Dublin: Irish Academic Press, 2007).

Hennessey, Thomas, *A History of Northern Ireland 1920–1996* (London: Macmillan, 1997).

Hout, Michael, *Following in Father's Footsteps: Social Mobility in Ireland* (Cambridge, Mass.: President and Fellows of Harvard College, 1989).

Jordan, Hugh, *Milestones in Murder: Defining Moments in Ulster's Terror War* (Edinburgh: Mainstream, 2002).

Kee, Robert, *Ireland: A History* (London: Weidenfeld and Nicolson, 1980).

Kumar, Krishan, *The Making of English National Identity* (Cambridge: Cambridge University Press, 2003).

Lawrence, Michael and Rowan Smith, *Fighting for Ireland? The Military Strategy of the Irish Republican Movement* (London: Routledge, 1997).

Magee, John and Jack Magee, *Northern Ireland: Crisis and Conflict* (London: Routledge, 1974).

McAll, Christopher, *Class, Ethnicity, and Social Inequality* (Quebec: McGill-Queens University Press, 1992).

McGarry, John (ed.), *Northern Ireland and the Divided World: Post-Agreement Northern Ireland in Comparative Perspective* (Oxford: Oxford University Press, 2001).

Merkl, Peter H. (ed.), *Political Violence and Terror: Motifs and Motivations* (London: University of California Press, 1986).

Moloney, Ed, *A Secret History of the IRA* (London: Penguin, 2002).

Moloney, Ed, *Voices From the Grave* (London: Faber and Faber, 2010).

Murphy, Michael A., *Gerry Fitt: A Political Chameleon* (Cork: Mercier Press, 2007).

Neumann, Peter R., *Britain's Long War: British Strategy in the Northern Ireland Conflict, 1969–98* (London: Palgrave Macmillan, 2004).

Northern Ireland Civil Rights Association, *We Shall Overcome: The History of the Struggle for Civil Rights in Northern Ireland 1968–1978* (Belfast: NICRA).

O'Brien, Maire and Conor Cruise, *From Ireland: A Concise History* (London: Thames and Hudson, 1999).

Patterson, Henry, *Ireland Since 1939: The Persistence of Conflict* (London: Penguin, 2006).

Prince, Simon and Geoffrey Warner, *Belfast and Derry in Revolt: A New History of the Start of the Troubles* (Dublin: Irish Academic Press, 2012).

Rafferty, Oliver P., *Catholicism in Ulster 1603–1983: An Interpretive History* (London: Hurst and Company, 1994). Courtesy of Wiley Publications.

Ripley, Tim and Mike Chappell, *Security Forces in Northern Ireland 1969–92* (London: Osprey Publishing, 1993).

Rose, Paul, 'Backbencher's Dilemma', Chapter 12 in: *The Northern Ireland Fiasco* plus 'Appendix' (A report by the Campaign for Democracy in Ulster on a visit to Northern Ireland in 1967) (London: Muller, 1981).

Taylor, Peter, *Brits: The War against the IRA* (London: Bloomsbury, 2002).

Taylor, Peter, *Provos* (London: Bloomsbury, 1997).

Tonge, Jonathan, *Northern Ireland: Conflict and Change* (London: Pearson, 2002).

Ulster: Sunday Times Insight Team (Harmondsworth: Penguin Books, 1972)

Van De Bijl, Nick, *Operation Banner: The British Army in Northern Ireland 1969–2007* (Great Britain: Pen and Sword Military, 2009).

Weitzer, Ronald A., *Transforming Settler States: Communal Conflict and Internal Security in Northern Ireland and Zimbabwe* (Berkeley: University of California Press, 1990); www.ark.cdlib.org.

Wichert, Sabine, *Northern Ireland Since 1945* (London: Longman, 1991).

Archival sources

NA PRONI FIN/30/P20 Minority Recognition and Representation.

NA PRONI HA/32/2/55 Letter about sending in the troops.

NA PRONI HA/32/3/3 Joint Security Committee Meeting at Stormont. Monday 6th July.

NA PRONI CAB/4/1535 Conclusions of a Meeting of the Cabinet held at Stormont Castle on Monday 20th July 1970 at 3.00 p.m.

NA PRONI CAB/9/G/89/2. Stormont Castle Meeting. Notes on points to be discussed with the GOC 22nd April 1970.

NA CAB/128/47 Conclusions of a Meeting of the Cabinet held at 10 Downing Street, SW1 on Tuesday 23rd June 1970 at 11 a.m.

NA CAB/128/47 Conclusions of a Meeting of the Cabinet 26 June 1970.

NA HA/32/3/3 Joint Security Committee Meeting at Stormont 4 July 1970.

NA PRONI HA/32/3/3 Meeting of the Joint Security Committee on 3rd August 1970 at Stormont Castle.

NA PRONI DCR/1/128 Meeting with Cardinal Conway 18th September 1970.

NA CAB/129/144.

NA CAB/4/1532.

NA PRONI CAB/9/U/6/1.

Civil Authorities (Special Powers) Act (Northern Ireland), 1922; www.cain.ulst.ac.uk/hmso/spa1922.

Criminal Justice (Temporary Provisions) Act (Northern Ireland) 1970, Chapter 22

Dáil Éireann, Vol. 248, 7 July 1970 (Private Notice Questions:- Northern Situation); www.oireachtas-debates.gov.ie.

Dail Éireann, Vol. 28, 28 July 1970; www.oireachtas-debates.gov.ie.

Dáil Éireann, Vol. 241, 23 October 1969 (Situation in Six Counties); www.historical-debates.oireachtas.ie.

Flags and Emblems (Display) Act (Northern Ireland), 1954; www.cain.ulst.ac.uk/hmso/fea1954.

Hansard Parliamentary Debates, HC Deb 13 October 1969 Vol. 788 pp. 47–164 www.hansard.millbanksystems.com/commons.

Hansard Parliamentary Debates HC Deb 7 July 1970 Vol. 803 pp. 494–6 www.hansard.millbanksystems.com/commons/1970/jul/07/northern-ireland.

Hansard Parliamentary Debates HC Deb 18 January 1971 Vol. 809 pp. 680–92 www.hansard.millbanksystems.com/commons.

Hansard Parliamentary Debates, HC Deb 3 July 1970 Vol. 803 pp. 201–92 www.hansard.millbanksystems.com/commons.

Herron, S. S., *The Great Conspiracy to Destroy Ulster* (out of print paperback, *c.*1971).

Ireland Act, 1949, Ch. 41; www.legislation.gov.uk.

People's Democracy, *Free Citizen*, issued on 7 July 1970.

Stormont Papers, Vol. 76 pp. 1619–1620.

Text of a Communiqué and Declaration issued after a meeting held at 10 Downing Street on 19 August 1969. Taken from www.cain.ulst.ac.uk/hmso

The Troubles (MacDonald Futura, 1980).

Three Days in July, TAL Productions.

Websites

www.cedarlounge.wordpress.com
www.cedarlounge.files.wordpress.com
www.dur.ac.uk/resources
www.grandorangelodge.co.uk/press/Orange-Standard
www.hansard.millbanksystems.com/commons/1971/jan/18/northern-ireland
www.historylearningsite.co.uk
www.nytimes.com
www.organizedrage.com/2010/04/1916-irish-proclamation
www.thepsychologist.org.uk/archive
www.pearsonhighered.com/assets/hip/us/hip_us_pearsonhighered/
    samplechapter/1405801352.pdf
www.saoirse32.dreamwidth.org/4767038.html
www.news.bbc.co.uk/1/hi/6923699.stm

INDEX

If you enjoyed this book, you may also be interested in…

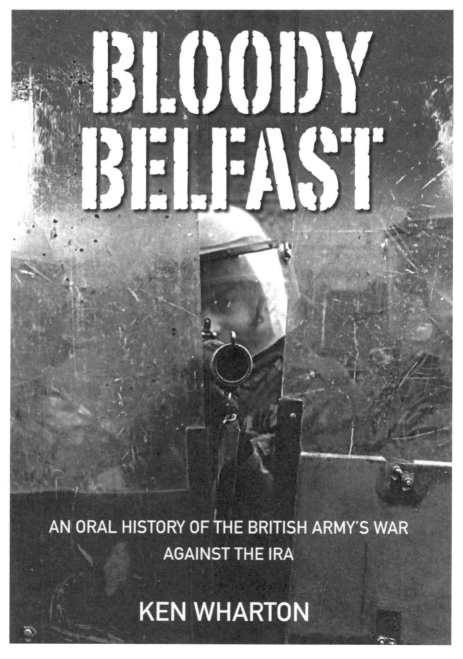

BLOODY BELFAST

AN ORAL HISTORY OF THE BRITISH ARMY'S WAR
AGAINST THE IRA

KEN WHARTON

9780752452494; £20